Mitch

W9-ADS-078

onn.

AMERICA AND EUROPE
IN THE POLITICAL THOUGHT
OF JOHN ADAMS

AMERICA AND EUROPE IN
THE POLITICAL THOUGHT OF

John Adams

BY EDWARD HANDLER

HARVARD UNIVERSITY PRESS

Cambridge, Massachusetts

1964

© *Copyright 1964 by the*
President and Fellows of Harvard College

All rights reserved

Distributed in Great Britain
by Oxford University Press, London

Publication of this book has been aided
by a grant from the Ford Foundation

Library of Congress Catalog Card Number 64–13422

Printed in the United States of America

973.4
H19

45103
Mitchell College Library
New London, Conn.

FOR SHIRLEY

PREFACE

---

*I*N THIS book I explore the theme of the American relationship to Europe as it appears in the political writings of John Adams. Although the European associations of Thomas Jefferson have received close scrutiny, it has been largely forgotten that Adams spent nearly twice as much time in Europe as Jefferson, and it has taken the devoted labors of Zoltán Haraszti to remind us that Adams interacted, if anything, more intensely with the ideas of European liberalism, ending as probably the one American of his generation who was most widely read in the political theory of the French Enlightenment. I have been concerned particularly with an almost entirely neglected element in Adams' encounter with Europe, his continuing preoccupation over several decades with the old continent's problems of revolutionary change. In his assessment of the foreign revolutions as in his political doctrine and its attendant social analysis, I detect a central paradox: perceiving the differences between America and Europe, Adams nevertheless applies American norms to Europe and transposes on America a set of fears derived from Europe.

PREFACE

However deeply it may immure him in the privacies of his cave, the scholar's activity carries with it also the everyday experience of his dependence upon others. The acknowledgment of accumulated obligation is one of the high amenities of his world, a symbolic homage to the truth that outside the community there is no individual life. I owe a special debt to Perry Miller, an early mentor and guide through some of history's cunning corridors. I have since drifted off into other fields of inquiry, but the subject of this work testifies to the enduring interest in the interpretation of American life that he stirred in me when I had the privilege during undergraduate days of spending many tutorial hours with him. I do not think I could have found my way around among the foreign revolutions that bulk so large in this study without the guidance afforded by R. R. Palmer's *Age of the Democratic Revolution.* Although I have ventured to differ with him a little about Adams, the frequency of my citations only imperfectly conveys what I owe to the spirit and tone and sheer intellectual grasp of his book. I am grateful, most of all, to Louis Hartz, who encouraged me to see that a task undertaken originally as an "extended term paper" to fulfill the requirements of a terminal degree in political science also could be conceived more ambitiously as a publishable work. The perceptive reader will grasp quickly that my book is an effort to apply some of the theses of *The Liberal Tradition in America* to the case of Adams. It goes without saying, however, that I alone bear the blame for any inadequacies that appear in the following pages.

The collections of a number of libraries were drawn upon during the research and writing; if I single out the Wellesley College Library for mention, it is because ac-

PREFACE

cess to its facilities saved me countless weary hours of travel time.

I am indebted to the trustees of the Adams Papers for permission to quote from the microfilm of the papers; the Historical Society of Pennsylvania for permission to quote from the Adams–Van Der Kemp correspondence; the Massachusetts Historical Society for permission to quote from unpublished papers in its collections; the Harvard University Press for permission to quote from Zoltán Haraszti, *John Adams and the Prophets of Progress*, 1952; and the University of North Carolina Press for permission to quote from the *Adams-Jefferson Letters*, ed. Lester J. Cappon, 1959.

My wife shouldered the burden of my despair during long years of drought, and the perhaps equally great burden of my enthusiasm when the rains came. She undertook stoically (I will not evade and say "cheerfully") the outrageous *corvée* imposed upon some academic wives, that of typing and retyping the several versions of the manuscript.

E. H.

"Southgate"
July 1963

CONTENTS

  I   Relativism and Universalism:
      Dual Perspectives   1

 II   Correct Principles of Political Architecture   30

III   On the Eve   73

 IV   Advent of Revolution   96

  V   Victory of the Bourgeoisie   126

 VI   American Anti-Jacobin   156

VII   Strait Is the Gate That Leads to Liberty   191

      Notes   229

      Index   243

AMERICA AND EUROPE
IN THE POLITICAL THOUGHT
OF JOHN ADAMS

CHAPTER ONE

RELATIVISM AND UNIVERSALISM: DUAL PERSPECTIVES

---

*H*ISTORY, as E. H. Carr has said, is a dialogue between past and present, with the events of the present continually posing new questions which must be asked of the past and altering our perspective on it. Not surprisingly, therefore, America's new world position has intensified interest in our historic relationship with Europe. Inevitably that relationship has been conceived in terms of polarities by recent interpreters of the American past. When Delmore Schwartz wrote that Europe was the "greatest thing" in North America, Philip Rahv felt bound in strict accuracy to point out that it was also the "most rejected thing" in North America. Nations like Russia and the United States, poised on the edges of the European civilization, have felt for it a "combined attraction and repulsion" expressive of the characteristic indecision of peoples at once linked to the "heartland" by innumerable ties of dependence which can hardly fail to be acknowledged and impelled to a repudiation of that dependence by the need to realize their separate identities. The conflict of Slavophile and

Westernizing tendencies familiar to students of Russian intellectual history has had its counterpart in an American tension between withdrawal and participation, estrangement and nostalgia. The "innocents abroad" have confronted the "passionate pilgrim," and frequently these contradictory impulses have warred within the same breast. One thinks instantly of the division in Jefferson's mind between his cosmopolitan love of Europe and his insular fear of its contaminations, although similar tensions are observable, if less written about, in other members of the founding generation.[1]

In John Adams' outlook on Europe, the polarities assume the special form of a conflict between what one writer has called relativist and universalist perspectives on the American relation to Europe.[2] On the one hand, Adams was acutely aware of the differences between America and Europe, picturing them as distinctive worlds with separate destinies. On the other hand, he submerged the disparities between America and Europe, with the consequence that he imposed European categories of experience upon America and American categories upon Europe: the two worlds were viewed as having a common destiny, which took shape in one aspect as a Europeanization of American political life and in another as an Americanization of European political life.

Europe's Revolutionary Age: The Relevance of American Experience

The tension between the universalist and relativist strains in Adams' thought appears with special clarity in his consideration of the problem of revolution in Europe. Long residence abroad stirred an enduring interest in foreign revolutionary struggles. For over forty years — from the Dutch Patriots in the 1780's to the abortive ef-

forts of the liberals of southern Europe in the early 1820's
— Adams followed practically every important manifestation of Europe's "age of the democratic revolution." A
major American revolutionary, he found it difficult to feel
genuine ties of sympathy with the foreign revolutions.
The grounds of his disaffection have little in common
with the tendencies of thought brought forward by the
European Reaction, having much more to do with his
conflicting conceptions of the relation of America to
Europe. Relativism and universalism alike pointed to conclusions antipathetic to the revolutions, leading him either
to discount in advance that foreign liberals could achieve
their objects or alternatively to impose requirements upon
them with which they proved unwilling or unable to
comply. Europe's revolutions, occurring hard upon the
American, raised for Adams the issue, which has come
alive again for our own generation, of the transferability
of America's revolutionary experience.

In the relativist world of John Adams America's special
social and historical exemptions were lovingly stressed to
the point of asserting American uniqueness. Adams' con-
trasting images of America and Europe grew largely out
of a powerful urge toward self-definition which expressed
a burgeoning sense of American nationality. Adams represented America and Europe as antithetical poles of
political reality, one pole embodying virtue and "liberality" and the other corruption and servitude. He was
tempted to consign the entire European world to political
perdition because it could not be brought easily to conform to American conditions assumed to constitute prerequisites for maintaining the liberal institutions that
alone comported with the "dignity of human nature." He
entertained despairingly bleak expectations about the
prospect of extending the area of freedom to precisely

those parts of Europe which subsequently have come to be regarded as strongholds of the "free world." Verging upon denial of the universality of liberty as a value, he erected it into an exclusive possession of the Anglo-American community. (England was included as the ancestral home of the institutions which the Americans enjoyed in a "purer" form.)

Fresh from a revolution in his own country, Adams, when abroad, displayed no messianic urge to explode the old order. Pride of inheritance blunted the impulse to proselytize for American degrees of liberty, as it smothered also his identification with the purposes and grievances of the middle classes, his own social counterparts in Europe. He attributed no special virtues to them, regarding them instead as partaking of a corruption that enveloped all European classes. He pictured an acute antagonism between American and European canons of behavior that stimulated strong inclinations on his part toward separateness and dampened his sympathy for European aspirations for liberty. "The refinements of policy in many of the courtiers in the Old World can scarcely be perceived by the plain genius of native Americans, nor can they be perceived without abhorrence of the heart." [3]

Abandoned to follies and depravities,[4] the Europeans, unlike the Americans, could not be expected to pass safely through the vicissitudes of revolution. Adams adjured the foreign liberals not to try to imitate American example. They must remember they were not Americans. Whatever moderate degrees of liberalization were possible in Europe must be accomplished by the most gentle and gradual means. He considered it wildly fantastic that any European liberals should think of overleaping monarchy and aristocracy to establish fully elective institutions. Monarchy and aristocracy were in his view indispensable in Europe, not because he had any particular affection for them, but on the contrary because he regarded them as a kind of punishment for Europe's sins. When a "great part" of a nation must be understood to be corrupted, elective institutions would produce an unimaginable venality.

When he encountered liberal opinion abroad, Adams experienced some initial difficulty in overcoming feelings of condescension and sheer incredulity. Could the citizens of these benighted lands really be serious in their commitment to liberty? The conditions of freedom were in his mind coterminous with America's peculiar social and historical circumstances, which could be found in like degree nowhere else. So it was an absolute conviction with him that Catholic peoples would never be able to achieve free institutions, and he was openly doubtful whether the French could operate republican forms among other grounds for the reason that they had lost "the modesty and domestic virtues of their women." [5]

When the European liberals began to take the road of revolution, Adams' mind surged immediately with forebodings. At a moment when only the earliest stirrings of revolution were visible in France, he already saw little reason to hope that any permanent gains for freedom's cause would result. Adams' relativist perspective expressed itself in a kind of political Calvinism that reserved the gospel of liberty for a happy few elect nations. It led him into exaggeration of American uniqueness and a too easy and complete pessimism about liberal reform in western Europe. If it produced an acute appreciation of the intransigent circumstances which nations subject to the feudal and clerical subordinations would have to sur-

5

mount in order to renovate their institutions, it also rendered him insensitive to the strength of the awakened European passion for liberty.

When confronted by actual full-fledged revolutions, however, Adams assessed them in universalist terms; that is, the assimilation of American institutional norms became for him in effect the condition of Europe's political salvation. His censures upon specific revolutionary acts assumed the direct relevance of an American model, which was projected abroad. Unhesitatingly he applied suppositions derived from his own revolution to Europe's quite different problems of political change. Adams' insistence upon the disparity of American and European circumstances never led him to the conception of plurality of paths toward the realization of liberal goals. He assumed the universal applicability of what were only American standards and transferred American preoccupations to Europe's revolutionary struggles. He came close to the rejection of friends of liberty abroad when they ceased merely to glorify the example of 1776 and attempted to apply it in their own way. To move toward American degrees of freedom required fundamental alterations of the structure of society in Europe, but Adams disclaimed the identity in purposes between the American and French revolutions when France's turned into a social revolution.

The impulse, implicit in Adams' criticisms, to reorder the European world in an American image suffered inevitable bafflement, because, as a more consistent relativist would have been compelled to acknowledge, differences in circumstances necessarily prompted differences in approach. The apparent rejection by Europe of the lessons that America had to teach and the contrast between the mixed results of Europe's revolutions and America's unequivocal success — two circumstances that were logically connected in Adams' mind — brought him back in the end to a reinforced conviction of an entire separation of destiny between the Old and the New World. In his treatment of the foreign revolutions Adams first fiercely asserted the contradiction between America and Europe; then he tried to resolve that contradiction on American terms; the defeat of his effort intensified the original sense of contradiction.[6]

Adams both affirmed and denied the relevance of American revolutionary experience. On the one hand, the Europeans were told that they must not attempt to make themselves over in the image of America, because they did not enjoy any of the special exemptions of the Americans; in this view the mistake of the foreign revolutionaries consisted in attempting to accomplish far too much too quickly. On the other hand, American preoccupations were transferred bodily to Europe without reference to America's special exemptions, and the liberals were told that their revolutions would have achieved a larger measure of success, if only they had followed the American precedent more closely. The evident incompatibilities of these perspectives should not obscure what they have in common: both are manifestations of the absolutism of the American political mind.

The assumption of the self-evident truth of American political norms in its relativist form could produce an urge to withdraw from Europe in the interest of preserving the norms themselves from contamination; it could also produce a skepticism about the possibility of transplanting them into alien environments. But relativist withdrawal could easily pass over into its apparent universalist contradiction, judgment of other peoples' efforts to transform their societies by the standard of conformity

7

to the American norms. Condescension about the likelihood of success of revolutionary ventures could coexist in the same mind with an unsparing severity in disapproving departures from the American model. Disappointment about revolutionary failures might be genuine enough, but they would be ascribed to political immaturity or irresponsibility, and these in turn were generally understood to mean inability or unwillingness to comprehend or follow American canons of behavior. Hopes for future success would rest on the belief that, given time, the foreign liberals would repent of their error.

In our own time when Americans live again in an age of revolution, centered primarily in the non-European world, the archetypal quality of Adams' conflicting perspectives on the problems of political change in foreign lands deserves emphasis. For the conviction of American uniqueness in combination with the assurance that nevertheless our patterns are relevant to others is a contradiction that has persisted to the present in American thinking. President Monroe in a preliminary draft of his celebrated message to Congress wished to proclaim at the same time an entire separation between the two hemispheres and American support for the Greek struggle for independence. The idea of two disaffiliated worlds could not quite blot out the vision of a single world unified by adherence to the republican doctrine brought forward by the United States. No one shared more completely the relativist sense of the eternal opposition between America and Europe than Woodrow Wilson before 1914, but he ended in his Fourteen Points and his peace program by making the United States the model for a reconstructed Europe. And an authentic spokesman for isolationism like Arthur Vandenberg could shift to advocacy of American partici-

8

pation in world affairs, and moreover a participation without easily ascertainable limits.

In the long perspective what may be remarkable is the relative ease with which the so-called revolution in American foreign policy could be accomplished. American isolationism, insofar as it is based on a belief in the absolute significance of American political experience, always contained an implicit interventionist premise. Even after the shift from isolation to involvement, Adams' antinomy has remained alive in some American minds. Those who have been most sensitive to the perils of alien subversion — in one mood most conscious of American uniqueness and most concerned to safeguard it — have also had a considerable problem in coming to terms with those institutional developments in western Europe and the new countries which appear to stray away from American political or economic patterns.

Such difficulties of adjustment testify to the vitality of Adams' disposition to universalize American norms; the full flowering of that propensity, including its crusading potential, has been reserved for a time when American power has grown to pre-eminent proportions and our security — psychological as well as strategic — has seemed to require the propagation of our system. Contemporary analogies to Adams' projections abroad of his constitutional ideas abound. One example may suffice to suggest the continuity of the response. A recent observer of the problems of state-building in tropical Africa, after commenting that "many people in the United States have tended to believe our brand of federalism can and should be easily transferred to the new states," points to the failure to understand the disrepute of the concept of federalism in an environment where federation too easily can degenerate into confederation or even Balkanization.[7] The parallel is close to Adams' burdening of the foreign liberals with his own constitutional obsessions without reference to differences of circumstance.

The crucial instance of Adams' imposition of an American institutional norm upon Europe appears in his insistence that the system of balanced powers — understood to mean a legislative authority shared by an upper and lower house and an executive with a veto — must provide the constitutional basis for renovation of the political order. Adams assumed that the European liberals must adopt the same attitude to sovereignty and the organization of public powers as the Americans. He was outraged by the uniformity with which the liberals in a succession of revolutions rejected his prescriptions about correct political architecture. He explained their persistence in error in terms of willful disregard of the teachings of history and the settled tradition of political thought. Without inquiring very seriously what strategic requirements must be driving them so consistently to the advocacy of unified sovereignties, he attributed the repeated setbacks of their revolutions to their failure to grasp that without the balance there could be no free government.

It was not, of course, disregard of experience and addiction to pernicious abstractions that impelled foreign liberals like Turgot or Condorcet to reject government by balanced powers and to desire instead the collection of state authority into a single center. In France Turgot had directly experienced the results of dispersion of governing power among constituted bodies when aristocratic privilege, barricaded behind the parlements, had overturned his reform program. Adams thought of the balance as procuring for society an indispensable element of "rest," but this value could have little appeal to liberals who had to innovate on a major scale to create the social basis for regimes of liberty. In nations confronting the problem of carrying through massive programs of social reconstruction, the system of balances could not be regarded as an acceptable basis for reconstituting the political order; a far greater degree of political centralization was required than in the United States. The foreign liberals understood that a sovereign power divided against itself would provide the forces of inertia with opportunities for obstruction. For this reason the members of Turgot's circle devoted major energies to dispelling "Anglomania" in France and exposing the oligarchic content in England's mixed constitution.

Adams saw as one virtue of his system its impartiality: it would give all major interests a veto on changes regarded as invading their essential rights. Foreign liberals found the claim of impartiality between the rights of the few and the many simply specious. In their societies the problem was that what the few regarded as indefeasible rights had come to be considered by the many as intolerable privileges. Adams missed the mischievous consequences for liberal goals that the system of balances could have under European conditions. In a society like the United States, which enjoyed equality of condition, the balance would not possess the reactionary implications that foreign liberals feared. Dispersal of the power to govern in America might at the most fortify the advantages of particular regions or economic interests. To balance offices of government against one another was a quite different matter than to balance classes of men.

The most important occasion on which Adams tried to apply the system of balanced powers to European constitutional problems was, of course, in 1789 when basic decisions were being made by the French National Assembly. With the zeal of the doctrinaire Adams urged the adoption of the system of tripartite participation in the lawmaking process. He had to pay a harsh penalty for pressing measures without due regard to the attendant circumstances. As will be demonstrated in detail later, none of the contending parties of whatever persuasion in France in 1789 found the system urged by Adams acceptable, as they conceived their interests. In transposing an American solution to an alien environment, he doomed himself to irrelevance. What Europe's constitutional problems required was to be thought about in European terms.

In his devotion to the system of balances, Adams reflected the fear of the despoiling propensities of the multitude aroused in American Whiggery by disturbances like Shays' Rebellion. The shattering finality with which the American middle classes had got out from under their "old regime" produced two observable effects on Adams, both decisive for their impact on his response to Europe's revolutions: his dislike of the feudal subordinations never acquired crusading intensity, and he was exposed all the more completely to fears about the danger of an unruly populace. In the theory of the balance Adams produced a tour de force transformation of industrious, property-minded American mechanics and farmers into the Athenian mob or the Roman proletariat against whom he sought securities in institutional surrogates for aristocracy and monarchy.

Curious results ensued when Adams transferred his absence of passion against feudal privilege and his preoccupation with the mob to the consideration of European political problems. Although his indignation against the "twin tyrannies" had been fiercely expressed during the Stamp Act controversies, he showed no wish to see them destroyed when he encountered them in the flesh in

Europe. Far from showing implacable hostility, he produced extenuations of the characteristic institutions of the old order. He was conspicuously silent on the matter of privilege, the major object of the Third Estate's animosity. Indeed Adams' constitutional solution would have rendered the privileges invulnerable and given them a fresh moral sanction. Without in the least manifesting Burkean reverence for institutions inherited from the age of chivalry, he found a political use in their preservation. He did not love them for their own sake, but he was convinced that untold horrors would follow if they were displaced. In his mind they assumed the guise of indispensable bulwarks of order and stability in Europe. In his advice to the foreign liberals Adams was insistent on the necessity to compromise with the old regime and to avoid frontal assault upon it. Steps toward increased "liberality" must be taken without exciting and unleashing the multitude.

Although he genuinely desired some reforms, Adams viewed the problems of renovation of Europe's political order from an entirely different vantage point than Europe's liberals. Socially of the Third Estate himself, he never entered into the feelings and shared the passions of Europe's middle classes. He had not been smothered by the incubus of a class exclusivism that denied equality before the law and the career open to talents. He was, therefore, free of class hatreds directed toward the rich and noble — a fortunate circumstance, but not one conducive to understanding the different historical fate of other peoples.

Adams wanted the European liberals to respond as if the main danger they faced came from the mob, but the strategic situation of Europe's middle classes did not correspond to that of the American. Europe's middle classes still had their initial victories over feudal subordinations to win; the hatred of privilege took precedence in their minds over fear of the people. To break the hold of aristocracy, they had to rally the masses and bring them into the political struggle. Where they failed to do so, they were put down easily by their enemies, as the Dutch Patriot experience showed. Had the French middle classes shown the caution which Adams required of them in 1789, they would have had to knuckle under to the upper orders. By struggling boldly instead for their own emancipation, they became the means for the release from bondage of others; in a great moment of history that is their glory, they brought forward new conceptions of political justice and became more than conspirators for a narrow class advantage.

The National Assembly's sweeping assertions on behalf of equality in 1789 worried Adams as much as its repudiation of balanced government. He lectured the leaders of the Third Estate severely about the impiety of seeking to abolish all distinctions. They were to understand that equality before the law, equality of rights and duties, was all that could be properly read into the revolutionary catchword. They must avoid talking about equality in such broad unconfined terms as would give encouragement to demands of levelers for equality of persons and property.

The French middle classes, however, exposed unlike Adams to the feudal ethos, were actually less egalitarian than he was. It was no part of their intention to do away with all social distinctions. If they did not take more forthright steps to discountenance possible misconceptions of equality in 1789, it was because they needed the people. The insurrectionary populace of Paris and the peasantry proved invaluable allies in destroying feudal privilege and cementing the rule of the bourgeoisie. The revolutionary middle classes were quite clear about the inequalities which they found intolerable. It was "unmeaning" distinctions of hereditary rank, and the perquisites which went with them, that they wished to destroy. Equality before the law and the career open to talents were for them as much as Adams the true substance of equality.

Before the Revolution Adams expressed hope that these values might ultimately prevail in Europe. But he was not prepared for the explosive effects of their assertion in a world riddled with class exclusivism. The equality of condition which Americans had received as a portion from their ancestors had rendered social revolution unnecessary in his own country. Agitations like that of Daniel Shays, furthermore, had aroused his fears of social radicalism. Frenchmen who desired to establish no more than equality of condition in his own sense came to assume the shape of dangerous social levelers in his mind. The simplifications of his social analysis contributed to this result. Without the need to worry about hereditary upper orders, he concentrated his attention on a presumed universal struggle between the propertied few and the propertyless many, mirroring a fear that arose out of the special circumstances of American Whig liberalism. Applied to Europe, his class analysis produced distortions, because it left out a whole dimension of social conflict without parallel in his own country. What was essentially a middle class struggle against the upper orders, with the assistance of the lower classes, was abstracted into a conflict between the few and the many. A comedy of mistaken identities ensued in which the leaders of the Third Estate, his own social counterpart in Europe, were transformed into followers of Wat Tyler and Daniel Shays. The men who later in the revolutionary decade ruthlessly suppressed the Conspiracy of Equals were treated by him as if they were potential or actual Babouvists.

Despite disagreements on many particulars which reflected the different strategic requirements of liberalism on the two continents, Adams' relations with European liberals were most comfortable in the period before they took the road of revolutionary action and while their liberalism chiefly manifested itself in fervent support of the American Revolution. If Adams found the foreign liberals bearable, despite their errors, before 1789, it was because they seemed to reflect an American image: of all Europeans in those years they were the ones most passionately devoted to America and its cause. When the French liberals turned from glorification of the "spirit of 1776" to what they conceived to be its application in their own country, Adams rapidly disclaimed identity with them.

Adams was not a reactionary, despite the apparent similarity of many of his strictures on the foreign revolutions with those of the Reaction; he developed a fierce hatred of the Reaction when it gained political mastery in Europe after 1815. He never denied the right of revolution; he was deeply committed to all the liberal values — equality of rights, free speech and press, toleration, elective institutions — for which the French bourgeoisie was struggling. The difficulty was that though he willed the liberal ends, he was unwilling to accept the means which appeared to be entailed in their realization in Europe. He pronounced anathema upon persons who in the name of liberty engaged in regicide, violated churches, confiscated property, applied the terror, and drove thousands into exile.

In assessing the revolutionary performance of foreign liberals, Adams forgot that all the world was not America. If there must be revolution abroad, he required in effect that it be conducted in the American style. He demanded the orderliness and sobriety, the avoidance of undue breaches of continuity, presumably exhibited by the Americans. He had himself pointed out that Americans had received their liberties as an inheritance from their ancestors and that the American Revolution was designed to repel innovations rather than to make them on a wholesale scale. These observations clearly implied that the Americans, if revolutionary in 1776, had been so in a special and limited sense. As Condorcet noted in a telling passage in his most famous work, the Americans unlike the French had not been required to change every social relation. Adams did not hesitate, however, to apply standards derived from an American example to the sterner necessities of less favored lands. He claimed for the American Revolution the prestige of being the genuine article, while at the same time asserting for it a unique respectability.

Adams denounced the execution of Louis XVI by the French revolutionaries as the disgrace of liberty, but the Americans had never had to destroy monarchy by outrage upon the person of a king. The Americans established republicanism by renouncing allegiance to King George. They explained why they considered themselves absolved from obedience in a long bill of particulars. They invoked the argument of the traditional theory of resistance which in other nations justified deposition of an unlawful sovereign. Adams himself spoke flamboyantly of the killing of an unjust king as no more reprehensible than destruction of an insect. But in America this violent language remained rhetoric; it never had to be translated into action. The Americans could have the luxury of talking like revolutionaries without having to enact the part.

Adams never had to confront the cruel dilemmas of Condorcet, for example, who, hating capital punishment, had to decide whether to vote for the King's death. The Americans detached themselves from monarchy with ease; no wounds were inflicted on the national psyche in the process. In France shedding of blood seemed required to dispel the sanctity which hedged a king, to reduce him to the status of mere citizen. Moralistic condemnation of revolutionaries who did not behave as decently and soberly as the Americans reflected inability to enter into the horrors and exaltations of a truly revolutionary experience.

Adams was outraged by the militant anticlericalism of the French revolutionaries, although he himself was accustomed to speak of the Catholic Church in terms as scurrilous as any Voltairean rationalist used. He was provoked into fervent anti-Jacobinism by actions which appeared to be based on convictions akin to his own often repeated one that a free government could not possibly coexist with the Roman Catholic religion. But the American liberals had not found it necessary to make war upon an established church to implement their values of religious toleration and separation of church and state. In several American states the clergy were zealots for liberty and major spokesmen of the revolutionary cause. There was no problem of a church with secular privileges, a church which was itself one of the upper orders. Adams appeared to expect from the foreign liberals the relatively benign conduct toward the churches exhibited by the Americans; he did not allow for Europe's difficulties in implementing the ideal of religious freedom, difficulties without parallel in American experience.

One of Adams' major reactions to the violence of the French Revolution was to deplore the "precipitation and temerity" of the foreign liberals. They had departed foolishly from moderate courses and by unnecessarily pressing the pace of change reversed many desirable trends. "The public mind was improving in knowledge and the public heart in humanity, equity, and benevolence; the fragments of feudality, the inquisition, the rack, the cruelty of punishments, Negro slavery were giving way. But the philosophers must arrive at perfection per saltum. Ten times more furious than Jack in the Tale of a Tub, they rent and tore the whole garment to pieces and left not one whole thread in it." [8] But he ignored the fact that on the central questions at stake in Europe, the aristocracies and their constituted bodies were not giving way. Even the modicum of change which the Dutch Patriots tried to obtain was met with fierce resistance, international intervention, and wholesale proscription of the defeated. The liberalism of a small segment of the nobility has obscured the fact that the great majority were not surrendering with quiet resignation, but were attempting to reinforce their privileges. Where their position was deteriorating, as in France, they were seeking a remedy by drawing the circle of class exclusivism more tightly. They succeeded in stultifying Turgot's effort at reform without revolution. Calonne's attempt to revive Turgot's reforms was met by full-scale aristocratic reaction.

Adams was entirely correct that many changes would have been possible in France without revolution; all classes were, for example, in agreement about the restoration of representative institutions. But on the matter of privilege, which was the focal point of contention in 1789, surrender not compromise was possible for the Third Estate. Never having experienced the class humiliations inspired by the feudal subordinations, Adams found less difficulty in counseling moderation about revolting against them. He never fully grasped the social issue which was at the bottom of Europe's disquiets.

Adams' response to the French Revolution affords one

of the first major examples of a persistent American difficulty, arising out of the special nature of the American revolutionary experience, in comprehending foreign revolutionary movements. Adams' own revolution had been little concerned with making sweeping social reforms. Its main energies had been devoted to removing an alien force conceived to weigh heavily upon an existing social structure that was considered in its main outlines to be entirely satisfactory. There was no counterpart in the American experience to revolutions aiming not merely at removal of political tyranny but at conscious reordering of society.[9]

Analysis of American Society

Adams' denial and affirmation of the relevance of American experience to Europe are paralleled by similar contradictory perspectives on the applicability of European experience to America. The latter duality, as much as the former, has had a continuing life in American political thinking. In his own lifetime Adams' assumption of the essential identity of political phenomena in America and Europe was met by Jefferson's rejoinder that inferences derived from European example had no necessary application to America. "Before the establishment of the American States, nothing was known to history but the man of the old world." [10] In the constitutional conventions of the 1820's advocates and opponents of the extension of the suffrage differed about the force of arguments based upon analogies to Europe. In the twentieth century democratic radicals and Whig liberals have reversed positions. The former have been tempted to emphasize the similarities between American and European experience in arguing the case for social or economic reform, while the latter have identified departures from the status quo with Europeanization of American political life.

When occupied at home in repelling parliamentary encroachments or abroad in interpreting his nation's purposes and achievements, Adams produced a picture of a benign and smiling American social landscape. Long before Tocqueville propagated the idea, Adams set forth his version of the proposition that the Americans differed from the Europeans in having been "born equal." In the *Dissertation on the Canon and Feudal Law,* his literary contribution to the resistance to the Stamp Act, Adams sought to convict Parliament of innovation upon settled institutions. He made his case in the terms of an original American purity now threatened by the introduction of European contaminations. In Europe institutions derived from the feudal past still held men in bondage. Americans, however, enjoyed an unparalleled degree of liberty as a portion from their seventeenth century ancestors who had detached themselves from Europe in revulsion against its clerical and feudal subordinations.[11]

In delineating the distinguishing features of the American social world to Europeans, Adams dwelt upon the high degree of equality of condition realized in America and the easier circumstances of its common people. Those "lofty subordinations" that in Europe placed the majority of men in a state of dependence upon the few had never taken root in the United States. Social distance between commoner and gentleman was not great enough to support a "spirit of pretension" among the few. No great church dignitaries victimized and intimidated the population; instead the entire clergy sprang from the people and were devoted to liberty. Some degree of education was possessed by all, not excluding "tradesmen, husbandmen, and laborers." The tax burden fell most heavily upon the "rich and higher classes." Property was not only widely distributed, but circulated rapidly in the absence of any considerable number of great estates that descended within the same families over generations.[12] If there were property qualifications for holding office, these were low enough so that multitudes were eligible. Above all, the Americans, a nation of proprietors, actual or would-be, were spared the presence of a proletariat. The people were not agglomerated in masses in the towns but thinly spread out over extensive territories. They were not easily excited to tumultuous commotion. During the War of Independence Adams stressed for the benefit of nervous European conservatives that "there has been more of . . . tranquillity and contentment, and fewer riots, insurrections, and seditions throughout the whole war, and in the periods of its greatest distress, than there was for seven years before the war broke out."[13]

To turn to the political theory which he elaborated in the last years of his European residence in order to answer French liberalism's attacks on government by balanced powers is to confront a remarkable alteration of emphasis. Adams rested his case not on the indigenous features of American life but on presumed analogies between America and Europe. The contradiction between America and Europe was dissolved again, but this time by imposing Europe upon America. Adams ceased to make the point that "the situation of our country is not like that of most of the nations in Europe"[14] and asserted instead that "we are like other men."[15] American advantages over Europe, it appeared, were chiefly geographical. "I see very little moral or political preference."[16]

In the pages of Adams' *Defence* one will seek in vain for the common man whose integrity, perseverance, and superior understanding enabled America to weather the storms of revolution. Adams has given us instead a portrait of people who have assumed the features of the sanguinary propertyless masses of Europe. Gone was the notion that with property ownership in the hands of the many, an unusual degree of confidence might be safely reposed in them; instead it was urged that even in the United States universal suffrage was unthinkable because it would mean that the poor would turn the propertied out of their houses. The emphasis on American exemption from feudal and clerical subordinations and consequent equality of condition was replaced by the assertion that all societies without exception had nobilities, whether marked out by hereditary legal distinctions or not. The gentlemen in the United States who were formerly without lofty pretensions were translated into relentless conspirators against the rights of the multitude. The same commentator who had made the pregnant social observation that General Washington elsewhere would have become a Caesar or Cromwell now discerned a uniform tendency on the part of society's pre-eminent figures to emerge as demagogues or tyrants.

In the world of the *Defence* the relativist perspective has become blurred, and discrimination of national differences has given way to an analysis of society and of political man couched in terms of universals. Not only was human nature the same in America as elsewhere, but the manifestations of that human nature in politics could be expected to be the same. All societies exhibited a similar differentiation into the one, the few, and the many. The natural tendency of each constituent social element, moreover, was to tyrannize without limit over the others. The struggle between the few and the many could be expected to assume furious intensity, with each pursuing its own interests with an exclusive single-minded class passion. The few eternally made war upon the great man who inevitably rose out of their ranks because they could not bear to acknowledge the superiority of one of their own number. When given their way, the few reduced the many to abjection and misery, and established a cruel aristocratic domination. When the many gained the upper hand, they attacked the property of the rich, being unable to accept or understand that the rich should have privileges from which they themselves were excluded. In their wish to thwart the gentlemen, the multitude repeatedly made common cause with the "one," enabling him to become a despot.

Because the passions expanded without limitation, and reason and conscience were frail reliances, there could be no effectual checks to men's power drives except those interposed by the external impediment of conflicting wills. The only remedy which could preserve both liberty and social peace was government by balanced powers. The function of the threefold participation in the legislative process was to tame the passions and produce social reconciliation. If men knew that their encroachments would meet a check, they would in the end learn to respect one another's rights. In Adams' thinking the right constitutional forms in the long run transform human nature itself. Faith in the efficacy of political mechanics has rarely been carried so far.

Adams represented his social analysis and political psychology as applicable in all times and places, but there is little difficulty in deciding that his conceptions bore a far closer resemblance to European than to American social circumstances. Adams' formal political theory in the *Defence* is in fact a projection of an image of Europe, itself drastically simplified, upon America. For the empirical evidence to support his universals Adams relied almost entirely upon European political experience. Considering the length of the *Defence* and its purpose to explain the necessity of the balance in the United States, it is noteworthy how little citation of American example occurs in the work. The longest passages dealing with American conditions were designed to minimize the special character of the American social order, by demonstrating that the same cleavage between the few and the many was found in America as elsewhere. The ferocious struggles of patrician and plebeian in the ancient and medieval city-states were rehearsed exhaustively as proof of the horrid consequences of unbalanced constitutions. But the relevance to American conditions of these elaborate historical parallels was assumed rather than demonstrated, although on the rare occasions when he confronted the problem of his reliance on historical analogies Adams saw some of the difficulties in their use clearly enough.

The duality that appears in Adams' accounts of American society raises the problem of his vaunted realism. Is it in universalist theses about man and society — as expressed in the theory of the balance — or in comparative perspectives on the differences between American and European circumstances that he approached more closely to American reality? Progressive historians like Beard and Parrington or a Marxist like Harold Laski (for whom Adams is the most important American political thinker) admired the universalist side of Adams, largely because they found in it a tendency parallel to their own to interpret American development in terms of European patterns of social struggle. The universalist Adams, however, lost sight of the true balancing forces in American society, while relying instead for order and stability on elaborate constitutional mechanics. The relativist Adams rightly sought the sources of American liberty and social peace in historical factors like the exemption from feudalism, in social factors like the absence of sharply drawn class lines, in ideological factors like the basic consensus centering on Whig principles in politics and Protestant ideas in religion.

The universalist Adams was obsessed with a constitutional remedy that would in effect organize deadlock into the machinery of government in all but the most unified societies. He would forestall class oppression by requiring the consent to legislation of all major social elements. But he overlooked entirely the mischief which might result from government inertia in societies where privilege was entrenched. His system of balanced powers could not possibly have worked if the few and the many in America were at one another's throats and if Americans were so full of the insatiable power drives he postulated in his psychology. The complicated organization of public powers that Adams desired could be adopted and perpetuated in America only because his social and psychological universals failed to describe America accurately. It was pure illusion to think that merely mechanical balances could contain urges to domineer as implacable and social conflicts as ferocious as those summoned up in the *Defence*.

In view of the universalist nature of Adams' formal theory of politics, it is all the more surprising that in recent years a group of new conservatives has perceived Burkean virtues in Adams' thought, one of them going so far as to celebrate the *Defence* as a masterpiece of Burkean conservatism.[17] It is doubtful that Adams himself would have been flattered by the coupling of his name with Burke's, especially if any implication of discipleship were intended. To the contrary, he maintained seriously that whatever was of value in Burke's thinking had been derived from his own ideas. Despite his opposition to the French Revolution his immediate feelings about Burke's *Reflections* were reserved and became positively virulent during the period of the Reaction. He lumped Burke with Johnson and Hume as subverters of Whig principles.

Adams never developed, as a Burkean theorist might have been expected to do, a philosophical defense of tradition and prejudice in vindicating the complexity of the American state constitutions. He was not content to argue in relativist terms, such as Burke might have used, that balanced constitutions were defensible simply as the ones most appropriate to American circumstances. Had he done so, he might have avoided his major mistake in respect to Europe, which consisted in imposing the balance in a most doctrinaire way as a solution applicable to societies very different from his own, and his major mistake in respect to America, that of blacking out his own clear-sighted awareness of the special features of American society. His theory of the balance was constructed in universalist terms on mechanistic analogies drawn from Newtonian physics, from which nothing could have been further away than the organicism of Burke. The central direction of Burke's political philosophy was profoundly incompatible with the abstract universalist style of thought about man and society cultivated by Adams. For Burke, the essence of wisdom was the recognition, above all, that in politics nothing universal could be safely affirmed.

Considered in its application to American social circumstances, the political theory of the *Defence* contains large elements of fantasy. What it embodies is less a description of American social facts than a nightmare vision of the potential for disorder that Adams feared was only too likely to prove endemic in a society with wholly popular institutions. As Adams was nervously aware and amply documented in the *Defence,* all previous trials of republican systems in Western history had been scarred by protracted and hideous civil wars, most frequently ending in the establishment of absolute despotism. In the United States the people possessed a degree of control over their government without parallel even in the ancient democracies. Where the populace was in a position to change everything, European example seemed to suggest that they had usually been disposed to do so.

Adams was haunted by the possibility of mass upheavals in a system which placed so few obstacles in the path of the popular will. During his years abroad a variety of manifestations at home which appeared to threaten order, decency, and the sanctity of property helped give credence to his fears. Too many in the United States in his judgment panted after equality of persons and property. Movements in favor of debtors had sprung up; attempts had been made to pass stay laws and to close the courts to prevent execution of judgments in favor of creditors. Disrespect for learning had taken the form of bigoted refusals to pay taxes in support of public education; there had been expressions of violent antagonism to lawyers and repudiation by religious enthusiasts of the need for an educated clergy. Several of these tendencies had reached fruition in the insurrection of Daniel Shays. In his native state demands for the abolition of senate and governor even appeared to threaten Adams' own handiwork, the constitution of 1780.[18]

The special circumstances of American liberalism provided the framework of preoccupation within which Adams interpreted these expressions of radical democracy. In the United States the middle classes had never needed to wage a massive struggle against entrenched feudal and clerical privilege. In its social aspect, the

American Revolution was largely a mopping-up operation against remaining feudal vestiges. The very ease and completeness of American liberalism's triumph, however, proved capable of inspiring its own peculiar anxieties. Hereditary institutions might weigh heavily upon the middle classes in Europe, but they could be regarded also as providing indispensable guarantees of order and subordination. With the antagonist from above simply obliterated, Whig liberals in America felt disarmed, conscious of the absence of sheltering bulwarks against eruptions from below. Without the anchors of safety provided by monarchical and aristocratic institutions, American society appeared cast adrift on a wild and turbulent democratic sea.

From this point of view the intensity of Adams' interest in the system of balances may be explained as an effort to find effective substitutes for the missing anchors. Although in the partisan struggles of the 1790's he was accused of advocating the introduction of monarchy and aristocracy, it was equivalents, not the institutions themselves, that he was seeking. If his relativism reflected estrangement from Europe, his preoccupation with the balance expressed a political nostalgia for the European-style securities not available to a society that had never known the feudal and the canon law. The wish not to cut loose completely from Europe found its source ironically in a distrust of the adequacy of those securities which his relativist perspective had designated as the peculiar resource of a congenitally republican society. In the terms of the anatomy of revolution, the *Defence* may be said to represent an effort to bring back the "old regime," although in the liberal guise alone possible in the United States, and Adams can be viewed as the political theorist of an American "restoration."

CHAPTER TWO

CORRECT PRINCIPLES OF POLITICAL ARCHITECTURE

*O*N THE EVE of revolutionary events that would transform the entire Atlantic community, a polemical exchange between Adams and the Turgot circle revealed the existence of a deep gulf of perspective and ideas between American and French liberalism. The encounter sharpened the awareness on both sides of differences that would prove persistent, despite a shared commitment to liberal values. The cleavage centered on constitutional ideas, but a clash was visible, in however fragmentary fashion, on economic and religious issues as well. Interchange of views generated a mutual incomprehension, exhibiting indeed some of the elements of high comedy and illustrating well the observation of Maurice Cranston that "liberals have sometimes been painfully surprised to find how little they have had in common with foreign gentlemen to whom they have been introduced as fellow liberals." [1]

The gap in constitutional ideas between Adams and Turgot and his followers cannot validly be explained as the product of the clarity of the one and the illusions of the other about the dangerous corrupting effects of absolute power. Given the nature of their aims, the French liberals were realistic enough — despite their metaphysical and abstract method — in assessing the situation which their nation faced and the requirements for dealing with it. One of their number, Condorcet, was sharp enough also in exposing the potential for inertia and deadlock inherent in his opponent's conception and the oligarchy it could conceal.

The conflict more simply reflected the divergent strategic situations of the two liberalisms. The formative experience of revolution gave a direction to the entire course of liberal thinking about political institutions in each country. The bias toward a divided sovereign displayed by Adams and toward centralization by Turgot and Condorcet were rooted in the differing requirements of the struggle for liberty in each country. In America the revolutionary spirit rose out of resistance to a centralizing tendency, out of a denial of the absolute claims to legislative supremacy made on behalf of Parliament. In France, on the contrary, revolution originated out of the effort to overcome the obstacles to emancipation of the individual from what were increasingly regarded as the intolerable restraints of a traditional corporate society. Distinctive liberal attitudes to the sovereign power inevitably emerged in the two countries.

Each party to the controversy committed the same error in prescribing for the situation of the other a constitutional remedy too exclusively drawn from a merely partial experience. Thus Turgot and Condorcet presumed to give advice to the Americans about their political institutions, although the character of the advice indicated that in their minds and hearts they had never for an instant left home. They accused the Americans of imitating the

English model, which they were very much interested in discrediting as possibly applicable to their own country, without seeming to understand that English example had been thoroughly assimilated into American experience by one hundred and fifty years of practice. They were nervously aware of the barriers to reform that a system of balanced powers could offer in a society riddled with legalized inequalities, but they failed to take into account that in the atmosphere of social equality prevailing in America, such a system would not have the reactionary implications they feared in their own country. Given the American social order, "balance" meant sharing of the sovereignty by different branches of government rather than by different hereditary status groups. Condorcet and Turgot did not admit the possibility that compositive government might suit a country not faced by the unresolved conflicts of France.

When it came to giving advice to the French about the renovation of their political order, Adams performed essentially the same operation in reverse as Turgot and Condorcet. He appeared unaware of the difficulties that his constitutional conceptions would create in a society struggling to surmount the feudal inheritance and create the social basis for liberal institutions. Failing to see that the system of balanced powers could give permanent securities against attack to interests already in possession of major privileges, he was vulnerable to Jefferson's forceful criticism that "mischief may be done negatively as well as positively." [2]

The tendency of both Adams and the Turgot circle to transfer their constitutional ideas without sufficient discrimination to the situations of other countries is traceable in part to their abstract and rationalist method. Invoking reason and nature, both universalized their constitutional preferences, representing them as "correct principles of political architecture" and claiming for them a validity akin to a mathematical demonstration. Neither proved capable of arriving at the conception of the merely conditional value of political machinery, an insight already brought forward by Montesquieu. Unlike Adams, Montesquieu, while finding the English constitution wholly admirable, specifically disclaimed that it embodied a generally desirable set of political forms for all of Europe.

The Battle Joined: Preliminary Issues

Adams may have become ultimately the most learned American of his generation in the writings of the French *philosophes*, but before he went abroad in February 1778, the liberal and reform ideas of the French Enlightenment had exerted minimum influence, whether by attraction or repulsion, on his mind. Pre-eminent in the arts and sciences, the arbiter of taste for all of Europe, France yet signified for him both in politics and religion not "liberality" but servitude. The existence of French liberalism, in all its boldness and variety, was a discovery made only when he took up residence in that country.

Within a few months of his landing in Europe, Adams, through Franklin's good offices, had met a number of France's intellectual luminaries.[3] That these "men of profound science" were preoccupied with speculation upon the first principles of politics and society came as a distinct shock to his preconceptions. Their attachment to the American cause immediately forged a common bond. For them the American Revolution appeared as nothing less than a turning point in the history of the human race. They were stirred to special excitement by the new American state constitutions. Something in the atmosphere of France made it electrifying to see another nation repudi-

ate its ancestral government and reconstitute itself by action of conventions subsequently ratified by the people.
The entire process aroused the hope that unsatisfactory
governments elsewhere might be remodeled by deliberate
choice and planning.[4]

When it came to the specific content of American political institutions, reactions were mixed.[5] Turgot and the
members of his circle were frankly disturbed at some features of these constitutions, especially the division of the
sovereignty among balanced powers to be found in all but
the constitution of Pennsylvania. The preliminary step in
what developed into an "international dialogue" between
French and American liberalism was taken by Turgot
himself, who wrote a letter to Richard Price in 1778 re-
cording his disappointment. This letter was published by
Price in 1785 after Turgot's death. Adams received a copy
from Price, which he proceeded to annotate in detail.
These annotations together with the three volumes of
the *Defence of the Constitutions of Government of the
United States of America* (1787–88) constitute Adams'
most sustained response to the political ideas of the
French Enlightenment. Adams in turn was answered in
a number of pamphlets written by members of Turgot's
circle, most notably Condorcet.

This interchange in the prerevolutionary decade was
conducted amicably for the most part as between friends
of liberty. Turgot's followers did not cease to praise
Adams as one who had showed "intrepidity and grandeur
of soul" in the first days of the American Revolution,
their attacks on his advocacy of government by balanced
powers notwithstanding.[6] Adams for his part — although
grace in turning a compliment was not one of his strongest points — paused in the midst of the labors of rebuttal
to salute Turgot as, unlike the "detestable Hume," a "lover

of liberty," and entirely well-intentioned in his interest in the United States, even if some of his opinions could not be reconciled with reason and the constitution of human nature.[7]

Turgot believed that the Americans had made mistakes in religious and economic policy, as well as in erecting a system of balanced powers, and in not providing sufficiently for a firm union of the several states. Each of his criticisms, while directed ostensibly at American arrangements, demonstrated his involvement with the issue of reform in France. He deplored that some states gave recognition to particular religious denominations and exacted tests for office. His complaint that a few even prohibited clergymen from standing for public office revealed his special awareness of the gulf between the position of the church in America and Europe. Americans failed to understand that the clergy were only dangerous when they were organized as a separate corporate body, thought of themselves as possessing special rights and interests, and presided over an official religion established by law. In presuming to regulate foreign and domestic commerce in detail, the Americans were as yet "far from realizing that the law of complete freedom of commerce is the corollary of the right to property." The passionate economic dogmatism aroused in Turgot by the impediments to the spirit of enterprise still prevalent in his own country was affronted by the makeshift, pragmatic character of American economic policy. The provisions for "coalition" among the states gave too little recognition of the need for a "fusion of all the parts to form a homogeneous body." [8] If Turgot was worried that the Americans gave too free rein to heterogeneity of local and regional interests, it was because he considered that his nation had suffered too long from such discordancies. In voicing a demand for centralization and the uniform principles of administration it would make possible, he was concerned with France, a composite but not unified country, pieced together over centuries by the reunion of detached areas and bedeviled still by internal customs barriers, provincial privileges, and an incredibly rich confusion of legal, administrative, and fiscal practice.

Adams appeared to agree fully with the general principles of Turgot's religious liberalism. "This enmity to test has my most hearty good wishes and prayers. I would try the experiment whether a state can exist without a shadow of a test." Although he was willing to pursue religious toleration even to the point of an entire disestablishment of religion, Adams nevertheless acquiesced easily in the contrary judgment of his fellow citizens. Article III of the Massachusetts constitution of 1780 enjoined the people to church attendance and provided for the use of tax money to support ministers and meeting houses, while allowing the citizen to have his contribution paid to the denomination of his choice. The provision is the most important one in the constitution not written by Adams, for his sentiments on this matter, as he explained, were not in conformity with the prevailing "taste of the public." Despite his preference for a complete separation of church and state, he generated none of Turgot's passion about the issue because in his state the Congregationalist ministry, while enjoying influence and prestige, was not a separate body of men with special corporate rights and privileges. There was not even political capital to be made from pursuing disestablishment in his state as aggressively as Jefferson had done in Virginia. The dominant church in Massachusetts was not tainted by association with loyalism. To the contrary, it was the loyalist Daniel Leonard who before the Revolution was "seized with a violent fit of anger at the clergy," while Adams, in the *Novanglus*, lauded the great majority of the ministers for preaching Christianity and informing the people they were not bound to submit to officials aiming at destruction of the ends of government.[9]

As late as the convention of 1820, held in Massachusetts to revise the constitution, Adams, who was a delegate, was uncertain about how he should vote on the issue of disestablishment. "An abolition of this law would have so great an effect in this State that it seems hazardous to touch it." Adams shared Turgot's devotion to liberty of conscience. "The rights of conscience are original rights and cannot be alienated." [10] But he was not aroused to do battle in their name against the historic privileges of an ancient church.

Adams, who confronted in his own country nothing like the restrictionism endemic in the French economy, would have none of Turgot's sweeping assertions in favor of laissez-faire. They impressed him as the product of a "headlong spirit of system and enthusiasm" and demonstrated that Turgot, for all his learning, was not a "judicious, practical statesman." While sharing, in general, Turgot's commitment to the removal of obstacles to freedom of enterprise, Adams found the great reformer's affirmation of his economic principles too unqualified and made without appropriate attention to circumstances. Agreeing entirely with Turgot about the sanctity of property rights, he was not willing to derive from them such stringent limitations on the scope of government.

The right of property is here carried a great length. It might as well be said that any exemption from taxes is a corollary from the right of property. Can we say that government had no right to regulate the commerce of individuals? Americans are, no doubt, involved in the mist of many European illusions; but I am not clear that this is so universally an illusion. An enemy to embargoes, prohibitions, exclusions, etc., in general, I cannot swear that they are always unlawful or impolitic.[11]

The appearance of doctrinaire antagonism to government activity in economic life was reserved for a later era of American development.

Although Adams again agreed with Turgot that a more perfect union among the states was desirable than that provided by the Articles of Confederation, he showed none of Turgot's passion for administrative centralization and imposition of uniformity upon the separate parts. He was willing to concede far more scope to regional particularisms than Turgot. They had not prevented joint action on issues of common concern in America. He had no acute sense of grievance about the matter. Union through creation of a composite of the several parts was the road he envisaged rather than through a dissolution or obliteration of them. "Americans must consider more soberly than Mr. Turgot did what is practicable and what is not. One homogeneous body cannot be made out of such heterogeneous parts scattered over such an immense continent. The parts are too distant as well as unlike."[12]

In the letter to Price, Turgot revealed himself as still an adherent of enlightened despotism as the best system for France. Adams could not resist the temptation to strike a blow against the unaccountable advocacy of absolutism by a writer so justly famous for his devotion to economic and religious liberty. A monarchy tempered by representative institutions, he pointed out, must possess great advantages over any simple monarchy. A senate, consisting of all that was "most noble, wealthy, and able" in the nation, with the right to counsel the Crown and to check ministers, was a security against abuses which a body of nobles who never met could not supply. Another assembly consisting of representatives chosen by the people would enable the communication of "all its wants, knowledge, projects, and wishes" to the prince.[13]

Adams was certainly correct in noting that Turgot, despite his economic and religious liberalism, did not grasp the virtues of free government. His own understanding of it was far surer, as he showed in emphasizing the necessity of "free communication" between government and subjects, if the subjects were to be secure against being "ridden like horses, and fleeced like sheep." Nevertheless Adams' reaction showed little comprehension of the functional imperatives which impelled Turgot to place his reliance on the enlightened despot. Turgot looked to the monarchy to exercise guardianship over the interests of peasantry and bourgeoisie and to implement liberal reforms in the face of the opposition of the privileged classes.

Even without political rights the "most noble" citizens in France had proved capable of stultifying reform. In advocating for France, as an alternative to simple monarchy, a system in which such persons advised the Crown and checked its ministers, Adams was intruding himself, with monumental innocence, into French politics, where in the eighteenth century two tendencies were in bitter opposition. Proponents of the *thèse royale* wished to strengthen monarchy and to annihilate intermediary bodies; advocates of the *thèse nobiliaire* proposed to limit the sovereignty of the king and give greater recognition to the autonomy of these bodies.[14] In France liberal reformers like Turgot necessarily desired enhancement of royal power. In England and the United States, on the other hand, liberalism traditionally meant support of intermediary bodies against monarchical centralization. Adams applied the Anglo-American pattern to France, where its implications were entirely different, and made it the universal form of the struggle for liberty. In America Montesquieu's defense of mixed government and separation of powers inspired admiration, because it confirmed existing prejudices against unified sovereignties; in France the liberals viewed the *Esprit des Lois* with misgivings as part of a reactionary trend in their country's politics.

"We Are Like Other Men"

To most of Turgot's censures Adams was content to reply in comments scrawled on the margins of his copy of the letter to Price. But one criticism briefly sketched by Turgot provoked an answer stretching into three volumes. Turgot was upset that the Americans who had given an example to the world in throwing off the British yoke were still enslaved to the mythical superiorities of the British constitution. Although the circumstances of Britain and America were utterly different, the revolutionary state constitutions established balanced governments on the English model. The tripartite division of powers in the English constitution was the result of historical factors from whose operation America happily had been spared. In America there was no hierarchy of ranks and orders, nor was there any necessity to create barriers against the power of a hereditary executive. Turgot professed bewilderment that in a new country where the possibility existed that constitutions according to nature could be constructed, the inhabitants had unaccountably followed the dictates of unreasoning prejudice. His preference was for a one-chamber legislature, no upper house, and a carefully restrained executive, such as had been adopted in Pennsylvania presumably under the guidance of the great Franklin.[15]

CORRECT PRINCIPLES

On the eve of the French Revolution Turgot's criticism, fleetingly made in the letter to Price, was taken up and fully elaborated by other members of his circle, notably Condorcet. In a series of polemical works Condorcet reflected the revulsion in France against the English constitution that had replaced the earlier celebration of it in works of Voltaire and Montesquieu. Condorcet urged the lack of utility and danger of dividing the legislative into different bodies and argued instead for a representative system providing for a single assembly dependent on free elections, initiative and referendum on the part of the voters, and a detailed declaration of rights. In his *Lettres d'un Bourgeois de New Haven* (to which Adams at one point meditated replying "at large") Condorcet, without mentioning Adams specifically, tried to rebut the *Defence*. Adams was surprised later that the experience of the French Revolution never persuaded Condorcet of his errors; for Adams the course of the Revolution carried its own confirmation of the necessity for government by equilibrium of forces. Condorcet, however, as late as 1793 stubbornly continued to echo his master in condemning the American constitutions as "tainted with the prejudices that those who drafted them had imbibed in their youth" and impaired "by the determination to preserve a balance of power in the state." [16]

Both Turgot and Condorcet argued that their constitutional preferences alone accorded with the requirements of reason and nature. They couched their demands for a unified sovereignty in the form of reflections on American experiences in state-building, but can anyone doubt that in reality they were exclusively and passionately concerned with the circumstances of France. Like so many of the French liberals who were caught up in the *rêve américain* in the years before the great Revolution, they were not so much devoted to America for itself, a country about which they knew little in any specific detail. The symbolic nature of the liberals' interest showed in their relative indifference to the innumerable errors of fact of which some were guilty and which people like Adams and Jefferson in despair repeatedly called to their attention. America was the mirror in which Turgot and Condorcet reflected their preoccupations with reform at home. Although they talked endlessly of America, their thoughts were entirely engaged with political and social struggles in their own country. They expressed their frustrated impatience with the American legislators, who, free of the restraints of the past, yet failed to recognize that reason and nature demanded unified sovereignties. What they meant to say all along, however, was that without a unified sovereignty social reconstruction in France would be stultified.

Turgot insisted upon the collection of authority into a single center not because he was incurably addicted to abstract metaphysics but because in 1776 he had directly experienced the effects of dispersion of power among several constituted bodies. France in the eighteenth century was more a centralized despotism in name than in actual fact. There were hereditary corporate bodies like the parlements, with important powers increasingly asserted with vigor by a resurgent aristocracy, which verified laws or taxes proposed by the Crown. The opposition of the parlements to his reform measures had forced Turgot from office. As France's comptroller-general, Turgot encountered aristocratic privilege entrenched behind constituted bodies possessing in effect a veto power on state actions. The political principle that Turgot distilled from this experience came to seem self-evident to most of the members of his circle: intermediary bodies provided a haven for particularisms hostile to the general interest. Only a fully centralized and unified power to govern organized by and receiving its sanction from the nation could successfully overcome the partial interests that baffled the general will.

In 1788–89 when Condorcet was writing one pamphlet after another exposing the fallacies of dispersing legislative power, the great question facing the French nation was how to organize the Estates General. Was it to meet and vote as a single body or by estates? Aristocratic and clerical interests that desired the formula of 1614 to prevail were in effect defending the idea of a sovereignty dispersed in several centers. What could be clearer therefore than that the system of balanced powers was a reactionary device which would give aid and comfort to the forces desiring to preserve France's hierarchic and corporate structure of society? Condorcet was compelled to insist that freedom must be organized on quite other principles.

The advocacy of simple constitutions by the French liberals seems best understood as a strategy of reform for a society bedeviled by deeply entrenched particularisms. But Adams can hardly be blamed for taking Turgot and Condorcet at their word when they presumed to give advice to American legislators. He was by no means willing to treat their argument as an elaborate façade behind which lurked an effort to resolve problems internal to France. The French liberals were not content to prescribe for their own country. They insisted upon generalizing their constitutional preferences into a system for which, invoking the sanctions of reason and nature, they claimed universal applicability as the "norm" for free institutions. What fascinated them about America was its freedom from the legalized social inequalities of Europe. America possessed that equality of ranks toward which Europe must move. They denounced checks and balances and wanted a centralized authority that would batter down the walls of hereditary privilege. The needs of their situation led them to the observation, which was certainly sound, that a government by dispersed powers would give special protection and opportunities to partial interests. They thought the Americans wildly irrational to establish political forms which had come into existence in Europe only as a result of the feudal inheritance.

If we turn to his rebuttal, what is most striking at the outset is the strategy of argument that Adams failed to adopt. He might have adapted his opponents' argument to his own purposes and pointed out that precisely because America had no hereditary privileged orders, the system of checks and balances had no such reactionary significance as in Europe. Such a system would not expose an already liberal society to the obstacles it could place in the path of a nation seeking to create the social basis for freedom. In France the balance of powers would counterpoise not merely different interests in opposition on matters of limited significance but interests separated by a gulf of fundamental values. In the United States there was no problem of carrying through a fundamental social reconstruction that would dispossess an entrenched aristocracy and a privileged church. All government officials were recruited from the same body of citizens who overwhelmingly were Whigs in politics and Protestants in religion. Even the American Tories did not really reject Whig principles, and in any case they had been excised from the social body. America could safely work constitutions that gave free rein to particularist interests, because the matters in dispute among her citizens no longer included the fundamental principles of political and social organization.

The line that Adams chose to pursue far from emphasizing American differences from Europe actually under-
played them. Rather than derive his case for the American
approach to sovereignty from American particularity, he
chose to found it on elements presumed to be common to
America and Europe. Instead of pointing out that the balance of powers could not produce the evils about which
the French liberals were apprehensive, Adams performed
the extraordinary operation of engrafting the social conflicts of Europe on American soil. He re-created in the
pages of the *Defence* the ferocious struggles between plebeian and patrician in the Greek city-states, ancient
Rome, and the medieval Italian republics. What sense
could it make to rehearse these horrors at such intermina-
ble length except on the assumption that the lessons to be
derived were directly applicable to American experience?

For the purposes of his argument Adams minimized the
uniqueness of America's social order. Despite American
exemption from the feudal inheritance and the consequent absence of hereditary distinctions, he insisted that
the three orders of king, lords, and commons existed in
reality, if not in name, in America as well as in Europe.
These were natural not artificial distinctions and therefore
not easily exorcised on any soil. The natural and eternal
divisions of society among the one, the few, and the many
were present in America as much as anywhere else. Plebeian and patrician in the United States would in the long
run (and already in the short run if reports from Berk-
shire County could be credited) exhibit the same propensities as their brethren in Europe, unless there was an effective balance in the constitution to restrain them and
compel them to virtue.

Adams has been praised by a few writers for his reminder that "there is no special providence for Americans,
and their nature is the same with that of others." Restored

to its context, the remark appears intended to underscore a conviction of the basic identity of political phenomena in America and Europe rather than to convey a profound religious sense of men as beings with a common destiny all alike under the judgment of God. As a rebuke to the arrogance of Americans it conveys nothing more serious than a warning that if they abolish upper chambers and try to subsist with unicameral legislatures, they must repeat the experience of unlikely places like Venice, Geneva, Biscay, and Poland and end up "in an aristocracy and an oligarchy." [17] On the plane of religious ultimates, the denial of special providence might represent a salutary reminder of the oneness of mankind; failure to acknowledge the possibility, however, that on the merely political level a special providence had been operative in the case of the Americans could spawn its own form of spiritual pride. It might lead to exaggeration by Americans of the element of autonomy in their achievements and engender a condescension that did not allow sufficiently for the difficulties of other nations not favored by special providences.

Turgot argued that it did not make sense for Americans to create constitutions that presupposed a European-style social order. In reply Adams raised American social conflicts to European levels of intensity and irreconcilability and wove a complex network of checks and balances to put them under restraint. Few intellectual encounters between major representatives of different political traditions have been so rich in ironies. The positions of both Turgot and Adams are confounded in separate ways by the fact that the system of balances worked relatively successfully in the United States because the kind of bitter social divisions that Adams postulated to prove the indispensability of his balances never really existed. Turgot urged the powerful unified sovereign in the United States which the absence of the feudal inheritance made unthinkable; Adams argued for a "tamed" sovereign, actually a reflection of American social peace, as a necessity to contain social strife. Turgot proposed for America a solution that fitted French requirements, while at the same time calling attention to the difference in American and French social-historical circumstances. Adams responded by defending a solution highly adapted to America's special situation with an elaborate disproof of American particularity.

In rejoinder to the objection that the Americans unaccountably imitated the English model when they could have chosen any system they wanted, Adams made one of his strongest and most briefly phrased arguments. Although it was true that the revolutionary state constitutions provided for a tripartite legislative along English lines, "It was not so much because the legislature in England consisted of three branches that such a division of power was adopted by the states, as because their own assemblies had ever been so constituted." The most important features of the state constitutions were borrowed from colonial practice, the major change being that the governors were no longer appointed by the Crown. The new constitutions reproduced to a remarkable extent the institutions under which the colonists had lived since the first "plantations." Even the apparent exception, Pennsylvania, confirmed the rule, because this state, the only one that had not known the tripartite legislative in colonial times, established a unicameral legislature.

Americans, then, were not entirely free to do as they pleased in the matter of constitutions. Substantial experience in working a particular set of political institutions had accumulated. Strong attachments to these institutions had grown up with the passage of time. In the absence of any compelling considerations to the contrary, was it not simple wisdom to preserve the inherited forms "rather than to endanger public tranquillity, or unanimity, by renouncing them?" [18] The revolutionary state constitutions were securely founded in the prejudices of the people, who preferred following the paths of their forefathers to making wholesale innovations in their old systems.

A whole world of political philosophy was latent in this particular reply to Turgot, but Adams never summoned that world into being. He was on the threshold of a defense of prejudice as the reason of history. He was close to saying that those constitutional arrangements were best which were most closely adapted to a people's circumstances, which grew organically out of its historical experiences and were most firmly rooted in its habits. If his political actions were governed by these principles, his political theory was grounded in quite different ones. For a moment Adams appears poised on the verge of a historical and organic conservatism such as was marked out by Montesquieu and Burke. Had he taken that road, it would have been much more appropriate for some current writers to salute him as the "American Burke." He might have avoided the excesses of an abstract universalism which assigned an absolute value to a constitutional machinery whose real virtue was its high adaptability to the special circumstances of the American states.

But instead he hurried on to the main body of his argument which was intended to demonstrate that if American constitutions were rooted in American prejudices, these prejudices were also in accord with reason. "It was not so much from attachment by habit to such a plan of power that it was continued, as from conviction that it was founded in nature and reason." [19] When he encountered

48

the fully articulate theory of prescription, prejudice, and tradition in Burke, he did not recognize its applicability as a defense of the American constitutions and tended to distrust the great English conservative as a subverter of true Whig principles. Adams' frame of discourse plainly had much more in common with his adversaries, Turgot and Condorcet, than with Burke.

A "Stupendous Fabric of Human Invention"

Having explained that the American constitutions were founded on long-standing indigenous usages, Adams then proudly acknowledged the resemblances to the English model. Adams was no unmitigated Anglophile, but he approached the English constitution with a reverence not to be outdone by any eighteenth-century Whig. The liberty and prosperity of the English were due to the perfection of the constitution.[20] The American constitutions were by no means exact replicas of the English, the essential difference consisting in not having made their first magistrates and senators hereditary. America's republicanism reflected the fact that the bulk of the landed property in the country was in the hands of the common people. But even as he pointed to the difference, he also depreciated it. In a passage of the kind that lent itself admirably to partisan exploitation in the 1790's as revealing his apostasy from republican principles, he then explained that at some point it might become advisable even in the United States to adopt the hereditary principle.

In future ages, if the present states become great nations, rich, powerful, and luxurious, as well as numerous, their own feelings and good sense will dictate to them what to do; they may make transitions to a nearer resemblance of the British constitution, by a fresh convention, without the small-

est interruption to liberty. But this will never become necessary, until great quantities of property shall get into few
hands.[21]

The criticism to be made of sentiments of this kind is not
so much what was said at the time, that they reflected
desertion of the republican standard, as that they minimized the organic character and special genius of American institutions. The republicanism endemic to the United
States was conceived as merely the peculiarity of a new
country, a difference from Europe likely to prove of passing significance.

Despite his constitution-worship, Adams was painfully
aware of certain English usages considered defective generally by American opinion and by a minority segment of
British opinion. He did not idealize the constitution exactly
as it was, although it must be said that he did not expend
much indignation on its defects. Adams cooled to the
English parliamentary reform movement when it fell into
the hands of leadership seeming to lack the appropriate
reverence for the essential soundness of the constitution
and espousing radical democratic ideas like universal
suffrage. He always acknowledged, however, that certain
improvements were required to counteract venality in
elections and procure a more equitable representation. If
certain constituencies were abolished, and "representatives proportionally and frequently chosen in small dis-
tricts, and if no candidate could be chosen but an established, long-settled inhabitant of that district, it would
be impossible to corrupt the people of England." In addition, the balance of the constitution was disturbed because members of the House of Lords were in a position
to dispose of a number of seats in the lower house. He
did not mention in the *Defence* the distribution of patronage, honors, titles, pensions, and sinecures by the Crown

to secure an amenable parliament. Jefferson, however, reports a conversation in 1791 in which Adams and Hamilton were participants and where the difference of opinion between the two about the results of royal influence was complete, Adams maintaining that if the constitution were purged of its corruption "it would be the most perfect . . . ever devised by the wit of man," and Hamilton echoing Hume's more penetrating view that without a Commons corrupted to the king's will, "it would become an impracticable government." [22]

The views of Condorcet on the nature of the English constitution deserve to be rescued from oblivion and do not by any means suffer by comparison with Adams'. Condorcet did not deny that the English enjoyed liberties beyond that of any nation in Europe. What he asserted was that this liberty was falsely attributed to the balance of the constitution. English liberties in reality were sustained by an "opinion happily united" in respect for matters like freedom of press, habeas corpus, and trial by jury.[23] If this view also begged some questions, especially in saying nothing about what had brought that unity of opinion into being, it was refreshing to see the point emphasized that the values of the community had an essential part in sustaining liberty. The dogmatists of the balance of powers often talked as if liberty was the mechanistically determined result of a stalemate between mutually encroaching interests.

Condorcet seized upon the same usages described by Adams as departures from the balance — the inequitable representation, the support organized by the king's ministers, the control of some seats in the lower house by the Lords — to make the point that the mixed constitution was a façade behind which an oligarchy drawn from the aristocracy ruled the nation. Although in the theory of the constitution the Commons represented the people, in Condorcet's view it really could not do so "because it is an aristocratic assembly which is controlled by forty or fifty ministers, peers, and commoners." Behind the balances of the system lurked the "authority of the rich, the noble, the magistrate, and the priest." According to theory, each power, to defend its own interests, became the defender of liberty against the usurpations of the others. In fact, the natural tendency of the system was toward deadlock. "The machine becomes so complicated that its actions are clogged." The result was that "alongside the legally established system there arises another one based on intrigue, corruption, and indifference. In a sense there are now two constitutions; one, public and legal, that exists in law books only; and another one, secret but real, which is the outcome of a silent understanding among the powers that be." The real constitution was to be found in such features as parliamentary corruption, which must be understood not as an excrescence but as essential to the working of the system. Given the separation between legislative and executive, the problem was to make them act together. In order to have parliament do his bidding, the king, through his ministers, used bribery and patronage to influence votes of the members. Condorcet even grasped that the English were, as came to be said later, a deferential nation, although he referred to the trait, which he despised in violently derogatory terms, as "a servile worship of . . . principles, which are in the interests of the rich and the powerful." [24]

In the textbooks of political theory Adams has always been represented as the realist and Condorcet as the prototype of the utopian ideologue. But the contrast between them is less starkly simple than that. Condorcet was intensely concerned as a supporter of the Third Estate to discredit the theory of the balance because he believed that applied in France it would fortify hereditary privilege. Given this animus, he was especially alert to the "ideological taint" in the theory and concerned to expose aristocratic predominance as the central trait of the English constitution. His awareness of the gap between the theory of that constitution and its actual workings led him to formulate a distinction between the legal and real constitution, a strikingly keen insight of permanent usefulness in the analysis of political systems.

In relation to the British constitution it was Adams who was incurably doctrinaire, showing an inability to absorb data incompatible with his dogmas. So, for example, his observation that "the lords return members of the house of commons" had dangerous implications for his whole argument. If both houses were recruited from the same class of persons, peers serving in the Lords and sons of peers in the Commons, what became of the theory that the lower house was to represent the many and act as a balance against the upper house which represented the few? One of his main arguments against single-chamber legislatures was that they tended to fall under the domination of notables. But the English example appeared to show that the notables could dominate a bicameral legislature as well. The stubbornness of the doctrinaire is apparent also in Adams' continued insistence that the royal veto was still a part of the English constitution after more than a century of disuse.

Rival Claims of "Rest" and "Motion"

The realism of Adams' political theory has nowhere been more praised, and nowhere more contrasted to Enlightenment thinkers like Condorcet, invariably presumed to have been led into error by excessive optimism about the "natural man," than in its view of the constitution of human nature. In demonstrating that the balances built into the revolutionary state constitutions conformed to reason as well as to the American tradition, Adams sought for a firm foundation in an answer to the question "what kind of beings men are." [25] Among those for whom it has become fashionable dogma to regard a political thinker as entitled to serious consideration only if he declaims sufficiently about innate depravity, Adams' frequent expressions about the wickedness of human nature win high esteem. The essential point to be urged here, however, is that Adams' view of human nature in its political applications was in its own way as incomplete and oversimplified as Condorcet's. Adams' view does not help very much to explain the varieties of political conduct observable in different societies. In its terms, for example, Adams could not really account for the relatively peaceable political behavior of his fellow Americans as well as the more optimistic Jefferson was able to do.

The picture of political man in the *Defence* is buttressed by a massive weight of empirical observation, derived almost entirely, however, from European sources. For evidence of the violent eruptions of political passions which he argued made balanced government a necessity, he resorted to the pages of the classical historians more than to the conduct of his fellow Americans, with the exception of the late wicked rebellion of Daniel Shays. It has already been noted that Adams tended to project the social conflicts of the Old World on American soil to justify balanced powers. It should be added that he also projected a human nature on American soil hardly likely to exhibit itself outside the context of the fierce social hatreds of less favored lands. It is difficult to believe that Adams' balances could contain social collisions of the intensity he described. So also if human nature were as obsessively predaceous as he postulated, it would break through the web of his balances like a shark caught in a net. It was no accident that one of the most complicated organizations of sovereign power ever devised appeared in a nation distinguished, in a comparative view at least, by the more benign manifestations of human nature in politics. Quite the reverse of the relation Adams sought to establish, muted predacity was more source of the balance than effect.

The idea of the exorbitancy of passions provided the psychological basis for Adams' theory. Adams viewed the limitless imperialism of the passions not pessimistically but in the framework of metaphysical assumptions provided by the cosmic optimism of the eighteenth century. Almost all the happiness of which man was capable arose from his "discontented humor." [26] The insatiability of the passions might be indispensable in the overall economy of human life, but in the political sphere it was attended with great inconveniences. It meant that men pursued power endlessly and were ever willing to encroach on one another's rights.

External restraints had to remedy the insufficiency of those internal to man, since he was so endowed that he could never remain at rest. "It is action, not rest, that constitutes our pleasure." Human nature "once in motion . . . rolls, like the stone of Sisyphus, every instant when the resisting force is suspended." The terms "motion" and "rest" suggest unmistakably the laws of mechanics which exerted so strong an attraction on the eighteenth century imagination. Adams' political science is constructed on an analogy drawn from the Newtonian law, cited approvingly at one point in the *Defence*, that "'reaction must always be equal and contrary to action,' or there can never be any rest." Of the value of such models he had no doubt. Fixed regularities were as much a feature of the social as of the natural world. "The vegetable and animal kingdoms, and those heavenly bodies whose existence and movements we are as yet only permitted faintly to perceive, do not appear to be governed by laws more uniform or certain than those which regulate the moral and political world." [27]

The central problem of politics in Adams' view was to produce "rest." By fashioning political machinery in which each active force was met by a counteractive force, the exorbitancy of the passions could be curbed. It was not safe for any of the great divisions of the community — the one, the few, and the many — to enjoy exclusive power over legislation, because each would be inexorably drawn to encroach on the others. A balance sufficient to hold each in check would be achieved if the consent of all three were required before a law could be enacted. In this system action was obtainable only when all the constituent elements of society moved in unison. Adams represented his tripartite sovereign as the universally required organization of liberty, but its correspondence to circumstances found in the United States, although rarely present elsewhere, is what strikes the observer. Only communities with exceptionally high degrees of political consensus sufficient to overcome the bias toward immobility inherent in the system or with exceptional levels of tolerance of government inactivity could successfully work government by "concurrent majorities."

A political machine fashioned in the Newtonian image had little appeal to French liberalism in the late 1780's. The problem of politics, as Condorcet saw it, was not "rest" but "motion." The issue that he faced was how to initiate change, not how to maintain stability, which he identified with the evils of the old regime. Animated by the passion of the reformer, he dreamed of a sovereignty that would possess the momentum to legislate the bourgeois order. France's equivalents of balancing powers had functioned to stifle the reform impulse of the monarchy. The experience with the parlements did not encourage belief in the efficacy of a government divided against itself.

Condorcet had no difficulty in formulating a series of formidable theoretical objections to Adams' tripartite sovereign. Such a system would have the greatest trouble in obtaining prompt decisions. The mutual resistance of the balancing forces would generate inertia. Condorcet disliked and scarcely understood government by parties, but he saw that their development would be encouraged by the need to overcome the "rest" inherent in a division of powers. Above all, he feared that balanced government would consecrate and preserve the divisions which existed in the community. The upper chamber in particular would become the haven of the "rich and powerful"; their power over legislation would be used to negate the popular will. Condorcet shared with Adams the essential liberal conviction that the powers of the rulers must be subjected to limitations in the interests of the rights of citizens. But he proposed to guard against oligarchic self-perpetuation by use of devices that would render the government more immediately responsive to the popular will.

Adams disparaged two kinds of checks which subsequent experience has shown to be efficacious in restraining the penchant of rulers to oppress. He took special pains first to minimize the value of the electoral process as sufficient to restrain officeholders without checks and balances within the machinery of government itself.[28] His views were formulated when direct experience of the way in which elections on the basis of a wide suffrage would work was fragmentary. Relying on deductions from the nature of man, and the dissensions between few and many in the Graeco-Roman world, he drew horrendous pictures of the oppressions which the majority would visit upon the minority in systems without balanced powers. He was an early convert among Whig liberals to the doctrine of the tyranny of the majority. "The majority has eternally, and without one exception, usurped over the rights of the minority." [29] As he conceived it, largely in terms of classical example, a permanent majority would confront a permanent minority, separated from one another by an impassable gulf of interests and opinions. In all matters at issue the majority would legislate "its private interest" without regard to the preferences of the minority. Elective officials, far from being governed by the psychology of anticipated reactions, would feel responsible exclusively to the majority, conceived as a monolithic entity, and would not have to fear repudiation in future elections. By favors, influence, services, officials could obtain a complete ascendancy over the majority who had voted them into power. The minority would be driven to rebellion by the endless oppressions to which it was subjected.[30]

Though this description was perhaps applicable to the parties of plebeian and patrician in ancient city-states, it had little relevance to the politics of his own society. Here fluctuating majorities and minorities would confront one another, divided on a basis of circumscribed interests and sharing a set of common values. The party victorious in elections would have to treat its supporters as potential defectors and its opposition as potential friends. The parties would reflect a disparity of shifting opinions, not a disparity of hereditary interests as in the ancient world. In one section of the *Defence* Adams devoted himself to

pulverizing the political errors of one Marchamont Needham, but this obscure seventeenth century English writer,
in pointing to the importance of "succession of persons"
in office and especially of "apprehension of coming elections" in restraining magistrates, showed a grasp of the
essential mechanism of political responsibility that ex-
ceeded Adams'.

Adams excluded also the possibility that values incul-
cated in the rulers could effectively set limits to their
"natural tendency to tyranny." Rulers would not be
checked by "anything within their own breasts" in the
absence of external impediments to their wills. Reason
and conscience, even as educated by religion and moral
teaching, proved insufficient to dissuade most men from
transgressions when they were tempted by the promise of
gain.[31] Adams assumed that internal restraints required a
degree of self-abnegation that was not possible for the
vast majority of men. But he was here confusing the kind
and the degree of virtue that was needed. To live by society's constitutional morality not extraordinary levels of
moral heroism were required, but a virtue which was the
product of socialization and which quite ordinary men
might be expected to possess. The permeation of the culture by certain assumptions about what was not done
could be sufficient. Cultural norms, by definition capable
of being upheld by the "average sensual man," could set
limits to the uses of political power. Without them indeed
no merely mechanical balances would suffice.

The Uses of History

Adams' system made little if any allowance for the
variety of social habit and cultural norm to be found in
different societies. That he could cite the experience of
fifth century Athens or thirteenth century Siena without

any sense of anomaly as affording evidence of how unchecked majorities could be expected to behave in eighteenth century America reveals much about the uses to
which he put history. He rehearsed with a heroic prolixity
the history of ancient and medieval republics to demonstrate the point that the punishment for lack of effective
balance in their constitutions had been violent death.

The paradox is that elaborate in his resort to history,
Adams was yet quite unhistorical. Reducing the variety
of history to a rigid pattern, he stressed uniformity and
constancy, rather than change, in the treatment of his
data. The uniqueness and special status of the particular
was hardly acknowledged; nor was history seen as bringing forth new things in uninterrupted succession, each
with its own shape and independent mode of existence.
He showed unswerving devotion to historical example as
a means of confirming postulates not historically derived.
He looked to history not to tell him what man was, but
for illustrations of an already formed view of man as a
fixed, unchanging entity. The passions in eighteenth century America operated in the same fashion and produced
the same results as in republican Rome. Divorcing human
nature from the integument of culture and history —
apart from which in fact it is never found — he could
hold with confidence that "All nations, from the beginning, have been agitated by the same passions," and feel
certain that his principles of politics would "go a great
way in explaining every phenomenon that occurs in the
history of government." [32]

For Adams following Bolingbroke, history was example
enforcing precept. Condorcet rejected the precept and
denied the force of the example as well. He boldly asserted that the historical evidence cited in favor of balanced powers proved nothing. The ancient republics had

not perished because of lack of knowledge of the art of establishing equilibrium among three powers. They had suffered through failure to grasp the principle of representation. Their violent social struggles had resulted from the collisions of patricians, accustomed over long periods to unchallenged authority, and the people, grown tired of submitting to this authority.

Impatient with historical analogies, Condorcet insisted that it was necessary to reason about politics "independent of examples." Political theory must be founded upon general principles derived from geometric not historical reasoning. His preference for a priori reasoning was in part a reaction to some of the uses to which history was put. He expressed intense dislike for the practice of citing historical examples and comparisons "to justify what is" rather than to show "what could be or ought to be done." Historical reasoning too often served to sanctify what reasoning from first principles established as unjust. Hating the institutions received from the past, he rejected history as the embodiment of the prejudices of mankind, although after the American and French revolutions he came to view it also as the record of the progressive emancipation of reason. Remorselessly abstract in his political method, he demonstrated nevertheless the rudiments of a historical consciousness in denying the force of the classical analogies used by the advocates of mixed government.[33]

At one point in the *Defence* Adams himself showed some concern about the validity of his citations of classical precedent. In commenting upon the political experience of Athens, he raised the question as to its applicability to America. Unlike the people in the ancient city-states, the Americans were sprinkled over large tracts of land and could not meet in a single assembly. They were, therefore, "not exposed to those tumultuous commotions, like the raging waves of the sea, which always agitated the ecclesia at Athens . . . The property required in a representative, senator, or even governor is so small, that multitudes have equal pretensions to be chosen. No election is confined to any order of nobility, or to any great wealth." [34] The tendency of this passage, if pursued ruthlessly enough, was destructive of major segments of Adams' argument. It suggested that the propensities of the multitude in Athens might not afford clues to what could be expected from the common people in the United States, that there were profound differences between the social orders of the ancient city-states and America.

The argument was rescued by the introduction of a subsidiary hypothesis, which had the effect of deflating the significance of the briefly acknowledged American particularity. He pursued a line of reasoning remarkably similar to that of some later analysts of the American scene — the Marxists are a good case in point — who have coped with American departures from expectations created by European-oriented social dogmas by emphasizing the temporary nature of American exceptionalism. American conditions were for the moment admittedly special, because they were the conditions of a new country. Initially the consequences to be apprehended from an absence of a correct balance in the constitution might not be produced in America. But it was of great importance to begin well. Misarrangements once entered into would have "great, extensive, and distant consequences." In a period not very far off, a hundred million people might fill up America's empty spaces. At this point the balance would be required to set limits to the passions which would display themselves in all their vigor, and produce the horrors which had occurred in all past republics where the necessity for an equilibrium in the constitution was not understood.[35]

The Universalist Mode of Social Analysis

Nowhere is Adams' absence of historical consciousness exhibited more completely than in his conception of social structure. The social analysis of antiquity — the one, the few, and the many — he defended as universally applicable. As he said later in answer to John Taylor's remonstrance, "Is there a nation, at this hour of the sixteenth day of June, 1814, on this globe, in which this analysis is not as obvious and undeniable as it ever was in any age or any nation of antiquity?" The distinction between the few and the many arose out of a fundamental condition common to mankind: the advantages accruing from exemption from physical labor were possible only for a minority. In every society the gentlemen, consisting of those who have acquired liberal education, must be relatively few, being persons of property and usually born of the more noted families. From among them a single pre-eminent individual destined to occupy the "first place" invariably appeared, on whom all eyes were focused in admiration or fear. The great majority in all nations must consist of persons pursuing occupations that required no knowledge of liberal arts or sciences, and who moreover were wholly destitute of property "except a small quantity of clothes, and a few trifles of other movables." [36]

Not only did the same differentiation appear in all societies, but each one of the constituent parts universally exhibited its own characteristic political propensities in its interactions with the others. "The envy and rancor of the multitude against the rich are universal and restrained only by fear or necessity. A beggar can never comprehend the reason why another should ride in a coach while he has no bread." The few were driven just as inexorably by their dominant passions to increase the advantages they possessed over the many and to augment wealth and influence at their expense.[37]

The eternal distinction between few and many, and the conflict it spawns, found political expression in Adams' assertion of the universal necessity of the bicameral principle. Two main lines of argument in favor of upper chambers are pursued in the *Defence,* one developed in the first volume and the other not making its appearance until the third. Adams began with the idea that in a single-chamber legislature the notables establish a thorough oligarchic domination; where two houses exist, however, the upper becomes the object of their ambition, and an "ostracism" is possible, which reduces the weight of their natural advantages.

To the extent that Adams developed an empirical foundation for this conception, he apparently had in mind certain aristocratic republics in Switzerland and Italy (Bern, Geneva, Venice) where a few rich and honorable families, not sufficiently segregated by the constitutions from the common people, had wrested from the people all right of participation in government.[38] English experience, however, showed that a double legislature could be controlled by the same order of persons. It provided instances, seeming to lend credence to the principle of ostracism, in which a popular figure in the lower house had been diminished in political importance by elevation into the upper chamber. But the support that Adams could derive from English example on this point was already equivocal in the eighteenth century, with major political figures much preferring the House of Commons as the theater for the exercise of their talents. Even in the United States the principle of ostracism was belied during the Federalist decade, when the balance of talent was found in the House of Representatives, not the Senate.

Adams' other case for upper chambers stressed their indispensability as "guardians of property against levellers for the purpose of plunder." Where the legislative power is undivided, the poor and vicious rob the rich and virtuous and spend their gains in debauch.[39] Whether as the theater in which the poor pillaged the rich, or the rich tyrannized over the poor, the single-chamber legislature appeared equally damned. The inconsistency in Adams' two postures is clear enough. What remains murky is whether the special prowess or the special vulnerability of the few worried him more. Without the least intention of accusing Adams of hypocrisy, one may hazard that the vulnerability was more acutely the object of his concern. The notion that to give the few their upper chamber reduced their influence bears a curious resemblance to another Whig conception, that it was necessary to deprive the propertyless of the suffrage to diminish the political importance of the wealthy, who otherwise would command the votes of innumerable economic dependents.

In 1788–89 Condorcet found neither of Adams' defenses of the bicameral principle convincing. In the context of French politics the theory that an upper house prevented aristocratic domination seemed ironical indeed. Condorcet would have undoubtedly agreed with Jefferson's classic objection: "I think that to give [the notables] power in order to prevent them from doing mischief, is arming them for it, and increasing instead of remedying the evil." [40] In France bicameralism would provide the aristocracy with an invincible weapon for the defense of its privileges. The necessity for an upper house to safeguard property was not an idea that was persuasive to Condorcet either. Hatred of privilege not fear of the people was his main preoccupation. To separate the bourgeoisie from the lower classes would only disarm them both before the common enemy. As a solution to the problem posed by Adams Condorcet considered it sufficient to debar the most impecunious persons from the privileges of active citizenship.

Adams' other distinctive political idea — that the executive, without exception for time or circumstance, must be armed with an absolute negative on legislative acts — was supported by two lines of reasoning as difficult to reconcile with one another as his contradictory statements of the virtues of bicameralism.[41] One position made the executive into an impartial mediator between the few and the many. In 1789 he had this conception in mind when he attacked the French National Assembly for granting the King merely a qualified negative. The notion of the executive as holder of the balance between the two great divisions of society won few adherents among delegates worried by the multiplying signs of the King's espousal of the nobility's cause.

Adams' other view, the one he more frequently stated, made the "principal personage" the champion and defender of the multitude, to whom he turned inevitably because the few were bound to be jealous of his eminence. For empirical support of this proposition Adams relied on the historic alliance between monarchy and people which had subdued the nobility in France. But in generalizing a tactical alignment into a permanent principle of politics and buttressing it further with psychological universals, Adams made a grave mistake. Very quickly in the French Revolution mutual sympathy between people and royal power was dissolved, and a threatened aristocracy became more royalist than the king. What proved of primary significance in producing these shifts was the consideration raised by Adams that the "principal personage" was himself recruited from the few. The conception of the natural affinity between the one and the many proved more applicable in a general way to the course of American political history but for reasons rooted in the politics of democracy and having little to do with Adams' psychological universals.

Adams' postulates about the political propensities of each of the three great divisions of society were intended to supply the basis for the system of tripartite legislative sovereignty provided in the American state constitutions. It is noteworthy, then, how little he drew upon American experience for the empirical foundation of his observations about the reactions of the three orders. In all the vast corpus of the *Defence* there are only fragmentary references to a century and a half of colonial political development. To take only one example: the evidence for the natural alliance of people and "principal personage" against the few was drawn from European history. The colonial experience of Massachusetts exhibited a quite different pattern. Here royal governor and lower house were chronically at loggerheads, with the upper house (the council) usually dominated by the lower. Indeed, as Adams himself admitted at one point, despite the balances in the colonial charter, including an executive veto, neither the one nor the few had proved able to withstand the pressures of the many when there were fundamental policy disagreements, and the many was determined to prevail. Where Adams discussed specifically American experience most fully was in passages designed to establish that the eternal differentiation and accompanying struggle between the few and many were as much to be found in his own country as elsewhere. Despite the absence of hereditary legal distinctions, nobility, based on inequality in wealth and advantages of birth, existed in fact if not in name in the United States as well as Europe.[42]

Arguments to the contrary by other theorists elicited elaborate protests from Adams. His response was devastating when Jefferson and John Taylor confidently asserted that in the United States the laws abolishing entails and primogeniture and dividing the lands of intestates among the children had "laid the axe to the root of pseudo-aristocracy." [43] He was contemptuous of the illusion that mere removal of feudal vestiges in land tenure prevented the accumulation of land in a few hands. The freer transfer of land ownership made possible would give immense stimulation to competitive forces, land speculation, and the consequent engrossing of vast tracts by a few. Adams was sensitive to the emergence of newer forms of wealth. He had visited the great Wedgwood pottery works while in England. The material for vast fortunes appeared available in commerce, in the building and operation of roads and bridges. In the fever for banks that swept America in the early nineteenth century, he saw opportunities for the rise of a financial oligarchy. He was savagely effective in reply to John Taylor's contention that "inhibitions upon monopoly and incorporation are remedies for aristocracy founded on paper wealth." How were these to be obtained in a democracy of cupidity where the "few are craving and the many mad for the same thing"? [44]

Adams was acute and forceful in his awareness of the fertility of the sources out of which inequalities spring. He had a far greater grasp than either Jefferson or Taylor of the tenacity of the forces which made for oligarchic influence in social organization. He verged at times on a theory of the inevitability of oligarchy.[45] This direction of his thinking was, however, in its ultimate tendency incompatible with his central emphasis on government by balanced forces. If the oligarchic forces in society were so united in the pursuit of power, if they possessed such immense advantages of wealth, birth, and talent, they would in fact govern despite the most elaborate combination of constitutional balances.

In a number of countries Adams noted that the few tended to divide, that horizontal differentiations created antagonisms within the oligarchy itself. In the United States, Virginia planters contested for power against the moneyed interests in the seaboard cities. In Holland the influence of the gentry in the inland provinces had prevailed over the interests of the cities, with the effect of annihilating the former astonishing commerce and naval power of the nation.[46] But he overlooked the consideration that the conflict among the few created opportunities for the many to acquire and extend their influence. One oligarchic interest in its contest with another summoned the many into action as an ally, as the Virginia planters rallied the small farmers or the French bourgeoisie relied upon the lower classes at critical moments in 1789. The divisions among the active political elements of a nation might constitute as potent a balancing force as any constitutional machinery. Such social balances were observed with great interest by Adams, but they were not incorporated into his system.

Admirably stubborn in calling attention to the persistence of social facts glossed over by others, Adams yet engaged in certain glaring oversimplifications and blurred certain essential distinctions in his own social analysis. The postulate of a single fixed form of social order was a fundamental error, epitomizing the lack of a historical consciousness. Unusual powers as a social observer were imprisoned within the framework of his universalism. Viewing widely diverse social structures as basically similar, he never found it in the least anomalous to consider the same set of constitutional arrangements applicable to the political problems of each. His system of balances was presumed to fit the conditions of France in 1789 as much as the revolutionary American states in 1776. It was with some justice that members of the Turgot circle like Condorcet and Dupont de Nemours grew impatient with Adams' tendency to prescribe one remedy for all maladies. "Whatever the state of the patient, or the cause of the illness, merely administer a dose of orders and balances." [47]

Even within the constrictions of the classical social analysis, it was possible to make greater allowance than Adams did for variation in the propensities of the few and many in different societies. Instead he portrayed the psychology of social classes as if it were everywhere similar. He rightly scouted the illusions of those who thought that because America had no hereditary legal distinctions, no other basis for permanent social differentiation between the few and the many existed. But even if, as he demonstrated, wealth and birth worked toward the emergence of "artificial aristocracy" in the United States, it did not mean that the resulting social order in the United States, and the collisions of the great interests within it, would exhibit the same character as that of the ancient republics or contemporary Europe. Where Jefferson's insight was surer than Adams' was in his recognition that the conflict between the few and the many must resolve differently depending upon the nature and composition of the constituent social elements.[48] The conflicts of ancient Rome could not be compared to those of repub-

lican America, Jefferson insisted, because the common
people in America were not the proletariat of ancient
Rome, nor were the American rich anything like the
Roman patriciate. Adams' own description of the Romans
as divided into parties "as jealous and distinct, and almost
as hostile as two nations" suggested how little that situation fitted American experience.[49]

If the few and the many in the United States shared
the same "canine appetite" for wealth, it was surely relevant to point out that the few might thereby have less to
fear from the despoiling propensities of the many. Both
interests might be expected to exhibit a basic respect for
the sanctities of property. If most Americans were possessed of property "in all the variety of degrees between
the extremes," the intensity of the struggle between rich
and poor might be affected. In the *Defence* Adams occa-
sionally mentioned with warm approval the "middling
portion" of mankind and indicated their presence in large
numbers among the common people in the United States.[50]
But he hardly made any room for this group in his social
analysis. Adams cited as evidence in favor of the persistent influence of birth the power of "illustrious names"
to carry American elections and the passionate devotion
to genealogy of some Americans. But what did the zeal
of every tradesman to establish a pedigree demonstrate
better than the overwhelming social democracy of the
country? It was a measure of how much the Americans
were really alike in social degree that some of them
sought so avidly for adventitious marks of distinction.
What did this passion for distinction have in common
with the anxious effort of a European noble to establish
the purity of his descent? If "illustrious names" could
carry elections in America, one reason was that they did
not have attached to them that massive weight of legal

immunities and privileges that set their bearers apart from the rest of the community in Europe. The differentiation between the few and the many existed undoubtedly in the United States, but the propensities of each group and their relations with one another were distinguishable from anything that Europe had known.

In the universalist mood which permeates his political theory, Adams related his case for government by balanced powers only fitfully to the distinctiveness of American social facts and historical circumstances. His system was urged as the specific against social disorder everywhere, but it was supportable in the United States only because the violent social strife he postulated to prove its necessity did not exist. He transformed an American politics of special interests into a European politics of class struggle. He disparaged the effectiveness of values instilled in the rulers by moral training and of the elective principle itself as safeguards against oppression of the citizen, declaring that internal division within the sovereignty was the only sure check. While he was dissolving American and European differences in a universalist theory of man and society, he was also making observations on the nature of the old regime and the prospects of liberal reform abroad that expressed an intense awareness of America and Europe as separate worlds. What he denied in vindicating the American state constitutions formed at the same time the root assumption upon which rested his analysis of Europe's political situation in the decade preceding the French Revolution. The theorist of divided sovereignty who disclaimed that the Americans were unlike other men quickly recovered his awareness of American particularity when he fixed his attention on the problems of European society.

CHAPTER THREE

ON THE EVE

*I*N HIS RETIREMENT John Adams admitted freely that
he had no inkling of coming revolution when he was
in France. "To be sure it had never yet entered my
thoughts that any rational being would ever think of
demolishing the monarchy and creating a republic in
France." His comments on the old regime at the time
contain no hint of expectation of an approaching crisis
in the life of the monarchy. To him it appeared safe and
unassailable, a permanent landmark on the European
scene. On the eve of the Revolution he was still speculat-
ing whether the "system of simple monarchy" after a few
modifications would "become stationary."[1]

The failure to anticipate cataclysm was entirely typical
of foreign observers during the prerevolutionary decade.
As H. A. L. Fisher has pointed out, "The sense of impending revolution was more acute during the despotic
anarchy of Louis XV's reign than in the years immediately
preceding the catastrophe . . . As the long uneasy reign
of Louis XV came to a natural end, and the ancient monarchy of France was found to have safely survived its
period of disorder and humiliation and to be refurnished

with a stock of good intentions, the presentiment of impending evil died away." [2]

Adams' colleagues, Franklin and Jefferson, who enjoyed as great opportunities of observing French affairs, were equally innocent of forebodings. Franklin thought that France was the most stable among the great states of Europe. All three considered England the more likely candidate for revolution, a belief more proportionate to desire than to evidence. None had any special insight into the developing political situation, and all were uniformly surprised by events. They were in touch with only limited segments of the French people. Although much has been made of their acquaintance with the liberal nobility and some of the more prominent French intellectuals, Adams and Franklin concentrated their attention, as diplomats on foreign embassy may be prone to do, on the views of governing circles. About the fall of Turgot, for example, Adams recited largely the opinions of a hostile court official. [3]

Adams was one of the first in a long succession of American diplomats who was under the necessity, upon arrival, of painfully acquiring the language of the country to which he was sent. Almost a year elapsed before he could read French with any ease, and an even longer period before he could really converse. He came to France without extensive knowledge of its political institutions; in his typically conscientious way he set himself to repair the deficiency, but as late as 1787 he showed some imprecision in his conception of the role of the parlements. In common with Franklin and Jefferson he tended to misgauge the state of feeling among the French on some crucial points. Although it is doubtful whether Louis XVI was ever the object of much veneration by his subjects, Adams considered that a "ruling passion [of the French] is a love of their sovereign." He might have been closer to the reality had he said that a ruling passion of the French was hatred of hereditary privilege. Adams did not catch the note of animosity in Mably's comment to him that "the nobles all believe that their nobility is from God. And . . . that the King cannot confer nobility."[4] Of this side of French opinion both Adams and Jefferson seem to have been unaware before 1789.

Crisis Symptoms

Failure to discern the essential drift of events was not due to lack of identification of crisis symptoms. In fact, Adams reacted sensitively to a number of phenomena that did not accord with the conventional picture of France as the most stable of European states. He was sure that the widespread enthusiasm in the nation for the American Revolution passed beyond mere desire to humiliate the ancient rival,[5] even though he did not suspect the depth of the longing for a new order of things that it embodied. Some at least of the inhabitants of the foremost absolute monarchy in Europe turned out surprisingly to be inveterate constitution-mongers.[6] He noted that Franklin gave audience to a stream of persons who importuned him with questions about specific articles in the new American state constitutions and offered innovations of their own. The passionate interest displayed in American political and social arrangements was gratifying. But the irritation soon aroused in Adams by the critical tendency of many of the suggestions and their often glaring inapplicability to American circumstances was little tempered by the realization that in actuality they represented a disguised demand for reform at home.

Adams witnessed the apotheosis of Franklin into the most famous man in the world of French opinion.[7] He forgave neither Franklin his popularity nor the French their extravagant praise of him. It was not until long after the Revolution that he penetrated to the core of the mystery of Franklin's reputation. Franklin was seen as one who "was to restore the golden age" by destroying soon all arbitrary governments.[8] Adams came to understand that for European liberalism in its revolutionary stage, Franklin was the charismatic herald of the new age to which it aspired, the incarnation of the reason of the Enlightenment. More conscious than most foreign observers of signs that could be read as indicating a deep social malaise in France, Adams discounted them heavily for the special reason that in his mind the gap between American and French circumstances was so complete as to make anything like a repetition of the late events in his own country unthinkable.

The alienated state of mind among French men of learning was not lost upon Adams. He discerned a marked tendency on their part to seek occasion on which to attack their institutions. At a meeting of the Academy of Sciences, he was struck by the penchant of the members to find hidden social meanings in the apparently most trivial circumstances. When one savant rose to read a paper on the art of making wine, the mere announcement of the choice of topic was enough to touch off a demonstration among his hearers. All the papers "seemed to search for opportunities to introduce hints and sarcastical allusions to the frivolities, vanity, affectation, follies, and prejudices of their own nation. This I should have expected would have been hissed at least, if no more. But on the contrary nothing was more loudly applauded, and nothing seemed to produce more gayety and good humor . . . More liberties of this kind were taken in France, I believe than in any other country." Tocqueville might have used

Adams' observations as one more source to support his conclusion that in the ten or fifteen years before the Revolution the "instinctive attachment and involuntary respect which men . . . are wont to feel for their own institutions, for their traditional customs, and for the wisdom or the virtues of their forefathers had almost ceased to exist among the educated classes." [9]

Adams confessed himself frankly in doubt about the meaning of the episode, but the display of an unrestrained spirit of criticism affected him disagreeably. In his own country nothing of the kind could have happened. It "would not have been endured." In Great Britain, too, although "some freedoms [might] be used with John Bull . . . you must be very careful to respect his essential characteristics." [10] He confronted the apparent paradox that in the Anglo-American world, where there was much more freedom of thought and expression permitted by the governments than in France, criticism was far less bold. The French academicians were not imbued with pious reverence for their own traditional values. There were no national sanctities that were removed from their pitiless gaze, no unquestioned beliefs that operated to discipline them.

Adams was here encountering the nakedly antitraditionalist bias of the French Enlightenment, and he reacted with instinctive dislike. Although a liberal, he was not antitraditionalist, because in his own country it was the liberal values that were traditional. The "libertinism" of the French thinkers — the suggestion that for them all the ultimate questions were still "open" — was repellent. His early suspicion ripened during the next decade into the accusation that they had produced "disorganizing effects." For a moment he seemed to sense the revolutionary implications in their denigrative urge and to see a danger posed for the stability of a society in which there were no longer any "absolutisms" beyond challenge.

But in the end he was inclined to treat the incident in the terms of his relativist perspective as one more indication of the corruption of French manners. Was it not a proof "of the last degree of depravity when a nation will laugh at their own vices and then go away and repeat them"? [11] Without ascribing to it the significance of a revolutionary portent, Adams recorded the French mood of disenchantment with long established patterns, the awakened conviction that "the world, and especially France, needs making over from the tiniest and more insignificant details to the most general moral and legal principles." [12] He had experienced briefly and felt alienated from what emerged as the animating spirit of the Revolution, its belief that society could be reconstructed from the foundations by conscious will.

Reform Expectations

Exposure to Bourbon France, if anything, softened Adams' hostility to monarchical absolutism. Before 1778 he had seen it through the medium of an already fully developed American myth as extinguishing all the rights essential to human nature. He could describe himself in Paris as "dwelling in the foul haunts of Machiavellian politics," but this was rather the ritualized language of republican virtue in which he felt obliged to cloak himself when writing to some of his correspondents than the true reflection of his position. In reality, he was impressed by the many respects in which French despotism departed from his stereotype. If, in the formal sense, the twin tyrannies of the feudal and the canon law remained intact, nevertheless certain substantial mitigations had taken place. Sharing fully in the eighteenth century's "complacent sense of living in better times," he found it highly gratifying that even despotism was proving responsive to the spirit of the age. France, in particular, appeared to be moving toward restoration of a degree of its lost liberty.

Even in the theory and practice of government, in all the simple monarchies, considerable improvements have been made. The checks and balances of republican governments have been in some degree adopted at the courts of princes. By the erection of various tribunals, to register the laws, and exercise the judicial power — by indulging the petitions and remonstrances of subjects, until by habit they are regarded as rights — a control has been established over ministers of state, and the royal councils, which in some degree, approaches the spirit of republics. Property is generally secure, and personal liberty seldom invaded. The press has great influence, even where it is not expressly tolerated; and the public opinion must be respected by a minister, or his place becomes insecure.[13]

In part this passage revealed some confusion in Adams' mind about the course of institutional development in France. He implied that the parlements represented recent innovation by the monarchy itself, when in actuality they were remains of the traditional constitution of France which the monarchy had not succeeded in obliterating. What he had noticed was the increased assertiveness of an old institution, whose very existence ran counter to mythical notions of the "simplicity" of absolute monarchy. He showed no reserve about the parlements, which enjoyed popularity at the time (1787) among all but a small segment of liberal opinion. To an adherent of the Anglo-American Whig tradition, the symbolism, invoked by the parlements, of constitutional opposition to government arbitrariness was highly congenial. He was not alone in missing the note of defense of aristocratic privilege that sounded in the parlements' remonstrances.

Adams' optimism about the future political prospects of France would be misinterpreted, however, if equated with that of the French liberals before 1789. In two important respects the mood inspired in him by the old regime differed from theirs. Behind French liberal despair about existing institutions lurked a tremendous confidence in future possibilities. Adams was neither so embittered nor so hopeful as they were, neither so unreconciled to the continuance in Europe of the feudal and canon law nor at the same time so confident about ushering in "Nature's simple plan of perfection in politics." [14] The old regime never became for him an intolerable reality, the antagonist that must be destroyed. If it denied the essential "dignity of human nature" when judged by an absolute standard of excellence, it was also a necessary accommodation to the prevailing state of manners and morals among the French.

His perspective on their problems must have seemed inordinately bleak to the French liberals, because there was a vast and unyielding condescension in his assessment of their situation. Palmer's observation about Jefferson applies equally to Adams: he was optimistic paradoxically because he expected so little. Having begun by consigning Europe to perdition, he conceded that some carefully limited improvements were possible. His own reform program, stated in 1787, fell far short of what French liberals already advocated. In this regard, he was in accord with his friend Jefferson, who as late as the end of 1788 thought that the newly summoned Estates General should settle for nothing more than some control of taxation and a right to register proposed laws. As Adams expressed it:

If religious toleration were established, personal liberty a little more protected by giving an absolute right to demand a public trial in a certain reasonable time, and the states were invested with a few more privileges, or rather restored to some that have been taken away, these governments [simple monarchies] would be brought to as great a degree of perfection, they would approach as near to the character of governments of laws and not of men, as their nature will probably admit of.[15]

His proposals were accompanied by stern cautions. "If the people should ever aim at more [than a share in the legislative], they will defeat themselves; as they will, indeed, if they aim at this by other than gentle means and by gradual advances, by improvements in general education, and by informing the public mind."[16] Like Jefferson he thought the French incapable of managing more than a limited degree of liberty, and he admonished them to avoid abrupt transitions and revolutionary means. The success of the American Revolution must not be misunderstood. It was no summons to other peoples to go and do likewise. The French could not easily break out of the prison of their past. A nation so long habituated to despotism could not quickly accommodate itself to the requirements of a constitutional regime. A main article of the liberal political creed required belief that no nation was ever so thoroughly corrupted as to be unable to recover its liberty.[17] But at particular moments he also doubted whether the capacity to operate free institutions might not be permanently impaired by a too prolonged experience of despotism. Europe then appeared to possess governments that could never be made much better or worse, and the difference between America and Europe in his mind emerged as one of elect and damned.

Adams assumed that the course of political development in France would reproduce the English Whig pattern. The political problem in France, as he saw it, was the overweening royal power, which ought to be curbed by introducing immediately a few of the more essential civil liberties and by restoring ultimately the political privileges it had destroyed. By patient strivings France might yet obtain constitutional arrangements on the English model.[18] Liberal opinion in France had come to see its task quite differently. The issue for it was the hereditary privileges of the nobility, not the power of the monarchy. The position of the monarchy was a secondary consideration. During the Revolution, the monarchy would forfeit the support of the nation and come under attack only because it made common cause with the nobility. A genuine social revolution was preparing in France, not a repetition of the events of 1688. Adams misunderstood the sentiments of the "enlightened portion" of French opinion, which did not desire a mere restoration of former political rights. A constitution along English lines would have prevented the changes most desired by the Third Estate, by augmenting the power of the nobility and entrenching it further in the possession of its traditional social and economic immunities. Even without political rights the nobility had been strong enough to frustrate the reform impulse of the monarchy.

Adams was advocating that France should follow the English example at a moment when French liberals were finding the visible embodiment of their hopes in newly emancipated America. The attraction of the American republic for them lay not so much in its specific political forms as in its freedom from the legalized inequalities of social situation characteristic of the old order. Touched by their devotion to his nation, Adams refrained from proselytizing among them for the adoption of American degrees of freedom. America and Europe were separate worlds. The republican system of a new country was not a suitable object of imitation for an ancient, wealthy, and corrupted nation. In this period Adams could not seriously credit that any European liberal thought otherwise. Europe could not — must not — aim at what was inherently best. The institutions that restored the full "dignity of human nature" were beyond reach.

In the *Dissertation on the Canon and Feudal Law* (1765) Adams inveighed against the "servile dependencies" of the European social order. Americans had taken up arms to prevent these "base services" from becoming implanted in their own country. In Europe, however, Adams displayed no destructive animus against the feudal inheritance. If he saw much in Europe that revolted his liberal sensibilities, he responded with an intensified conviction of the superiorities of his own nation. He pitied the benighted citizens of such corrupted lands without identifying with them. His feelings about the old regime became almost benign. Considerable progress had been made — more might be expected — in mitigating the severities and more obvious injustices of absolute monarchy. His reform program might urge certain carefully confined constitutional changes, but it was conspicuously silent on the matters of deepest interest to the Third Estate. His liberalism was of a socially quiescent kind. Seemingly unaware that they were burning issues in France, he expressed no indignation about corporate monopolies, fiscal exemptions, or feudal dues. He contemplated no social reconstruction, no reordering of the class relations, even though acknowledging that the common people were still "subject . . . to aristocratical domination." [19] The equalitarianism of the great Revolution at its first appearance assumed the shape in his mind of dangerous social leveling. His writings of the prerevolutionary period, though in particulars critical of the dominant institutions of the old order, do not at any point question their legitimacy.

Aristocracy, Church, and People

R. R. Palmer has found an "angry irritability," a "sense of downright outrage," in Adams' discussion of the European patriciates, akin to that which "animates the Abbé Sieyès' eloquent diatribe, 'What Is the Third Estate?'" [20] It would seem on the contrary that the gulf between Adams and the French liberals is nowhere more strikingly displayed than in the different attitude assumed toward the nobility. Precisely missing in Adams is the exacerbated feeling of a Beaumarchais or a Sieyès that the prevailing "class distinctions are . . . unjust privileges, established by wicked men against the express intention of . . . nature." [21] His position is more accurately conveyed in the statement that "the objection to [absolute monarchy] is not because it is supported by nobles, and a subordination of ranks." [22] Deeply bourgeois in his habits, moral opinions, and outlook on the world, yet Adams did not share French middle class hatred and envy of the aristocracy. In fact, the absence of such violent animus well illustrates the thesis of one writer who observes that "the Americans, though models to all the world of the middle class way of life, lacked the passionate middle class consciousness which saturated the liberal thought of Europe." [23] As a leading spokesman of a victorious middle class which had never had to cope with the challenge of an entrenched aristocracy, Adams was free of one of the class obsessions of the French bourgeoisie. He was more just in recognizing some of the positive merits of the aristocracy, some of the historic services it had performed. He was easily reconciled to the preservation of the institution.

If Adams' state of mind was not identical with that of

the French liberals, neither was it in accord with Europe's conservatives. From the perspective of what was ideally best, he always insisted that "artificial aristocracy" was to be despised and the nations subjected to it pitied. He felt no Burkean reverence for the institution. He did not "glorify, in an ideal light, the chivalry of the nobility of France." When later he read Burke's threnody on the departed splendors of the "age of chivalry," he was unmoved, commenting dryly that "in his description there is more of the orator than the philosopher." [24]

Admittedly Adams' writings before the French Revolution contain many harsh strictures upon the European patriciates. His Yankee moralism was offended by the libertinism and the religious infidelity of the nobles. He despised their cult of honor, did not share their taste in the arts, and found their exquisite courtesy overelaborate and insincere. They were luxurious and too exclusively devoted to pleasure. The nobles had long since been reduced to political impotence in France, but in former times when they ruled unchecked, intolerable evils had been the consequence. They had permitted commerce and manufactures to languish, reduced executive power to a shadow, and exercised a cruel dominion over the people. They tried to inspire the common people "with so mean an esteem of themselves and so deep a veneration and strong attachment of their rulers as to believe and confess them a superior order of beings." Adams' justification of absolute monarchy was that it had rescued states like France from the horrors of rule by a feudal nobility. The people in their misery had turned to an alliance with the monarchy to subdue aristocratic pretensions.

Adams was stung especially by the nobility's condescension toward the middle classes, its disdain of those who lived by the product of their own labor. It was "aristocratic dogma" to consider "husbandmen, merchants, and tradesmen" beneath notice and to advocate their exclusion from government. "There is no doctrine . . . which goes so far as this towards forfeiting to the human species the character of rational creatures." Every monarchy, despotic empire, and aristocracy adopted this "unphilosophical" and "wicked position." Except in Switzerland, England, and the United States, no nation allowed the "middling elements" to be citizens.[25]

The class resentments expressed in these passages are unmistakably reminiscent of similar sentiments repeatedly voiced by the French liberals and might easily lead to an identification of the two positions. As a matter of fact, Adams' repudiation of aristocratic values had a more self-confident quality than that of the French middle classes, who were divided in their attitude to the nobility between contradictory urges to destroy and to emulate. But Adams espoused the cause of the middle classes in a far less intransigent way than the French liberals.

Adams voiced two political demands on the liberals' behalf. He asked for the career open to talents. "The moral equality that nature has unalterably established among men gives these [the talented] an undoubted right to have every road open to them for advancement in life and in power that is open to any others." He seemed unaware of the explosive possibilities of such a demand in a society riddled with class exclusivism. The middle classes also ought ultimately to be given their proper political weight through representation in an assembly that would be "an essential part of the sovereignty."[26] He did not conceive that the bourgeoisie might aspire to anything more; the aristocracy as well must acquire its own independent role in the government. What the Abbé Sieyès expressed for the Third Estate was a desire to become the nation, to claim the entire sovereignty, and thereby to submerge the aristocracy.

Unlike the liberals, Adams assumed that all the elements of the historic social constitution of France ought to be preserved. The problem, as he saw it, was to work out a more acceptable balance among them. Refusing to regard the nobility as a merely parasitic class that had outlived its usefulness, he even contemplated restoring its political vitality, a conception which seemed mischievous and reactionary to the liberals. He declined to condemn the principle of hereditary rank as repugnant to reason and nature. "All governments, even the most democratical, are supported by a subordination of offices, and of ranks too." [27]

Despite his strictures, he sounded also on occasion certain notes of extenuation and apology that have no counterpart in the views of the liberals in the prerevolutionary decade. Thus he observed that the aristocratic prejudice against trade had at least the merit of countering the ascendancy of pecuniary values. "It may prevent, in some degree, the whole nation from being entirely delivered up to the spirit of avarice . . . It may prevent the nobility from becoming too rich, and acquiring too large a proportion of the landed property." During the Revolution he returned to this point and argued that in destroying their nobility the French were paving the way for the rule of the least meritorious form of aristocracy, that of wealth. Adams was even willing to justify aristocratic pride and social exclusiveness, qualities that had become so galling to the Third Estate. "Those other hauteurs, of keeping the commons at a distance, and disdaining to converse with any but a few of a certain race, may in Europe be a favor to the people, by relieving them from a multitude of assiduous attentions and humiliating compliances, which would be troublesome." The nobility despite its reduced political importance played an indispensable role in making absolute monarchy tolerable to the nation "by checking its ministers and preventing them from running into abuses of power and wanton despotism." By resistance to executive power they reconciled "the monarchical authority to the obedience of the subjects." Otherwise "the people would be pushed to extremities and insurrections." [28]

Adams completely misjudged the forces and sentiments at work in France. The success of aristocratic resistance to the reform efforts of the monarchy was in fact a major precipitant of revolution. The Third Estate saw the nobility as the defenders not of common liberties but of exclusive privileges. Adams was again thinking in terms of the English model. Conceptions drawn from the role of the English nobility had little application to the very different conditions in France.

The French middle classes before the Revolution were filled with a sense of moral superiority to their nobility. Their spokesmen viewed the confrontation of the classes as a kind of elemental clash between virtue and corruption. They nursed an image of themselves as embodying the worth and ability of the nation held down, ignored, and despised by an aristocracy riddled with affectations and depravities. The central fact is that Adams did not enter into this state of mind at all. He held to the contrary that the corruptions of French society were not confined to its ruling orders. They permeated all ranks. "It may gratify vulgar malignity and popular envy, to declaim eternally against the rich and the great, the noble and the high; but, generally and philosophically speaking, the manners and characters of a nation are all alike." All classes grew "vicious, vain, and luxurious, exactly in proportion." Considering nations as a whole, "We shall find that intemperance and excess are more indulged in the lowest ranks than in the highest." [29]

As he saw them from the outside, Europeans of all classes were much more alike than they appeared to one another. The worst traits of the aristocracy were only reflections of more general evils of European society. His apology for the nobles assumed ultimately this negative form. If they escaped censure at his hands, it was because he included them in a condemnation directed to Europe as a whole. While he sympathized with some of the grievances of the Third Estate, he was not stirred to passionate indignation. He did not see the middle classes as they saw themselves, as innocent virtue unjustly assailed. His experience abroad stimulated an intensified sense of the impassable gulf between Europe and America rather than a revolutionary urge to eradicate ancient wrongs. Consciousness of national differences submerged feelings of class solidarity.

The ambivalence in Adams' attitude toward the nobility appears as well in his treatment of the Catholic Church. His writings of the period are punctuated with angry condemnations of the pretensions of the "Romish clergy." They have persuaded Catholic Europe "to believe . . . that God Almighty had entrusted them with the keys of heaven, whose gates they might open and close at pleasure; with a power of dispensation over all the rules and obligations of morality; with authority to license all sorts of sins and crimes; with a power of deposing princes and absolving subjects from allegiance." They have reduced the minds of the people "to a state of sordid ignorance and staring timidity . . . infusing into them a religious horror of letters and knowledge." In his journey through northern Spain in the winter of 1779, Adams was struck by the misery of the peasantry, which he largely ascribed to the exactions of the Church. He saw no one "rich but the churches, nobody fat, but the clergy." He observed villages in a state of decay. Each "has churches and convents enough in it, to ruin it, and the whole country round about it, even if they had nothing to pay to the king or landlord." The monastic establishments were "so many hives of drones." [30]

All this scurrilous comment can be easily misunderstood because of the apparent resemblances to the anti-Catholic spirit of the French Enlightenment. Adams' sentiments, however, were rooted in the Protestant prejudices of his Puritan forebears rather more than in Voltairean rationalism. The essential difference with the French liberals is that while he was anti-Catholic, he was not in the least anticlerical. His denunciations did not issue out of a will to do battle against the secular privileges of the Church in the name of liberty. His desire for reform would have been satisfied by the establishment of religious toleration in France, and he thought that the country was on the threshold of accomplishing this change. He wrote home to reassure colleagues who hesitated to associate the United States with the most powerful Catholic monarchy in the Old World, "The spirit for crusading for religion is not in France. The rage of making proselytes which had existed in former centuries is no more. There is a spirit more liberal here in this respect than I expected to find." It was almost possible to conclude that France was a "tolerant nation." [31]

As in the case of the aristocracy, Adams was silent on exactly the matters that most concerned the French liberals. He voiced no demands for separation of church and state. He saw the Catholic clergy as an inveterate enemy of free institutions, but, in saying so, he did not mean to encourage attacks on its property holdings or measures for the secularization of education. He was content instead to contrast American felicity with European decadence; in his own country "sacerdotal ordination" was established "on the foundation of the Bible and common sense." [32] In Europe unreason in religion made it all the more unlikely that reason in politics might come to prevail. Adams himself has sufficiently accounted for his own lack of anticlericalism in observing that in New England at least the clergy were "jealous partisans of liberty." French liberals, sharing his view that the power of the Catholic Church was a major obstacle in the path to liberty, unlike him drew the conclusion that the Church would have to be frontally attacked. Even before the Revolution Adams noted with irritation, if not yet dismay, the prevalence of deism and atheism among this segment of French opinion. For him Catholicism was the most "corrupted" form of Christianity, but it was still Christianity, and as such infinitely preferable to infidelity. On this point there opened the deepest of all the chasms between him and the liberals.

Insofar as he espoused the cause of the Third Estate, Adams always distinguished clearly between its respectable and solid segments and the petty bourgeoisie and proletariat. All calculations about the prospect of political reform in France had to take account of the fact that the poor were far more numerous there than the propertied. In most of Europe the "preponderance of property had passed from the many to the few." Adams expressed some sympathy for the miseries of the unpropertied whose plight he had observed at first hand in the great European towns, but predominantly they inspired him with dread. Their existence seemed, of all portents, the one most unfavorable to liberty. The urban poor included depressed categories like the "manufacturers" in England, the street-walkers in Paris and London, and the swarms of beggars who had marred the scene for him in his first journey from Bordeaux to Paris in 1778. He recorded his horror at the "panics and transports, [the] contagions of madness and folly, which are seen in countries where large numbers live in small spaces, in daily fear of perishing for want." [33] The Lord Gordon riots were a compelling instance of the depths of bigotry and destitution to be found among London's common people. [34] In Europe's city populations he could easily imagine that he saw the reincarnation of the mob whose riots and seditions had distracted the life of the Greek and Italian city-states. The *Defence* cites as authoritative the description given by the Scottish historian Adam Ferguson of the rabble, which

in great and prosperous cities, ever sinks, by the tendency of vice and misconduct, to the lowest condition . . . that dreg . . . actuated by envy to their superiors . . . by abject fear . . . ever ready to espouse the cause of any leader against the restraints of public order; disposed to vilify the more respectable ranks of men, and, by their indifference on the subjects of justice or honor to frustrate every principle that may be employed for the government of mankind, besides fear and compulsion. [35]

The fear of the mob entered into Adams' assessment of the political situation in France in the most crucial way, leading him both to qualify his hopes about political liberalization and to accept the legitimacy of the dominant institutions of the old regime. His unwavering assumption was that under no circumstances were the unpropertied to be allowed to become an active factor in politics. Their characteristic political expression could be expected to take the form of violent assault upon property. Relaxation of the rigors of absolute monarchy must not be too sudden or complete, if the danger of unleashing the multitude was to be forestalled. The problem in France was to extend political liberty without activating the masses and adding to their political weight. Constitutional changes in the system of absolute monarchy would have to be accomplished without recourse to revolutionary means. With their unruly proletariats no European states could safely undergo revolution. In America revolution had succeeded, but there was no mob. "What would have become of American liberty, if there had not been more faith, honor, and justice in the minds of their common citizens, than are found in the common people in Europe?" [36]

He envisaged for the future the establishment in Europe of "democratical branches" of the legislature to take their place beside hereditary branches in checking absolute monarchy, but political liberty was to be extended only to the nobles and the propertied elements among the Third Estate. It would be essential to exclude the propertyless from the franchise. He held the conventional Whig view that such persons must be presumed to be dependent upon others and incapable of exercising the rational foresight necessary for participation in politics. Adams cautioned the French liberals against excessive boldness, against attempting to accomplish too much. They must understand that republican institutions, in particular, were beyond reach. To make all offices elective was always a "hazardous experiment," but in Europe, where the preponderance of property was in the hands of the few, it was unthinkable.

In Adams the note of middle class animosity against aristocratic privileges was muted by the uneasy awareness of the mob. His justification of the hereditary principle must not be confused with the admiration of it for its own sake that was characteristic among European conservatives. Adams' fear of the people outweighed his dislike of the feudal subordinations, and he consequently looked upon the aristocracy as a necessary ally. It is not really surprising then to find him conspicuously silent on the question of the traditional prerogatives of the nobles and insistent that the nobles must be included as an essential component in any new constitutional structure in France. To make common cause with the people in an assault upon the "prejudice of nobility" would in his view place property and order in jeopardy. His divergence on this point from the spokesmen of the French middle classes was a fundamental one. As a sympathetic observer has remarked, "They had not yet learned to tremble before the power of the people." [37] They were obsessively preoccupied with hatred of aristocracy and willing for the moment to give leadership to the entire Third Estate. Not until after their initial victories over the nobility, for which the active assistance of the people would be required, would they learn to fear the masses and make their peace with the forces of order. Then they would be willing in moments of crisis to pursue a policy of alliance with what remained of traditional institutions.

The absence of obsessive preoccupation with hereditary privilege on the part of the American revolutionaries like Adams has been interpreted in psychological terms as the response of a satiated middle class without need to wage a bitter struggle against an entrenched aristocracy.[38] The analysis of Adams' relatively benign attitude toward the French nobility confirms this view. But it suggests also the additional consideration that a victorious middle class was not without its own special obsession directed in particular to the groups below it on the social scale. From the time at least of Shays' Rebellion, America's middle classes have reacted with fierce indignation to the major political manifestations of these groups. The phantom that haunted the minds of the Founders was the idea that hitherto in history popular institutions had proved incompatible with order and security of property. Their special nightmare was the possibility of the eruption from below. It was from this angle of vision that Adams surveyed the European political scene. In his view the condition of Europe's common people loomed as the largest factor limiting what could safely be attempted.

The essentially conservative solution to France's political problems considered desirable by Adams included even enlargement of the political rights of the nobility. His advice to the liberals was all on the side of caution and the avoidance of major innovations. He did not sense that French society was on the eve of fundamental reconstruction. French liberalism saw its task as the creation of a society in which liberty would be more than a name for the privileges and immunities of entrenched corporate hierarchies. It exhibited of necessity a social radicalism absent in the liberalism of a society that had the good fortune to be "born equal." There was little in Adams' own revolutionary experience to prepare him for the restless innovative energy of French liberalism in its heroic age. Although he envisaged liberalization, it was always within the bounds permitted by the received social order, upon which he did not anticipate or favor full-scale assault. His friend Jefferson shared his modest expectations about the prospects of political change in France up to 1789, but in the face of unanticipated revolutionary events, when it became necessary to make a choice, Jefferson embraced the Revolution, including even the terror. Confronted with the same choice, Adams, from the beginning, withheld his sympathy. He became, in the philosophical sense, America's great anti-Jacobin.

CHAPTER FOUR

ADVENT OF REVOLUTION

A STRIKING PASSAGE in the preface of Adams'
major work takes note of an increasing disequi-
librium in European society resulting from the
weight of its achievements. It was experiencing a "reformation of manners and improvement in science" that
would have astonished "the most refined nations of antiquity." But on the other hand the "knowledge of the
principles and construction of free governments" remained
at a full stand.[1] Much later historians would find in this
asymmetry — although they might express their sense of
it in different terms — the source of the revolutions that
engulfed western Europe. Awareness of Europe's uneven
rate of development led Adams, however, not to predic-
tion of political upheavals but to the expectation that the
spirit of improvement which in his view constituted the
special glory of the age would permeate the political
realm and without radical discontinuities gradually and
peacefully produce more "rational" governments. The
movement of events at the end of the century disap-
pointed these hopes. There ensued instead an "age of
revolutions and constitutions." The United States "began
the dance" with the "greatest revolution that ever took
place among men." From there the "contagion" spread

into Europe and Latin America, bringing into question all existing authorities.[2]

The American Revolutionary: A Peculiar Breed

At first glance there appears every reason to suppose that Adams would welcome and extend his full sympathy to the revolutions of his time. Himself the product of revolution, in his own native state he was a "new man," who had raised himself into political prominence from a family that had known only respectable obscurity for several generations. The revolutionary agitations afforded him a first major opportunity to display his talents. In the controversies with the mother country he consistently took up positions in advance of more hesitant American Whigs. To invoke the terminology of a later radicalism, he was in the vanguard of the revolutionary movement, prodding his compatriots along the path toward open breach with Great Britain. His *Thoughts on Government* in 1776 was a clarion call to the colonists to establish new state constitutions to implement their newly declared independence. Deeply imbued with the Whig tradition in English politics that always insisted on the community's inherent right of revolution, he considered that the right to kill a tyrant in cases of necessity could "no more be doubted than that to hang a robber or kill a flea."[3] A sober Braintree lawyer suspicious of rhetorical flourishes, he spoke with apparently fierce indignation of those feudal subordinations shortly to be assailed by the European revolutionaries:

Nature has not made this discrimination [between patricians and plebeians, nobles and simples] . . . I want to see nations in uniform. No church canonicals, no lawyer's robes, no distinctions in society, but such as sense and honesty make. What a fool! What an enthusiast! You will say. What then? Why should not I have my hobby-horse to ride as well as my friend? I'll tell you what. I believe this many-headed beast, the people, will, sometime or other, have wit enough to throw their riders; and if they should, they will put an end to an abundance of tricks with which they are now curbed and bitted, whipped and spurred.[4]

To turn to the attitude which Adams exhibited in reality is to confront a central paradox in his political thinking: a major American revolutionary, he was not a champion of revolutions. Greeting Europe's revolutions with reluctance (with one or two exceptions to be noted), he watched their course usually with mounting dismay. Professing during their course to hope for little in the way of permanent gains for the cause of liberty, he found his pessimism amply justified in the result. He was particularly proud of his assessment of the French Revolution, conceiving himself to be one of the few Americans who had seen through it at once and had never even momentarily succumbed to its attractions. He was in fact unique among American statesmen in never having given his heart to that Revolution at any point. Acute jealousy gave an edge to the satisfaction with which he noted that even the cautious Washington had indulged extravagant hopes about it. From the beginning, as he said, he himself had viewed it not as a "minister of grace" but as a "goblin damned." [5] In his retirement he received the capitulations of many of his former associates from whom he had been alienated by the party struggles of the 1790's. They now praised him for the views on the French Revolution which were formerly deplored as the "effusions of a splenetic mind." [6] He thought mistakenly that even Thomas Jefferson had conceded unreservedly that he was right.

Adams' distrust of the foreign revolutions was the characteristic product in the first instance of his conviction that America and Europe were separate worlds. His sense of the immeasurable distance between them inspired a certainty that what the Americans could safely do would overtax the capabilities of Europe. A singular concurrence of circumstances accounted for American success. The objects in view were well understood by the entire nation, because the animating principles traced back to the "first plantations." Despite differences in religion, law, and customs the colonies were alike in the great essentials of government and society. They had not divided. There had been retained throughout "a decency, respect, and veneration for persons in authority of every rank." The good sense and integrity of the body of the people had not failed.[7]

Readily agreeing that there was much in Europe's social order to provoke revolutionary discontents, Adams tended at the same time to discount in advance the likelihood that the revolutionaries could succeed in substituting anything more satisfactory. In some essential way, he appeared to imply, it was Europe itself and not a given social order that was beyond redemption. His attitude to the old regime was curiously ambivalent. Without valuing it for its own sake, he had no wish either to see it destroyed. The subordination essential to society could not be maintained in Europe without hereditary institutions. He upheld the right of revolution, but he doubted whether it was prudent for European liberals to exercise it. In every European country the people were sunk in illiteracy and superstition and prone to wild disorder when unleashed.

Adams was without confidence also in the political capacities of the revolutionary leaderships. Even the best of them, like the liberal nobility in France, although humane and high-minded, were utterly devoid of political experience. He accused the liberals of a vast innocence about the difficulties they must surmount, while at the same time condemning them for failing to apply constitutional measures which ironically took no account of some key difficulties which they actually faced. When the revolutions were in progress, Adams dropped his relativist insistence on American and European differences and repeatedly sought to impose an American constitutional absolutism. His distrust flowered into acute hostility when this universalist impulse suffered inevitable frustration. If the more moderate liberals lost control of events and gave way to the "men of blood," it was, he maintained, because they had been unreasoning enemies of mixed constitutions and advocates of unified sovereignties. The first reason why Adams was something less than hopeful generally about the cause of liberal revolution abroad was that he found American and European conditions so disparate; it is also true, however, that when he damned the foreign revolutions in specific terms, it was largely because they failed to conform to an American image.

For some the age of revolutions represented the fulfillment of the best hopes of the Enlightenment. Adams did not see it that way. For him it seemed rather a repudiation of the distinguishing qualities of the eighteenth century, measure and good sense, immunity to political or religious frenzy. The revolutions brought back again into the life of Europe the enthusiasm and fanaticism last seen during the Reformation. They must therefore be considered a retrograde step. They had divided Europe, which was previously becoming "more and more like one community, or single family." [8] Behind his dislike of the revolutionary developments lived a frustrated conviction that gradual transformation into liberal institutions without a breach of continuity would have been the more appropriate path for history to have followed. The innovative energy which the French Revolution displayed, its obliteration of ancient landmarks, brought out by way of counterresponse the socially conservative side of his political thinking. He disliked many of the new institutions the Revolution created, the temper of mind it inspired in its adherents. Its militant secularism, its ability to grip the masses and to marshal the resources of a nation, all seemed to portend the coming of a new age for which he felt little affinity.

In many particulars the strictures which Adams passed upon the French Revolution bear so close a resemblance to the opinions of the counterrevolutionaries that it is easy to make the error of identifying his position with that of the Reaction. Despairing of the Revolution, he still did not wish to smother the reform impulse. It must not be forgotten that he criticized always from within the camp of liberalism. Acknowledging that there were generous impulses and genuine grievances behind the revolutionary urge — it was not merely the product of envy and the desire to "pull down" — he thought the revolutionaries were doomed from the start by their blind ignorance of constitutional mechanics and their unwillingness to concede sufficiently to the intractability of the historical inheritance they were striving to alter.

The truth is that if Adams was a revolutionary, he was so in a sense very different than that produced by the other great modern revolutions. He exhibited little of the political messianism or apocalyptic fervor of the French or Russian revolutionaries. On occasion during the War of Independence he spoke the language of enthusiasm in proclaiming the universal significance and promise of the American Revolution. It was the "most complete, unexpected, and remarkable of any in the history of nations."

The Americans had taken up arms "as much for the benefit of the generality of mankind in Europe as for their own." He agreed with Franklin that America's "cause is the cause of all mankind," and that "we are fighting for [Europe's] liberty in defending our own." [9] American exertions must confer untold blessings upon posterity. "The progress of society will be accelerated by centuries by this Revolution. The Emperor of Germany is adopting, as fast as he can, American ideas of toleration and religious liberty, and it will become the fashionable system of all Europe very soon. Light spreads from the dayspring in the west, and may it shine more and more until the perfect day!" [10]

These expressions would be misunderstood, however, if they were taken to imply any sense of obligation to proselytize directly for American liberty among other nations. "It can never be the duty of one man to be concerned in more than one revolution, and, therefore, I will never have anything to do with another." Adams did not take up the position of a professional revolutionary. Uncharged with crusading zeal, he was not in the least inclined to see his own as the first link in a chain of revolutions destined to achieve the immediate liberation of all existing societies. Unlike Tom Paine or Joel Barlow, he did not conceive of revolutions as cosmic changes far transcending the local historical circumstances of any particular state. As he wrote to Lafayette, "I am not . . . an enthusiast who wishes to overturn empires and monarchies for the sake of introducing republican forms of government, and, therefore, I am no king-killer, king-hater, or king-despiser." [11]

If Americans were not themselves to instigate revolutions in other lands, how then was their achievement to contribute to the enlargement of liberty elsewhere? No very clear reply was given by Adams' generation. Franklin suggested that simply by existing a free America would exert pressure on Europe's rulers to mitigate their tyranny, because otherwise the common people would emigrate in large numbers.[12] In Adams' opinion America would exert influence through the massive radiance of her example without direct intervention.

But here again there was an ambiguity. For what was America to exemplify in European eyes? Adams was deeply concerned that European liberals not make wrong inferences from the American experiment. He did not want them to pay the American Revolution the ultimate compliment of direct imitation. He found no contradiction in arguing both that the Revolution was for all mankind and that it must not be misconstrued as a license to subvert existing societies. Other nations might choose to follow America, but it would have to be at a safe and respectful distance. In terms of the opportunity to enjoy the blessings of liberty, mankind was not one. Adams was not alone among his countrymen in the opinion that republican institutions were suited only to the special environment of a new country. In 1778 the Reverend Samuel Cooper cautioned a group of French officers visiting Boston against letting the triumph of liberty "on this virgin soil" too much kindle hopes for what might be achieved in their own country. "If ever you attempt to propagate [the sentiments of the Declaration of Independence] on your own soil after so many ages of corruption you will have to surmount far other obstacles." [13]

When the age of revolutions dawned in Europe, Adams was clear that the American Revolution had been one of the seminal influences. The example of the United States had infected Europe with revolutionary enthusiasm even in the absence of active propaganda by the Americans.

American complicity in Europe's revolutions had been unintended, but Adams was troubled nevertheless by the consequence he had helped unwittingly to further. "Have I not been employed in mischief all my days? Did not the American Revolution produce the French Revolution? And did not the French Revolution produce all the calamities and desolations to the human race and the whole globe ever since?" [14]

Unlike the European revolutionaries Adams was unable to entertain millennial expectations about any revolution, including even his own. He could invoke the sanctions of nature and historical necessity in favor of revolution. "Universal history was but a series of revolutions. Nature delighted in changes, and the world was but a string of them." [15] But he never conceived of revolutions as culminating points of the historical process, cataclysmic events which inaugurated the final eras in which the perfections of the natural order would be realized. A liberal Protestant, verging on Unitarianism, he was nevertheless wedded to the traditional Christian distinction between the transcendental and mundane realms. These were necessarily disparate and would remain so to the end of time. On this earth there could be no surcease from human troubles. The final era would be realized outside time. Political perfectionism was a species of impiety; whatever else revolutions might be, they were not the moments in which humanity was reborn. Adams belongs to the revolutionary type who thinks of himself as defending principles present in his society from the beginning. A mood of sober satisfaction with prevailing social arrangements did not induce the quasi-religious states of exaltation at the prospective realization of an entire new order of things such as is found in men like Condorcet. Ecstatic social visions are the product of class humiliation; they were foreign to the mentality of a middle class which was never afflicted with a sense of intolerable grievance.

Viewing them in terms of pragmatic consequences, rather than as integral elements in a religion of history, Adams approached all revolutions in a spirit of diffidence. Steeped in the historical literature dealing with popular overturns, from Thucydides to Clarendon, he considered that they were always hazardous experiments to which many unavoidable evils attached. Most often they failed to accomplish their objects, ending in despotism. They were sanguinary and cruel, marked by frequent displays of the mob spirit. Loosening the bonds of society, they gave free rein to the lawless and wicked portion of mankind who always waited for an opportunity to profit from relaxations of authority. His *Autobiography* recalls the melancholy into which he was plunged in 1775 by a "common horse jockey" who thanked him for creating a situation in which

'there are no courts of justice now in this Province . . .' Is this the object for which I have been contending? said I to myself . . . Are these the sentiments of such people, and how many of them are there in the country? Half the nation, for what I know; for half the nation are debtors, if not more, and these have been, in all countries, the sentiments of debtors. If the power of the country should get into their hands and there is great danger that it will, to what purpose have we sacrificed our time, health, and everything else? Surely we must guard against this spirit and these principles, or we shall repent of all our conduct.[16]

Revolutions were not lightly to be engaged in because they unhinged societies from their accustomed habits and opened the way to endless changes. "Innovations, though often necessary, are always dangerous." On the eve of the Declaration of Independence he took alarm at the "rage for innovation which appears in so many wild shapes in

our province. Are not these ridiculous projects prompted
. . . by disaffected persons, in order to divide . . . the
attention of the people . . . Many . . . that I have heard
of are not repairing, but pulling down the building, when
it is on fire, instead of laboring to extinguish the flames."
With the connection to the Crown about to be severed
formally, he urged the necessity of making state governments and forming a confederation, but he wished also
that as few changes as possible be made in the political
forms inherited from the colonial period. He was afraid
that the new legislature in Massachusetts would attempt
a "material alteration in the qualification of voters. This
will open a door for endless disputes and . . . number-
less corruptions." [17]

Adams' experience had nothing in common with the
concept of revolution as a total renovation of existing institutions previously condemned as denials and perver-
sions of the natural order. For him revolution consisted
in the exercise of the traditional right of resistance, which
arose according to Whig doctrine where there are "manifest intrenchments, either in design or in being, by men
of power, upon the fundamentals or essentials of [the people's] liberty." [18] The Whig pattern of the American Revolution did not generate in Adams the receptiveness to
change which was required in order to enable him to as-
similate easily the quite different European pattern of
social revolution.

Adams' preference was for placing reliance on historic
constitutional liberties instead of abstract natural rights
in justifying resistance to Parliament. He always disparaged the Declaration of Independence as a mere "theatrical show" [19] and professed to be unable to understand
why Jefferson had received so much credit in the world
for a paraphrase of Locke. He recalled that in 1773 Haw-

ley, Samuel Adams, and Dr. Joseph Warren had prepared a draft reply to Governor Hutchinson's defense of Parliament's right to make laws for the colonies in all cases.

It was very prettily written, but filled with that silly democratical nonsense which at that time, and ever since, has poisoned so many of our newspapers, and produced such a black catalogue of horrors in the French Revolution . . . I reasoned . . . with the committee till I convinced them of the many errors, and induced them to expunge them; and, instead of them, introduced that discussion from legal and constitutional authorities which was adopted by the committee . . . and which convinced the whole people of North America . . . that by law and constitution Parliament had no authority over us.[20]

Nothing affords more certain indication that the Americans underwent a special kind of revolution than the peculiar breed of revolutionary typified by Adams who carried it through. In the absence of a wide range of traditional institutions to be attacked, Adams' reluctances about innovation and an unconfined language of abstract rights were understandable. With the Christianity he knew in his native state enlisted on the side of revolution, he was under no pressure to develop a secular and millennial counterreligion. Because of the limited extent to which he was called upon to act the part of revolutionary, he missed the characteristic experiences, with their accompanying states of feeling, common to the great foreign revolutions.

Happy the people so circumstanced as to be able to forego these experiences. The favor of history, however, could engender its own kind of absolutism and disqualify the possessor from entering easily into the situations of those not so favored; unless, that is, sufficient discount were made for one's own particularity. Before the Europeans turned to revolution, Adams was inclined to urge that the American revolutionary example was not to be imitated because the factors accounting for its success were special to the point of being unique. With the spread of revolution, Adams projected his own experience abroad with an entire confidence in its applicability as a standard for measuring the performance of foreign liberals. The American Revolution began to be treated by him as special only in the extraordinary degree of its success, Providence having prospered it exceedingly out of benevolent intention to procure an enlargement of liberty. Adams dispensed judgment in the assurance that his own was the model revolution, and he was grimly sardonic and incredulous when he met Condorcet's perception that the Americans had been revolutionary only in a restricted sense. Without distinctions as to objects to be attained and obstacles to be overcome, the means and measures used to accomplish his own revolution were assumed to be directly relevant to the situation of the vast portion of mankind seeking to be free.

The Dutch Patriot Movement

Before the developments in France in the late 1780's increasingly engaged his attention, Adams witnessed the surge of the revolutionary spirit in Holland, where during that decade middle class groups challenged the rule of constituted bodies "which claimed sovereignty for themselves [and] were self-perpetuating in a limited number of families."[21] He observed closely the rise and progress of the Patriot Movement among the Dutch, its initial successes and subsequent eclipse by a triumphant reaction. In some respects his personal involvement with the events in Holland was greater even than with those in France. Holland was the theater of his most successful diplomatic initiatives. These he considered as not less important for his nation's independence than Franklin's mission in France, and afterwards he felt that his exertions there had never been properly valued by his countrymen.

Adams spent most of the period between 1780 and 1782 in Holland seeking recognition from the government and loans from Amsterdam bankers. In April 1782 he became America's first accredited ambassador at the Hague. Thereafter until his return home in 1788 he made several additional trips to the country principally to negotiate fresh loans. Unlike the situation in France where the monarchy was sympathetic to the American cause because of imperial rivalries with Great Britain, the House of Orange was strongly pro-British and distinctly cool to the struggling American colonies. To further his diplomatic purposes, Adams found it necessary to engage in a considerable propaganda effort to influence opinion among the Dutch along lines more favorable to the United States. "To this end he . . . bent himself by industriously employing the press, and by seeking to extend his personal acquaintance and influence as far as possible in useful directions." [22]

Inevitably he gravitated toward those persons who were most troubled by the political conditions in their own country and who were shortly to become the leaders of the Patriot Movement. Among these people enthusiasm for the American Revolution was easily aroused. Some of the bankers and merchants among them were willing to lend their funds to America, even before their government granted official recognition. Their newspapers provided an opportunity to disseminate American public documents, including the Massachusetts constitution of 1780, and to publish material relating to trade opportunities and political and social conditions in the United States. [23]

The mere imparting of such information had an inflammatory effect on the incipient Patriot Movement and undoubtedly contributed further to arousing demands for political change in Holland. Adams was drawn into close personal association with a few of the chief leaders of the Patriot Movement, and he expounded some of his major political ideas to them. "My friends in Holland were much employed in revolutions. In several conversations there, I had occasion to mention some things respecting governments which some of these gentlemen wished to see on paper." [24] Their promptings, he maintained, supplied him with part of the impetus to write the *Defence*. They in turn offered suggestions, which he appears to have considered hasty and ill-considered, to be incorporated into the American state constitutions.

In Holland, as nowhere else while abroad, Adams functioned as a catalyst of revolutionary enthusiasm. On one occasion when provoked by the indifference of the Dutch government to the purposes of his mission, he even uttered directly subversive sentiments, in advocating to Patriot friends that the power of the Prince of Orange (the stadtholder) ought to be reduced and Holland separated from her excessive dependence on Great Britain.[25] If he came close in Holland to exerting direct influence on a revolutionary movement, his activity was prompted less by a missionary impulse to propagate revolution as such than by zeal to promote his country's interests.

The Patriot Movement, whose agitations were at their peak between 1784 and 1787, consisted of a coalition of "Democrats" and "Aristocrats" (regents) voicing common opposition to the stadtholder. The former were largely well-to-do burghers excluded from state affairs because they were not members of the Dutch Reformed Church or did not belong to the regent families that monopolized positions on the town councils, the provincial estates, and the Estates General. The anti-Orange regents, while possessing full rights of participation in Holland's town councils and estate assemblies, wished to reduce the prerogatives of the stadtholder (principally his power of recommendation for state offices). They also opposed the House of Orange's traditional policy of close alliance with Great Britain.

Originally in the hands of the regent Patriots, the initiative passed to the Democrats, who desired not only to curb the Prince of Orange but also to make magistrates responsive to the popular will. The Democrats "formed themselves into militia companies, held a National Assembly of such companies . . . talked of equality of rights for persons of diverse religions, protested at the hereditary monopolizing of office in certain families, repudiated the three-estates system in Utrecht, and believed that they were imitating the American Revolution." [26] In rejecting both "a government by one man rule, or any system of independent family rule," the Democrats found themselves suddenly deserted by most of the regent Patriots who, not being able to "strain their principles to this pitch" and taking fright, began to make their peace with the House of Orange. [27]

Holland's internal struggles were complicated further by rivalries among the great powers. The House of Orange was favored by Prussia and England. France, in order to thwart English influence, for the second time within a decade, encouraged a popular movement. In 1787 the Prussians, on the pretext that the Patriots had given affront to the dignity of the Princess of Orange (sister of the King of Prussia), intervened with military force, routed the Democrats, and restored the power of the House of Orange. A proscription of the Democrats followed; many took refuge in France and a few emigrated to America. The French monarchy, heavily beset with financial difficulties, made no serious move to counter the Prussian intervention despite previous indications to the Democrats of support.

Adams followed the efforts of the Patriots with special excitement, approving evidently the desire of the Democrats to renovate a political system that "was a self-created, self-continued, and self-preserved aristocracy, in which the people had no more share than they had in France; no more, indeed, than they had in Turkey." He was deeply troubled by the failure of the Patriots and their subsequent humiliations. "I tremble and agonize for the suffering Patriots in Holland." The country appeared ruined beyond remedy. It was likely that the Dutch republic would be extinguished, or that if "the old forms are . . . preserved, the Prince will be so much master in reality, that the friends of liberty must be very unhappy, and live in continual disgrace and danger." He hoped that the best among the Patriots would have "sense and spirit enough to go to America," [28] and he assisted the Mennonite pastor Van Der Kemp to emigrate.

Sympathetic to their aspirations and their personal plight, Adams was severe when it came to assessing the qualities of the Dutch Patriots as revolutionary liberals. He indicted them as "unskillful and unsuccessful asserters of a free government." [29] They "were little read in history, less in government; knew little of the human heart and still less of the world. They have, therefore, been the dupes of foreign politics and their own indigested systems." Too confidently dependent on the support of the French, they had unwisely provoked the Prussian intervention. The revolutionary leaders had failed to understand "the necessity of uniting and combining the great divisions of society in one system." [30] They had been too inattentive both "to the sense of the common people in their own country," [31] who were devoted to the cause of the House of Orange, and to the conservative wing of their supporters, whom they alienated by pushing too far and too fast for a broadening of the basis of political participation.

Adams was not alone among liberal observers in his adverse judgment of the Patriots. Lafayette charged that they had been unable to agree on any plan and that they had been almost as opposed to one another as to the stadtholder.[32] Jefferson wrote that it would be "worth a great deal of blood" to reduce the power of the stadtholder and to place the happiness of the Dutch people on a ground more "within the command of their own will." [33] But he thought that the Democrats had grossly mismanaged their affairs by raising demands that frightened their regent allies into the arms of the Orange party.

Adams' remarks on the abortive Dutch Revolution take on major significance as the first of a long series of commentaries by him on the struggles of revolutionary liberalism in western Europe. The prospects of liberalism abroad became at this point one of his continuing preoccupations. The attitudes that appear in his discussion of the Patriots prefigure in many essential respects those assumed later toward the French revolutionaries. His derogatory reference to their "indigested systems" anticipates his subsequent opinion that the French liberals would have fared better if only they had understood balanced powers. As a liberal himself, it must be emphasized, Adams conceded the necessity for reform of Holland's stiflingly oligarchic constitution. But he turned harshly upon the reformers, charging that they were unequal to the occasion and deficient in the necessary political understanding.

His condemnation was little tempered by recognition of the painful difficulties of the situation with which the reformers had to cope. The Dutch Patriots were beaten because of foreign intervention, their own military inexperience, lack of popular support, and deep division in their own ranks.[34] Adams was fond of referring to the "fiery trials" through which the American Revolution had to pass, but the range of unfavoring circumstances confronted was meager compared to the problems faced by the Dutch liberals. Geographical factors and the international balance of forces both contributed to the success of the American Revolution. America was not like Holland a tiny country, readily accessible by land and sea to great powers deeply concerned about the outcome of the nation's internal struggles and determined to prevent them from being resolved in a manner unfavorable to their interests. The American Whigs, in addition, were not beset by the variety of contradictory interests within their own ranks that bedeviled the Dutch Patriots. The Americans were able to secure crucial support from France at a time when that nation was not yet exhausted and overwhelmingly preoccupied by its own developing internal crisis. The purposes of the Whig leadership were understood and supported by a large part of the common people. Given the circumstances of life in a new country, the right to possess arms and the ability to use them were widely dispersed among the Americans.

Adams shared with Jefferson the view that the Dutch Patriots had not been sufficiently moderate. But it is difficult to see how they could have been any more so without surrendering the substance of their demands. These were people, after all, actuated by the sense of intolerable grievance. They considered themselves indistinguishable in quality, in wealth, in achievement, from the few persons in their country who alone possessed political rights. The Patriots made no suggestions about universal suffrage or anything even remotely approximating it. They asked no more than enlargement of the tiny oligarchy that governed Holland. By one estimate, had their efforts in Utrecht succeeded, only one-fifth of the adult population in the city would have possessed political rights.[35] If the Democrats had gone only so far as their supporters among the regents were willing to follow, they would at best have made themselves the instrument of the victory of people whose program promised, if anything, to strengthen oligarchic domination of the Dutch political system. Limiting the power of the stadtholder — the heart of the Patriot regents' demand — would have submerged the force that at least acted as a counterpoise to aristocracy.

The cruel dilemma of the Democrats was that they were compelled to attack both one-man government and family rule. To accomplish both aims was impossible without the support of the common people, who in the towns still favored the stadtholder and in the countryside were still deferential to their regent superiors. In one respect, it can be argued, the Democrats were far too moderate. They made no effort to enlist popular support.[36] To stir the people into political activity required a much more revolutionary program than this upper middle class group was willing or able to envisage.

Adams' verdict that the Patriots were "dupes of foreign politics" seems on the harsh side, just as his assertion that they relied too much on French support was after the fact. A country like Holland, because of its strategic location, was hardly in a position to isolate its domestic struggles from the concerns of the great powers. As Adams himself later put it, Holland was a "frog between the legs of two fighting bulls." [37] The Orangist enemies of the Patriots were supported to the hilt by English money and Prussian arms. Desperate necessity and not mere inexperience or unsound judgment prompted the Patriots to rely on French support. They had received assurances from the French government, and they supposed that the French must react vigorously to the threat of vastly increased English-Prussian influence in Holland. They were not alone in their miscalculation. Much of Europe was astonished at the feeble French response when the moment of decision came. Action was forestalled by the onset of a profound crisis in the life of the French monarchy to which participation in a war on behalf of the American states contributed.

Adams' assessment of the Dutch Patriots provides a classic instance of his imposition on the vastly different situation of a foreign revolutionary movement of standards and expectations drawn from an American model conceived as an absolute. As the exponent of one successful revolutionary liberalism evaluating the failures of another, he conceded little to the stringency of the alternatives confronting his less fortunate foreign brethren.

Aristocratic Resurgence in France

The beginnings of the "fermentations" in France increasingly diverted Adams' attention from the desperate state of the Dutch Patriots. When early in 1787 the King's finance minister, Calonne, summoned an Assembly of Notables, seeking its help in relieving the financial distresses of the government, and precipitated the aristocratic resurgence that was to form the first phase of the Revolution, Adams was in London, occupied with the *Defence,* while fuming inwardly at the sterility of his efforts to improve relations with Great Britain. For information and commentary on the developing crisis in

France, he relied chiefly upon Jefferson and Lafayette. Lafayette, perhaps remembering the chilling skepticism with which Adams had responded to his earlier expressed hopes for major political reform in his country, indulged himself in predictions that must have confirmed Adams' opinion about the immaturity of his political judgment. "Affairs in this country considered in a constitutional light are mending fast." The prospect Lafayette held out was that France would arrive at a constitution within a decade certainly not comparable to the American, which was "the only one truly consistent with the dignity of man," but better in some respects than the English.[38] Jefferson was more guarded in his optimism. His expectation was that the French were about to remedy the "cruel abuses" of their government and to prepare a new constitution, which would give to this people "as much liberty as they are capable of managing." [39]

Adams judged the summoning of the Notables "one of the most important events of the age." He saw nothing amiss, as a few in France already did, in the monarchy's confining its consultation of the nation to "personages of the first dignity." In common with most liberal opinion he was not sympathetic to the reforms of Calonne, attributing the financial troubles of the Crown to its own extravagance and maladministration rather than to the more basic inequalities in the tax structure. Impatient for news of the results of the Assembly, Adams begged Lafayette to send him an account of whatever was communicable about the deliberations. His appetite for political reconstruction would have been satisfied with modest accomplishments, and his first impression was that this was all that was likely. "A little more liberality in religion, in commerce, in letters, and in politics would not only augment the felicity of France but be a good example to the rest of Europe." [40] Observing the deepening paralysis of the government and the growing self-assertiveness of the nobility during the course of the year, Adams concluded that the French had become "impatient under the yoke of servitude . . . imposed upon them, and disposed to compel their governors to make the burden lighter." The gathering agitation for the summoning of the Estates seemed to promise "improvements of various kinds. Superstition, bigotry, ignorance, imposture, tyranny and misery must be lessened somewhat." [41]

Although hopeful expressions appear in Adams' comments at this stage, they are already surrounded with qualifications and have almost a perfunctory quality, as if they were concessions to the more sanguine expectations of the persons with whom he was sharing impressions. The major emphasis in his developing attitude to the political awakening of the French is contained in the apprehensions he was already voicing as early as the fall of 1787 at a moment it should be noted when, although in an increasingly fluid situation everything was becoming possible, nothing decisive had as yet occurred. Pressures were mounting for the convoking of the Estates, but the monarchy did not capitulate to them until the following year. Effective political opposition was still the monopoly of the nobility. The newly organized provincial assemblies had met, enjoying vaguely defined powers over local administration, with aristocratic domination assured by the method of voting by orders. There had been some popular demonstrations chiefly in support of the insurgency of the parlements, but neither the bourgeoisie nor the people had entered the political struggle. [42]

At this point it would have been premature to have concluded that a revolution would take place. Outside of France there was hardly any awareness that major politi-

cal change impended. Yet the fact is that Adams' mind
surged with forebodings. Even as the momentum of events
intensified and he became convinced late in 1787 that
"the present conjuncture appears the most critical and
important in Europe, of any that has ever happened in
our times," [43] he never for a moment lost his sense of the
difficulties that the French must surmount to achieve constitutional government. During this very year he had formulated in the *Defence* his considered view that
political reform in France, although necessary, must proceed by gradual and gentle measures, and he easily took
alarm as this no longer seemed to be what the situation
promised. To the unprecedented occurrences among the
French he brought his not easily shaken conviction that
this was not a country providing a congenial soil for successful revolution.

Admittedly improvements were "much wanted in all
the institutions . . . ecclesiastical and civil," but how or
when they would be achieved was shrouded in doubt.
Representative government would require the coopera-
tion and understanding of the common people. But "what
dependence can be placed upon [them] in any part of
Europe?" [44] When Lafayette sent him an account of the
proceedings of the Auvergne Assembly, Adams congratu-
lated the young nobleman on the "progress . . . towards
a good representation" being made in the province. The
constitution of the parochial assemblies was conceived
"upon a very large and liberal scale." Accustomed to think
that America led the way in such matters, he was astonished that the property qualification for choice of electors
was smaller than the "forty shilling freehold or forty
pound fortune" prevailing in his native Massachusetts.
Reluctant to offer advice, he nevertheless hoped that the
provincial assemblies would not prove overassertive. "If

they act only as councillors of the King [they] must operate for the benefit of the nation." The great issue that pressed to the fore at the end of the following year in connection with the Estates General already worried him in its application to the provincial assemblies. He questioned Lafayette, "Do the three estates sit all together in the same room and debate together? Is the vote determined by majority of members or by the majority of estates?" He gave no indication that he opposed separate seating of the orders, even if this should entail aristocratic domination of the proceedings.[45]

The growing certainty that the Estates General would be summoned raised the question in his mind as to how such a project would "mix with simple monarchies." It appeared an effort "to reconcile contradictions," which could conceivably develop into a threat to the existence of the monarchy. He already worried about persons in France who dreamed of "reinstating republics, as absurdly constituted as were the most which the world has seen." The likelihood then would be a revival of "confusion and carnage, which must again end in despotism." If his memory served him accurately, Lafayette had suggested the possibility of a republic in France as far back as 1785. The French in Adams' view would require a long apprenticeship to install elective institutions even on a most limited scale. Their national character had not hitherto exhibited the solid and unspectacular qualities indispensable to the effective functioning of a representative system. He conjured up unflattering visions of meetings of future French legislatures. "The world will be entertained with noble sentiments and enchanting eloquence; but will not essential ideas be sometimes forgotten in the anxious study of brilliant phrases?"[46]

The representatives of the high nobility, who in 1787–88

led the resistance to the King's proposed tax revisions and demanded the revival of representative institutions, evoked his open contempt. He suspected they would prove as inept in asserting the nation's rights as, in his view, the Dutch Patriots had been. The failure of the one movement helped to condition his mood about the other. An aristocratic revolt was in progress in France, and Adams might have been expected to distrust it. In the *Defence* he described in detail the political propensities of nobilities, picturing them as permanently unreconciled to strong executive power and eternally conspiring to reduce it in order to establish ascendancy over the people. In these terms the events in France in 1787–88 could be viewed as an effort by the nobility to create a "status state" in which it would dominate both monarchy and people. In fact Adams did not see it that way, any more than most liberal opinion in France as yet did.[47] His analysis of the political behavior of aristocracies also pointed out that in their struggles to limit the power of monarchs they had often become spokesmen and defenders of popular liberties. In this light the notables and parlementaires might appear as the legitimate leaders of the nation in a movement to curb despotism. The reactionary character of the aristocratic resurgence did not become clear to liberal opinion in France until in the fall of 1788 the parlements formally demanded that the Estates General "be regularly convoked and composed . . . in accordance with the forms observed in 1614."[48]

If Adams was suspicious of the high nobility, who were leaders in the opening phase of the Revolution, it was not because he thought of them as vehicles of a feudal reaction, conspirators for narrow class advantage. He doubted their political capabilities and moral fiber, not the sincerity of their intentions or the legitimacy of their claims to speak on behalf of the nation. Pleasure-loving, elegant aristocrats were not the stuff out of which devoted revolutionaries were made. "Will the Duke of Orleans make a sterling patriot and a determined son of liberty? Will he rank, with posterity, among the Brutuses and Catos?" [49]

In April 1788 Adams returned home, happy, as he said, to remove himself "out of the noise of all these speculations in Europe." [50] By temperament immune to enthusiasm, he had expressed guarded satisfaction that some of the worst abuses of monarchical absolutism appeared on the way to being amended. Circumspect about offering advice, he was nevertheless certain about the direction in which constitutional reform should proceed. Apprehensive about some future possibilities that he dimly discerned, he avoided as yet anything like outright opposition to the emerging trend of events.

He did not comment again upon political issues in France until the fall of 1789 with one exception, in which, however, he sufficiently revealed the tenor of his developing opinions. On this occasion he gave a savage rebuff to one French liberal who expressed extravagant claims that his country was about to establish institutions comparing favorably with those of America. In the summer of 1788 Brissot visited him at Quincy and reported the substance of their conversation in a book of impressions of America published a few years later. For Brissot, Adams was a visible embodiment of American freedom from "meaningless" class distinctions. Adams represented republican virtue and the career open to talents. Brissot described Adams as now retired like Cincinnatus or Fabius to his farm upon the conclusion of "difficult embassies," after having raised himself to the "first dignities" from the humble station of a schoolmaster. He took special pride in talking with this celebrated American liberal about the surge toward free institutions that the French were making. Expecting approbation and sympathetic understanding of his hopes, he encountered instead a blunt disapproval that puzzled and affronted him. "I don't know whether he has an ill-opinion of our character, of our constancy, or of our understanding, but he does not believe that we can establish freedom even such as the English enjoy; he does not believe that, according to our ancient States General, we even have the right to demand that no tax should be imposed without the consent of the people."[51]

Years later Adams recorded his own memory of the conversation. His version coincided largely with Brissot's, although in retrospect he may have exaggerated somewhat the grimness and finality of his observations. At the moment of recollection (1805) France had entered a period of unrelieved despotism under Napoleon, and it seemed to Adams that all his harshest judgments on the Revolution had thereby been vindicated. He had remarked that

the French . . . were not capable of a free government and they had no right or cause to engage in a revolution. By this I did not mean that a nation has not a right to alter the government, to change a dynasty, or institute a new constitution in the place of an old one; for no man is clearer on these points than I am; but I know that the nation was not disposed to a revolution, and that it never could be made a national act; as indeed it never was.

The revolutionary initiative had originated with noblemen "not one man of whom knew what he was about." Their purposes had been neither understood nor approved by the bulk of the French people, who at that time were still deeply attached to the monarchy.[52]

The responses to Brissot are symptomatic of the progressive alienation of sympathy between Adams and the French liberals that took place during the revolutionary decade. The asperity of certain of his expressions brought about a breach also with the Rational Dissenters in England like Price and Priestley, who had been the group among all Europeans with whom he had developed the most cordial relations while abroad. It produced as well a coolness of feeling between him and many former friends and associates in the United States, among whom the idea gained currency that he had changed his political doctrines and turned apostate from the "good old Whig principles." The supposed alteration of his sentiments was attributed to his prolonged residence in Europe, where it was suggested he had been "blinded by the glare of monarchy."

Actually his view of the French Revolution did not represent any fundamental change in his political orientation, as he tried for the rest of his life to explain. It was rather an extension and development of the assessment of the prospects for political change in Europe worked out in the prerevolutionary decade. The opinions he then held were shared in varying degrees by many Americans. Scholars like Palmer and Malone have shown, for example, that well into 1789 Jefferson doubted that the French were prepared for any fundamental alteration of their political and social structure and that he exerted his influence while ambassador to persuade French liberals to settle for modest gains. The direction that the Revolution took was not something that Jefferson anticipated. Its impact, however, was to deepen and extend his liberalism and especially to enlarge his sympathies for foreign liberal movements.[53]

The individuality of Adams' response to the Revolution, pursued to an extent that some considered an "affectation of singularity," consisted in his complete immunity to the enthusiasm that the Revolution inspired in the liberal camp everywhere in the Western world. Adams was never gripped by the sense of new possibilities that the Revolution evoked in most other liberals. The Revolution confirmed him in the positions he had earlier adopted, and he persisted in them with a rocklike immobility through its course. In reality a former associate like Jefferson was affected by the French revolutionary experience more fundamentally than he. The essence of the change was that Jefferson came to think that the freedom established by the American Revolution had a universal meaning and promise for all mankind, that it was a proper object of aspiration by other peoples, even though other nations might have to follow a different or more difficult path to its realization. Adams remained a liberal in the limited sense in which he had always been one. He persisted in the earlier tendency to consider liberty the peculiar possession of a very few peoples, and he never acquired any confidence that nations like the French could succeed in mastering its secrets.

Adams' rigidity in a period of massive change paradoxically led to the result that he was misunderstood as a turncoat in the liberal cause. He approached the Revolution with the limited expectations born of his relativist perspective; in this view the French simply did not constitute suitable material for a free government. As the Revolution deepened, however, he began to be alienated, and unlike Jefferson disclaimed kinship, because it moved along lines that diverged sharply from American patterns. He found it difficult at first to believe that the French could have serious revolutionary intentions, because they were so unlike the Americans, but once convinced they had, he plied them with advice which overlooked how different from the Americans their situation actually was.

CHAPTER FIVE

VICTORY OF THE BOURGEOISIE

*B*EGINNING in the autumn of 1789 and continuing through the next two years, a second stage in the development of Adams' attitude to the Revolution may be discerned. To the earlier general misgivings inspired by his relativist perspective, there were now added criticisms in universalist terms of specific acts of the Revolution. Rejecting with special scorn the new political institutions the National Assembly was creating, Adams repeatedly offered advice about the alternative course it ought to have pursued. As much as at the Revolution itself, he took increasing alarm at its international impact, at the spirit of undiscriminating enthusiasm its progress evoked in the liberal segment of opinion in England and universally in his own country. In correspondence and in the most curious of his productions, the *Discourses on Davila,* he attempted to counteract these fervors without, however, repudiating the Revolution outright or associating himself directly with the counterrevolutionary current of opinion launched by Edmund Burke.

In the *Defence* Adams replied to the attacks of French proponents of unified sovereignties upon the balances in the American state constitutions. Instead of grounding his case primarily in the special features of American life, he sought a more general sanction for the tripartite legislative in the insatiability of human passions and the horrors exhibited in the history of unmixed governments. The system of balances emerged in his theory not merely as institutions whose virtue was their adaptability to American circumstances but as institutions possessing an unconditional value as the sole appropriate method of realizing free government. The universalist nature of his derivation of the balances left no room for necessary distinctions between societies. With American political behavior and social structure assumed to be in all essentials similar to those of Europe, the same constitutional strategy could be advocated as suiting the needs of both. What was in reality a distinctively American solution or evasion of the problem of sovereignty was transposed to other societies with an entire confidence in its relevance to their problems. Adams brought to the political experiments in France an obsessive and doctrinaire commitment to particular constitutional forms which largely ignored the attendant political circumstances in that country.

1789: *Constitutional Renovation*

The first and most crucial revolutionary development — the reunion of the orders, enforced by the intransigence of the Third Estate — provoked Adams' open dismay. As he saw clearly, the position of the aristocracy would be completely undermined by this momentous decision, if it were allowed to stand. With the three orders sitting together, decisions would be made by a majority of the members, considered as individuals, and nobility and clergy would cease to exist as distinct corporate entities.

The staunch republican Yankee, who three years before had written to Count Sarsfield about his hopes of preserving an "empire of liberty" in America without "such artificial inequalities as are prejudicial to society," saw no inconsistency in expressing fears to the same correspondent about the possible extinction of such "artificial inequalities" in France. "Mixed in one assembly with the commons, will not the nobles be lost? Outnumbered and outvoted on all occasions?" [1] Far from urging on the revolutionary bourgeoisie, he appeared to side with Louis XVI in insisting on the preservation of hereditary standing powers.

Adams did not understand the frame of mind of the Third Estate in 1789, and indeed he was never afterwards to understand it. "Privilege" was a word that never made its appearance in Adams' political vocabulary. In one important respect he even lagged behind what the monarchy was already willing to admit. In June the King had offered a program that included consent to legislation and taxation in periodic future meetings of the Estates General.[2] In September Adams did not envisage the establishment of constitutional monarchy — which the King had already conceded. He was doubtful whether it would be wise for the Estates General to claim authority to control the Crown, and he thought it preferable that they "be contented to advise it." [3] As late as the autumn of the year he found it difficult to believe that the French could be serious about the renovation of their system, after so many generations of despotism. He approached the Revolution with an incredulity born of his already formed estimate of French national character and political capabilities.

By the early months of 1790 the outlines of a new French constitution were becoming clear in the United States, with reception of the news that the National Assembly had decided to repudiate the bicameral principle and limit the king's power over legislation to a suspensive veto. Adams' response was immediately hostile. "But I will candidly admit that the form of government they have adopted can in my humble opinion be nothing more than a transient experiment. An obstinate adherence to it must involve France in great and lasting calamities." The French, it appeared, were following the dubious authority of Franklin and imitating the "miserable crudities" of the Pennsylvania constitution of 1776. Ignorant of "the true elements of the science of government," they would inevitably find themselves under the "necessity of treading back some of their too hasty steps." Unhesitatingly he urged the French to inaugurate the system of balanced government that had proved conducive to liberty in the Anglo-American world. It was indispensable to "methodize" and "rationally digest" the traditional three orders into an upper and lower house. "If in earnest a constitution is to be established you must separate the nobles by themselves and the commons must be placed in another assembly; and the clergy divided between the two. In short your legislature must have three branches [including the King], and your executive and legislative must be balanced against each other, or you will have confusion." [4]

Adams' opinion as to the position that the King must occupy in the revised system can be sufficiently inferred from the criticisms he was offering of the fledgling United States constitution. In his view (summer 1789) the equipoise of power in the federal government was not adjusted with the "necessary accuracy." Because his veto could be overridden, if only by extraordinary majorities, the "president's independence as a branch of the legislative" was dangerously limited. The weakness, if not amended, promised the "destruction of [the] constitution." The sovereignty was tripartite in the American system. "The house and senate are equal, but the third branch, though essential, is not equal. The president must pass judgment upon every law; but in some cases his judgment may be overruled . . . it is . . . certain he has not equal power to defend himself . . . as the senate and house have." [5] The adoption of the suspensive veto by the National Assembly seemed no better than a miserable expedient to one who appeared convinced that even the Americans could not avoid dire consequences without an absolute executive veto. The King, confronted by a "vast legislature in one national assembly," was like a "gladiator in a pit without arms to defend himself against an hundred lions." He "could resist nothing." [6]

In the National Assembly's constitutional debates (August-September 1789), the arguments for an upper house and an absolute veto were thoroughly canvassed and rejected by large votes. It was not because these arguments were little known that they had no appeal. What seemed elementary wisdom to Adams proved quite unacceptable to the National Assembly. Even Louis XVI did not desire an absolute veto on legislative decisions, because he thought such a power politically too dangerous ever to use in practice. [7] A major figure in the Assembly, Mirabeau, pointing to the historic role of the French monarchy in curbing the nobility, argued for an absolute negative on the ground that the King represented the nation as much as the legislature. [8] But Adams seems to have had no advocates among the French for the absolute veto in the sense that he meant, that the executive could simply block the legislature's acts without any further recourse. Even Mirabeau had in mind something quite different. His proposal called for immediate dissolution and appeal to the electorate when the King negatived legislative action.[9] The voters would then express themselves as to whether they preferred the views of legislature or King.

The suspensive veto, as actually adopted by the National Assembly and treated with such scorn by Adams, was a very considerable power. It was immediately interpreted to mean that a measure passed against the King's veto by two successive biennial legislatures in addition to the one in which the measure originated could become law without his approval. The King was thus empowered to block for as long as six years legislation repeatedly sanctioned by the Assembly and presumably by the electorate.[10] There were grounds for maintaining that this was a dangerous provision, but not surely on the basis urged by Adams, that it left the King no power of resistance. The suspensive veto encouraged the King to take the antagonistic course toward the Assembly which ended by alienating the country from the monarchy. Adams contended that the King should have been given a veto that could not be overridden and that royal power should have been buttressed further by a second chamber. He disapproved particularly the argument used by Mirabeau in support of an absolute negative, because its direction was so pronouncedly antiaristocratic. With the dominant temper of the National Assembly hostile to the nobility, Mirabeau had to defend a strong executive on the ground that the king, equally with the people, was concerned to prevent re-establishment of aristocratic privilege. In Adams' view Mirabeau imperfectly understood the necessity of providing against the tyranny of the majority in a single assembly, not recognizing that an upper chamber as well as an executive veto were necessary to accomplish the desired result.[11]

A majority of the National Assembly's constitutional committee, including Mounier, strongly favored an upper

chamber. But their ideas about how it should be constituted differed markedly from Adams'. Although Mounier
and his adherents were dubbed "Anglomaniacs" by their
opponents, they were far from being slavish advocates
of the English model. They specifically excluded the
notion that the higher clergy and nobility should be
seated in the upper house, unlike Adams, who spoke of
confining it to the two privileged orders. Maintenance of
the hereditary principle along the lines of an English
House of Lords proved unacceptable even to the more
moderate liberals in the Assembly, who were more attracted to the American model of an elective senate with
the addition of a high property qualification for office-
holding. Mounier tried unsuccessfully to reassure the Assembly that an elective senate would not bring back
aristocracy, that it would not be composed exclusively of
nobles.[12]

In September 1789 all segments of middle class opinion
in the National Assembly were much more revolutionary
than Adams was prepared to be, and his suggestion for
"methodizing" the three estates would have been considered dangerously reactionary. Even the French Right
at the time did not want a "rationally digested" system
in the English fashion. The bulk of the nobility desired
instead the traditional system of orders as the only secure
basis for its social position. In a House of Lords the
smaller nobles would be obscured by the wealthier and
more prominent members of their class. In an elective
senate they would have to go into politics to contest for
the votes of plebeians.[13]

Adams was puzzled and affronted at the hostility to
balanced government displayed by the National Assembly. The views of men like Mounier or Mirabeau, although
not completely coinciding with his own, seemed at least

on the right track in their recognition of the need to counterpoise other centers of power to the will of the Assembly. But how to explain the repudiation of the soundest opinions expressed in the deliberations? In part it must be put down to ignorance of the correct principles of political architecture. The French revolutionaries might be sincere in their devotion to the "principles of liberty," but they had not yet learned the "principles of government." [14] (The time of the unprincipled and desperate adventurers had not yet arrived.) The "Anglomaniacs," who came closest to understanding the balance, had been defeated by well-intentioned but politically inexperienced men, who too frequently gained ascendancy in periods of stress. "I know by experience that in revolutions the most fiery spirits and flighty geniuses frequently obtain more influence than men of sense and judgment, and the weakest men may carry foolish measures in opposition to wise ones proposed by the ablest. France is in great danger from this quarter." [15]

Adams was nettled that his own contribution to the understanding of balanced government was ignored or brushed aside by the National Assembly. As he wrote to one admirer of his political writings, "With all your compliments and elogiums of my *Defence* would you believe that neither the whole nor any part of it has been translated into French? At this interesting period; at such a critical moment, would you not have expected that every light and aid to the national deliberations would have been eagerly embraced?" [16] Although Jefferson had promised to make efforts to procure its publication, the *Defence* did not appear in a French edition until 1792. In oblique fashion, however, his work was known to some members of the Assembly. In 1787 John Stevens of New Jersey published a rejoinder to Adams which castigated the *De-*

fence as too partial to ranks and orders and to the government of England. Early in 1789 Stevens' pamphlet appeared in a French version with annotations by Condorcet
and Dupont, who used it to mount an attack on balanced
government which had considerable persuasive effect on
the National Assembly.[17] Paradoxically, Adams played
a role in France in 1789 in the form of a rebuttal to his
own views.

What made it possible for a refutation written by an
obscure American, even if accompanied by the "clarifica-
tions" of distinguished members of the Turgot circle, to
outweigh the deeply considered views of one of the most
illustrious figures of the American Revolution was, of
course, the deep animus against hereditary privilege
nursed by the Third Estate. The opposition to an upper
chamber arose out of the belief that it would provide an
asylum for aristocracy, just as the opposition to an absolute veto arose from the well-founded suspicion that the
King would support his nobility against the Third Estate.
To establish a balance, it was felt, would place the gains
of the Revolution in jeopardy.

Given this dominant state of feeling, the advocates of
an upper house like Mounier were obliged to exercise
caution and argue that an elective senate would not become an instrument of aristocratic influence. Similarly
those who urged a strong executive found it expedient to
place their emphasis on the long-standing alignment between the royal power and the Third Estate in the struggle to curb the nobility. Adams, who understood the
importance of this historic alliance better perhaps than
any other American of his day, raised it to the level of a
dogma in postulating that popular interests everywhere
required a powerful executive as a protection against an
encroaching aristocracy.

VICTORY OF THE BOURGEOISIE

The abstract universalism of Adams' theory of executive power took no account of the specific circumstances of the Revolution and could hardly recommend itself to the National Assembly, confronted already by the hesitations of the King about giving his sanction to the "abolition of feudalism" of August 4. Since June the King, as the first gentleman of the realm, had taken up a new position as the defender of the nobility, and the nobility had also begun to find new virtues in the throne. In the face of rapprochement between monarchy and nobility the National Assembly did not think it possible to create a powerful hereditary executive whose loyal acceptance of the "new order" could not be trusted. The constitutional alternatives available to the "friends of liberty" were narrowly circumscribed ones, and it is pure myth to ascribe their adoption of unmixed government to inexperience or lack of realism. As one historian has put it admirably, "In France the essence of the revolution of 1789 was the revolt of the Third Estate against the nobility. With a hostile nobility to overcome, and a king sympathetic with the nobility to contend with, the creation of an upper house and a strong independent executive was simply not among the possible choices for men interested in furthering the French Revolution." [18]

Adams affected to believe that the National Assembly was bewitched by an unreasoning preference for simple as against complicated governments. As he later (1796) commented:

The word 'simplicity' in the course of seven years has murdered its millions — and produced more horrors than monarchy did in a century. A woman could be more simple if she had but one eye or one breast; yet nature chose she should have two as more convenient as well as ornamental. A man would be more simple with but one ear, one arm, one leg. Shall a legislature have but one chamber then, merely because it is more simple? A wagon would be more simple if it went upon one wheel; yet no art could prevent it from oversetting at every step.[19]

These analogies, to which Adams was so much addicted, were not found compelling by French liberal opinion in 1789. Another kind of analogy, perhaps, would have found more favor, such as the description of France under the old regime as "like an attic stuffed full of all kinds of old furniture."[20] Simple government — another name for an undivided legislative authority — would enable the attic to be swept clean of "unmeaning" encumbrances. The majority of the National Assembly was quite explicit in voicing the considerations that governed its preferences as to constitutional forms. As even the "bicamerist" Lally-Tollendal remarked, "It is not doubtful at present that a single chamber is preferable. There is so much to destroy and almost all to create anew."[21] Others pointed out that years of basic reconstruction lay ahead, in which there would be no means of separating ordinary from fundamental laws. There must be no royal veto or upper chamber to obstruct the work of remodeling French institutions.[22]

Adams preached a system of class reconciliation to be achieved by giving the major social interests vetoes on the actions of one another and by erecting an independent executive strong enough to hold the balance between them. He thought his constitutional mechanics could create social peace when the truth is that it could function only on the basis of an already existing social peace. France in 1789 was full of radical social disharmonies and class hatreds. In this environment the balances were viewed in terms of their effect on the class relations. For the Third Estate a constitution on the English model was biased in favor of aristocracy. It would give a fresh sanction to privilege and provide the nobility with a political haven. It would make the realization of the nation's demands dependent upon the will of an entrenched minority. For classes impatient for far-reaching reforms a system with such ample potential for stalemate seemed to favor the interests most hostile to change. The very purpose of social reconciliation was suspect where there was "so much to be destroyed." Although no country was more admired by the French in 1789 than America, the dominant opinion in the National Assembly regarded advocates of America's mixed constitutions as possessed by the "devil of aristocracy."

On one occasion, which is therefore of special interest, Adams showed himself explicitly aware of the political circumstances governing the constitutional decisions of the Assembly. In the *Discourses on Davila* he took note of the argument of friends of the Revolution like Richard Price that a single assembly was required in order to prevent the upper orders from reversing the Revolution. As Adams himself neatly summarized the position: "If a senate had been proposed, it must have been formed, most probably, of princes of the blood, cardinals, archbishops, dukes, and marquises; and all these together would have obstructed the progress of the reformation in religion and government, and procured an abortion to the regeneration of France." [23]

Adams may have been willing to concede that the "best apology" to be made for a "sovereignty in one assembly" was that it was "only intended to be momentary" during a period of extensive reform. But he was very far from accepting the expedient, so defended, as desirable; the "best apology" was not in his view a very good one. One writer has recently cited the passage just noted as indicative that Adams would have opposed advocates like Mounier in the National Assembly debates and that he would have joined with the Left in accepting the temporary necessity of simple government.[24] Adams has often enough been presented as a conservative, and in recent years has emerged even as the "American Burke," but this is perhaps the first occasion in which he has been portrayed as a man of the Left. The interpretation urged here to the contrary is that Adams emphatically thought that the National Assembly had taken a wrong turning in its constitutional decisions of August-September, and that the members he respected most were the "bicamerists" like Mounier and the advocates of "King veto" like Mirabeau, even though their views were not identical with his own. He cited the argument in favor of a single house to show that even ardent advocates of the Revolution like Price conceded the *ultimate* desirability of an upper chamber. In another place in the same work he alluded to the dangers of even momentarily straying from the true path. "When [the balance] is once widely departed from, the departure increases rapidly, till the whole is lost."[25] Again in *Davila* he explicitly counseled that the common people must not aim at the entire sovereignty.[26]

Once before in the case of the Pennsylvania constitution of 1776, Adams had met the same apology for a single sovereign assembly. On that occasion "an apprehension, that the Proprietary and Quaker interests would prevail, to the election of characters disaffected to the American cause, finally preponderated against two legislative councils."[27] Pennsylvania had found by experience the necessity of a change and had adopted a new constitution in 1790. At no point was Adams ever willing to extenuate the first Pennsylvania constitution on the ground of temporary necessity. From the beginning he condemned it roundly.

> I fear I was mistaken when . . . I foretold that every colony would have more than one branch to its legislature. The Convention of Pennsylvania has voted for a single Assembly. Such is the force of habit; and what surprises me not a little is, that the American philosopher [Franklin] should have so far accommodated himself to the customs of his countrymen as to be a zealous advocate for it. No country ever will be long happy, or ever entirely safe and free, which is thus governed. The curse of a *ius vagum* will be their portion.[28]

Adams rejected the argument that the expediencies of the moment, however pressing, should be the governing consideration in establishing a constitution, which by its very nature was intended to set forth the fundamental pattern of a nation's government and to embody its idea of political justice. A constitution shaped by passing exigencies would embody the will of dominant partisan interests. It would not prove lasting, because it would not win the allegiance of all segments of the nation. It was likely, in addition, to function as the instrument of one part of the nation to despoil and oppress the others. Only the system of balanced powers was truly impartial, because it armed each division of society with the necessary power to secure itself against attack.

There can be no doubt that in this light Adams saw the first revolutionary constitution in France as a grossly partisan document directed toward the destruction of the aristocratic interests which he regarded as a necessary and permanent part of the social scheme. It is a misunderstanding of Adams' thinking to believe that he would have approved of the men who voted for a single assembly on the ground that only in this way could opposition to the will of the Third Estate be overcome. In Adams' view the Third Estate was the "people," but not the entire nation. What he really thought of the constitutional strategy of the Left is perhaps best revealed in the following passage: "The popular leaders have views that one assembly may favor, but three branches would obstruct. Such is the lot of humanity. A demagogue may hope to overawe a majority in a single elective assembly; but may despair of overawing a majority of independent hereditary senators, especially if they can be reinforced in case of necessity by an independent executive." [29]

To have favored the Left's constitutional views, Adams would have had to respond more sympathetically than he did to its substantive purposes. The crux of the matter is that he did not share the end in view of the "popular leaders," a waging of effective war on the privileged classes. His quarrel with the French liberals about constitutional issues was ultimately also a quarrel with them about the content of the Revolution itself. He disliked not only the concentration of power in a single center, but also what the advocates of that power seemed to wish to do with it. He drew back before the massive social upheavals of the great Revolution. At first incredulous about the seriousness of the revolutionary liberals, he next took alarm at their appetite for innovation. Adams' tripartite sovereignty would have excluded the conquest of equality of rights which was, above all, the achievement of 1789.

1789: Social Revolution

The animating impulse of the Revolution, the struggle against hereditary privilege, from the first appeared to Adams as no more than "vulgar malignity" against the nobility, a "pernicious policy" inspired by "false philosophy." The National Assembly would have cause to repent that it had stirred up popular resentment against the "great families" by representing them "as scourges, as blind and mechanical instruments in the hands of divine vengeance, unmixed with benevolence." Noble families were "sent to be blessings" and "they are blessings, until, by our own obstinate ignorance and imprudence, in refusing to establish such institutions as will make them always blessings, we turn them into curses." It could have no "good tendency or effect, to endeavor . . . to make them objects of hatred . . . to the common people. The way of wisdom to happiness is to make mankind more friendly to each other." The existence of such families was not their fault. "They created not themselves. We, the plebeians, find them the workmanship of God and nature, like ourselves." His reply to the complaint of the Third Estate about privileges was to explain that neither conspicuous birth nor hereditary wealth was reasonably the object of censure, even though conferring influence, popularity, and power. Long before his famous interchange in retirement with Jefferson, Adams formulated the idea that the distinction between artificial and natural aristocracy was not well founded. "It is fortune which confers beauty and strength, which are called qualities of nature, as much as birth and hereditary wealth, which are called accidents of fortune; and, on the other hand, it is nature which confers these favors as really as stature and agility." In pursuing the design to uproot hereditary privilege, the French National Assembly was dangerously close to adopting the "contracted and illiberal" doctrine of Machiavelli, that nations desiring to establish free government must ruthlessly extirpate their great families. To the contrary, Adams urged, all countries had their beloved families, and it was a wild idea to seek to annihilate them.[30]

Adams' reaction to the news of the reunion of the

orders was initially to express fear that the nobility would be lost. At one point in the *Discourses on Davila,* however, he developed the very different idea, a reiteration of what he had earlier said in the *Defence,* that the Third Estate in instituting a single assembly did not understand its own self-interest. A single assembly augmented the influence of nobility and must therefore be considered the "highest flight of aristocracy." Five-eighths of the National Assembly were noble. "The first fresh election will show the world the attachment of the people to [the noble families]. In short, the whole power of the nation will fall into their hands, and a commoner will stand no chance for an election after a little time, unless he enlist himself under the banner and into the regiment of some nobleman." [31] In so arguing, Adams was assuming that the common people, still attached to traditional superiors, would vote them into office in any electoral contest to the exclusion of upstart competitors. If there were only a single chamber, the nobles would thereby monopolize political control.

The remedy, of course, was Adams' familiar one of ostracizing the "great" into an upper house. Adams' position was not merely a disingenuous effort to disarm opposition to upper chambers. It undoubtedly rested upon a misjudgment of the state of popular opinion in France that was entirely understandable in view of some features of his experience while abroad. In Europe he observed the common people apparently unshaken in its "ancient prejudice" in favor of distinguished families. The Dutch Patriots foundered on this very point. If the French Revolution had a different outcome, it was in large part because outraged feelings against aristocratic pretensions were found among the people as well as the bourgeoisie. Adams was not alone in being unprepared for the new state of mind of the larger part of the French peasantry and townspeople. In the elections for the Estates General, French liberals demanded that each order be required to choose its representatives from its own members, fearing the prestige of the nobles and supposing them capable of being elected to represent the people.[32]

Adams is more legitimately open to criticism for erecting his limited observations of popular deference to superiors into an abstract universalist argument for the absolute necessity of second chambers. He can be charged also with adopting contradictory positions. The establishment of a single chamber could not be both the "highest flight of aristocracy" and a measure promising the destruction of nobility. It is highly probable that it was the latter possibility about which he was most concerned. The new mass insubordination evoked by the Revolution frightened him and presented him with problems of reinterpretation. His first conclusion, that it was deliberately fomented by the National Assembly, underestimated the extent of spontaneity in the expression of popular grievances and aspirations. In a later phase of the Revolution he attributed the insubordination to the pernicious activity of men of letters, accusing them of reasoning the multitude out of its habitual social attachments.

In the effort to demonstrate that the nobles must retain an essential part of the sovereignty in any new constitution adopted in France, Adams, as previously in the *Defence*, strongly emphasized their historic services on behalf of liberty.

These families, thus distinguished by property, honors, and privileges, by defending themselves, have been obliged to defend the people against the encroachments of despotism. They have been a civil and political militia, constantly watching the designs of the standing armies, and courts; and by defending their own rights, liberties, properties, and privileges, they have been obliged, in some degree, to defend those of the people by making a common cause with them.

The defects in Europe's traditional political order were not rightly to be ascribed to the existence of nobility. To this institution "Europe owes her superiority in war and peace, in legislation and commerce, in agriculture, navigation, arts, sciences, and manufactures, to Asia, and Africa." The problem was that hitherto the common people had possessed no adequate means of defense of its interests against nobles or courts. Deprived of political rights, the common people had supported kings against nobles. The progress of "reason, letters, and science" had strengthened the commons, and it was now possible for them to win a "share in every legislature," beyond which, however, if they were prudently led, they would not attempt to go.[33]

Adams was aware of the class resentments which led representatives of the Third Estate to speak of the nobility in the new hostile fashion of the time as the "privileged classes." Far from sharing such feelings, he tried to combat the extremes of class passion that had come to the surface. Nobility rightly understood was not properly an object of envy. "The noblesse of Europe are, in general, less happy than the common people," as was demonstrated by their inability to maintain their own population. "Families, like stars or candles . . . are going out continually; and without some fresh recruits from the plebeians, the nobility in time would be extinct." Its economic plight in particular was often a desperate one. "If you make allowances for the state, which they are condemned by themselves and the world to support, they are poorer than the poor; deeply in debt; and tributary to usurious capitalists as greedy as the Jews." [34] They were forbidden by law to trade. The nobles "derogated" or fell into the common mass if they went in for business or a profession.[35] Considering them as a group, Adams felt justified in concluding that "they were debarred from more privileges than they enjoyed."[36]

To those middle class spokesmen who complained of the insincerity and immorality of the nobles, he replied that the "degeneracy of the higher orders" was no "greater than that of the lower orders."[37] He refused utterly to condemn the nobility in the class-conscious terms adopted by the French bourgeoisie. The bourgeoisie's wounded self-esteem, its rage against what had come to seem meaningless distinctions, was hardly comprehensible to him.

He was no doubt correct in noting that ugly resentments and a self-conscious sense of its own virtue entered into the passion for equality manifested by the Third Estate. But he gave little credit to this passion as expressive of genuine grievances. He had observed accurately that many of the nobility were laboring under increasing burdens which made it more difficult for them to support their station. But he missed the intensity with which they pressed for the reinforcement of class exclusivism as the remedy for their deteriorating status. In pointing to the stringent economic pressures to which the nobility was exposed, some privileges from which it was debarred, he was filling in some essential details but at the cost of minimizing more glaringly evident parts of the total picture. Nowhere did he acknowledge the detailed lists of abuses of which the Third Estate's *cahiers* were full. He made no mention of the immunities of the upper orders, their virtual monopoly of higher offices in church and state, the seigneurial relationship between landlord and tenant, manorial forms of income and property, the differences between nobles and commons in the penalties inflicted by the law for the same offenses, the vestiges of serfdom, hunting rights and game laws, property in office. The social measures of the Revolution — for example, the "abolition of feudalism" of August 4 — never roused any great enthusiasm in his breast. He thought that this action had been taken too hastily, that the consent of some of the deputies had been obtained by unscrupulous means, that the necessary respect for property had not been present.[38] The National Assembly in seeking to reform one system of feudalism might, he thought, by unwise measures contribute to the establishment of another.[39]

In destroying the distinctions attaching to birth, the National Assembly ran the danger of raising unduly the consideration attaching to wealth. The distinction of property would outweigh all the rest, especially in commercial countries, if it were not rivaled by some other. The prejudice in favor of birth moderated and restrained the prejudice in favor of wealth. Adams called attention to certain aristocratic virtues that were worthy of admiration and ought not to be allowed to pass out of the world. They included "patience, courage, fortitude, honor . . . service of the public." To destroy respect for birth merely set all passions on the pursuit of gain. A "sordid scramble for money" ensued whose fruits were "treachery, cowardice, and a selfish unsocial meanness." [40] Although fiercely insistent on appropriate provision for the security of property and for a time closely associated as a rising lawyer with New England's mercantile-shipping interests, he had limited affection, if always respect, for men of money. In Holland he had observed a society that seemed more given over to commercial values than any other in Europe. While expressing admiration of the "many excellent qualities" of the Dutch, he complained also of a "general littleness arising from the incessant contemplation of stivers and duits, which pervades the whole people." [41]

As a reflective and generalizing type of mind, struggling to find the meaning of the great political events of his age, Adams was attracted to the idea that increasing accumulation of wealth among the commons was one of the deeper sources of the French Revolution. In the *Defence* he made handsome acknowledgment of the debt which political speculation owed to James Harrington's "noble discovery" that empire followed the balance of property. He made his own special application of the principle — close to constituting "the foundation of all politics" [42] — to the events in France. As he explained, "The aristocracy of wealth is now destroying the aristocracy of birth."

But in approving the description of the temper of mind of the French bourgeoisie as "eager by overgrown riches to partake of the respect paid to nobility," [43] he disparaged openly the generosity of the emotions inspiring that class. His "economic interpretation" contained little suggestion that he considered the movement from rule by birth to rule by money as in any sense a necessary progress toward a higher order of things. Birth was more favorable to an "emulation in knowledge and virtue" than money. "As avarice is a meaner passion than ambition, is there not danger of corruption, depravity, and ruin from the change?" [44] In Adams' country the bourgeois order of life had triumphed easily and completely; the paradoxical result was that he espoused middle class values without militancy and was able even to experience some nostalgia for an alternative order of life whose virtues the struggling, class-conscious French bourgeoisie felt constrained to deny.

In his studies of French political institutions Adams encountered the work of Boulainvilliers, who founded the traditional system of orders upon racial differences. In this theory the nobles were represented as descendants of the early Germans, who had established themselves as lords over the persons and lands of the Gallo-Romans. Boulainvilliers extolled the nobles as a distinct race of men, "heroic and military, made for command and insistent upon the marks of respect assured by honorific distinctions." [45]

If Adams had no sympathy for this kind of apology for hereditary rank — "the generality of rulers have treated men as your English jockeys treat their horses, convinced them first that they were their masters, and next that they were their friends" [46] — neither did he approve of the position of a liberal like Condorcet, who asserted that nobility, because founded in conquest and usurpation, was without sanction in reason. Adams turned to one of the "sacred phrases" of eighteenth century Tory apologetics for defense of the idea that hierarchic gradation was not repugnant to reason, invoking the "great chain of being" against French equalitarianism. "Nature, which has established in the universe a chain of being and universal order, descending from archangels to microscopic animalcules, has ordained that no two objects shall be perfectly alike, and no two creatures perfectly equal." [47] He leaned also upon the authority of Scottish moral philosophy to find a sanction in nature other than force for orders and ranks. He was deeply impressed especially by Adam Smith's account of inequality among men as grounded psychologically in certain supposedly unalterable universal dispositions of human nature. [48]

Adams' charge that money was getting the better of birth in France did not prevent him from maintaining as well on some occasions, without any sense of inconsistency, that the Revolution was making war on all necessary social distinctions, not merely birth, and that in particular it threatened the security of property. Not only did he not approve the attack upon hereditary aristocracy in itself, but especially he considered that the sweeping language used in making the attack gave credence to more general misconceptions. Unqualified assertions on behalf of equality inspired false inferences tending to the destruction of "decorum, discipline, and subordination." [49] If the National Assembly seriously contemplated the "abolition of all distinctions and orders," it would be difficult to vindicate it from "an accusation of impiety. God, in the constitution of nature, has ordained that every man shall have a disposition to emulation, as well as imitation, and consequently a passion for distinction; and that all men shall not have equal means and opportunities of gratifying it." [50]

Adams was at pains to discriminate the legitimate meaning which alone in his view attached to equality. The French revolutionaries might properly aim at "restoring equal laws." Among men "all are subject by nature to *equal laws* of morality, and in society have a right to *equal laws* for their government." Equal rights and equal duties could be inferred from the "common nature" of men, but, he warned, not "equal ranks and equal property . . . any more than equal understanding, agility, vigor, or beauty." From the events of 1789 he had caught an implication that "too many Frenchmen . . . pant for equality of persons and property. The impracticability of this, God Almighty has decreed, and the advocates for liberty, who attempt it, will surely suffer for it." [51]

The National Assembly had failed to provide adequate security for property, security without which liberty could not be maintained. To place property at the mercy of a

majority who have no property was to commit the lamb
to the custody of the wolf. The controversy between rich
and poor was as "old as the creation" and "as extensive as
the globe." [52] Where the pendulum vibrated too far to the
popular side, "horrid ravages [were] made upon property
by arbitrary multitudes or majorities of multitudes." In
his view this vibration had occurred in his own country
and "France [had] severe trials to endure from the same
cause," [53] unless an upper house and an independent executive with an absolute veto were established. The National Assembly had resorted to exhortations to the people to maintain order and respect property, but without
the necessary institutional checks these addresses would
be regarded "no more than the warbles of the songsters of
the forest." [54]

In criticizing the National Assembly for failure to safeguard property, Adams, so often vaunted as the realist in
politics, showed that he hardly understood the dilemmas
of that body. The representatives of the solid bourgeoisie
who dominated the Assembly did not fail to show great
solicitude for property rights. They did more than issue
feeble calls to the populace to wait quietly for reforms.
Shortly after the abolition of the privileges, they sternly
reminded the peasantry that manorial payments must be
continued pending redemption. In some parts of the country the newly formed National Guard repressed disorder.
As early as December 1789, six months before Adams'
strictures, the Assembly divided the population into active and passive citizens on the basis of differences in
wealth, confining the right to vote and to serve in the
National Guard to the active category. [55]

If the members of the Assembly deplored assaults on
the persons and property of citizens, they also recognized

that the insurrectionary violence of the Paris mobs — the "mutinous rabble of Paris," as Adams referred to them — had twice within a few months preserved the gains of the Revolution. If they found peasant uprisings embarrassing because the bourgeoisie also were owners of manors and because attack on feudal property might give countenance to disrespect for property in its other forms, it was also clear that the peasantry was putting the axe to the basis in land for aristocratic predominance. Adams' system with its concentration on providing a remedy for the perennial controversy between rich and poor was primitive equipment for coping with the complexities of social struggles in France. The confrontation of "the rich who are few" and the "poor who are many" was only one element in the situation. The multitude — who were in fact almost all Frenchmen — included discordant interests, both rich and poor, united for the moment against an aristocracy that consisted of a few very rich and many poor, but all privileged.

In 1789 the primary class enemy for the bourgeoisie was the aristocracy not the people. Adams' independent executive and upper chamber could have prevented the pendulum from swinging too far to the popular side, but the chief beneficiaries would have been the aristocracy and the old regime. Because the main part of the French bourgeoisie could not be stampeded into making peace with the old regime out of fear of horrid ravages of arbitrary multitudes, an enlargement of freedom became possible for France and the entire Atlantic civilization. Adams also had known his moment of revolutionary courage. In 1774 he responded to "ministerial party" declamations against mobs with ambiguous feelings much like those of the National Assembly. It had to be granted that where mobs went unchecked, the populace became insolent and disorderly, but what then? "Shall we submit to parliamentary taxation to avoid mobs?" [56]

Adams was afraid that the French revolutionaries had confused equality of rights, a legitimate aspiration, with equality of means, a species of impiety. But in the short run he erred in thinking that the Revolution was undermining property. In fact property was being consolidated more firmly than ever, on a far more diffused basis, than it had ever been before in France. Adams himself recognized this in his occasional interpretations of the Revolution as the triumph of wealth over birth. For the long run, however, there were senses in which the Revolution pointed in the direction of equality of means despite its enthronement of the bourgeoisie. From the sweepingly general way in which the Assembly formulated its belief in equality of rights, having in mind hereditary distinctions, the basis for attack upon distinctions other than birth could be found. In countenancing expropriations of feudal rights, the National Assembly could engender disrespect for the claims of property in general. In refusing to condemn the popular uprisings, the National Assembly had conferred a new legitimacy on the direct action of the masses.

Adams cannot really be said to have been mistaken in catching in the language and actions of the National Assembly implications for the future which went far beyond the immediate intentions of the bourgeoisie in 1789. His political imagination reached beyond the events themselves toward the immensity of their portent, in alarm, because he had limited affection for that future which he dimly perceived. For his part Adams loathed the abstractions of declarations of rights with their capability of arousing expectations that ought not and could not be fulfilled. He was certain that property rights had to be acknowledged without equivocations and that all mobs without exception must be discountenanced. "It is sometimes said that mobs are a good mode of expressing . . . the resentments . . . of the people. Whig mobs to be sure are meant! But if the principle is once admitted, liberty and the rights of mankind will infallibly be betrayed." [57]

The members of the National Assembly, if acquainted with Adams' assessment of their work, would no doubt have been bewildered to find themselves exhorted to aim at equality before the law and at the same time condemned for abolishing hereditary distinctions. Just as the connection between concentrated sovereignty and reform of "feudalism" seemed to them inescapable, so also appeared the linkage between equality of rights and reduction of the nobles to the status of mere citizens. How could there be equality before the law without the elimination of the privileges that went with inherited rank? The preamble to the first revolutionary constitution made the connection. It declared that "no privilege or exception to the common law for all Frenchmen any longer exists for any part of the nation." At the same time it proclaimed that "nobility no longer exists, nor peerage . . . nor feudal regime . . . nor patrimonial courts . . . nor any other superiority than that of public officers in the exercise of their functions." [58]

Because it aimed at equality of rights in a society not born free or equal, the Third Estate was driven to carry out the social revolution that had never proved necessary in America. Approving of the goal of equality of rights, Adams never drew the conclusion implicit in his relativist contrast of American and European circumstances, that the French would necessarily have to follow a different path to its achievement than the Americans. Instead he recoiled before the explosive effects of attempting to reorder a social system pervaded by inherited status inequalities. To shy from social upheaval was to make the social freedom essential to the "dignity of human nature" the peculiar birthright of his own nation, because practically speaking it would be unrealizable anywhere else. There was little in Adams' revolutionary experience to prepare him for acceptance of a social revolution abroad, and postrevolutionary disturbances in the United States had inspired him with a dread of mass insubordination and disrespect for property, against which he sought for securities in second chambers and executive vetoes.

Although his own society exhibited a high degree of equality of condition, he took alarm at a revolution that was attempting to move European society in the same direction. In seeking to obliterate the aristocratic principle, the French bourgeoisie appeared to him to be undermining a chief support of decorum and order, clearly indispensable in Europe and possibly even required in the long run in the United States. He brought to the events in France the American Whig preoccupation with the danger of an unleashed multitude. Free of class animosity against hereditary privilege, whose burden was never directly felt in the United States, he showed some nostalgia for missing aristocratic virtues and a lively appreciation of the usefulness of aristocracy as an anchor of social stability and a barrier to the uninhibited sway of pecuniary values.

The constitutional measures he advocated as universally applicable, however much they might fit American conditions of social peace, were entirely unsuited to the reform aspirations of the Third Estate in France. With an executive veto and a second chamber, only those changes acceptable to the upper orders could have been carried out. While these changes would have been considerable, because all classes demanded a constitution and a regime in which individual rights would be respected, what was found most intolerable by the Third Estate, orders and privileges, would have been rendered untouchable and conceivably given a fresh lease on life. Adams was prepared to see a Whig revolution cast in the Anglo-American mold take place in France, which would have left the existing pattern of social relations essentially undisturbed. His response to the upheavals of 1789 would prove not the last occasion on which Americans showed themselves willing to accept foreign revolutions only on American terms.

CHAPTER SIX

AMERICAN ANTI-JACOBIN

BY EARLY 1790 Adams had formulated his fundamental objections to the course of the French Revolution. His protest was directed both against the equalitarian content of the revolutionary purpose and the constitutional forms adopted to implement that purpose. He sought to impose a constitutional formalism, the essence of which was the assertion that the system of balanced powers was universally both a necessary and sufficient condition of liberty. "I still hold fast my scales and weigh everything in them."[1] His misgivings did not yet assume the form of open denial of the legitimacy of the Revolution itself. Of the need for political regeneration in France he professed no doubt, however much he might deplore the means and measures used to accomplish it. He avoided outright denunciation of the acts of the National Assembly, preferring rather to express the hope that on mature consideration that eminent body would tread back some of its hasty steps. The tone of his commentary was still that of admonition addressed to patriots who through inexperience were in danger of choosing wrong courses. His criticisms of the first year of the Revolution were essentially a continuation of the dialogue with French liberalism initiated earlier and conducted amicably as between friends of liberty, although the tone of acerbity with which he responded to the enthusiasm of some defenders of the Revolution was producing a coolness in his relations with many old friends at home and abroad.

The "American Burke"?

A problem that arises in view of Adams' early critical tone toward the Revolution is the extent to which his opinions coincided with those of Burke. In view of the fact that Adams began to publish the *Discourses on Davila* several months before Burke entered the lists, it can be presumed that he was initially not much influenced by Burke's work. The first number of *Davila* appeared in Fenno's newspaper in March 1790, whereas the *Reflections* was not published until late in the year.

There is no single place in Adams' work in which he ever indicated very fully his impressions of the *Reflections*, and his attitude must be inferred from a number of incidental comments. In Maclay's *Journal* Adams is reported as follows: "Mr. Adams . . . came . . . and told me how many late pamphlets he had received from England; how the subject of the French Revolution agitated English politics; that for his part he despised them all but the production of Mr. Burke." [2] Burke's work was detested widely in America in the early 1790's by Federalists and Anti-Federalists alike (Jefferson spoke of the "rottenness" of Burke's mind), and Maclay duly recorded his shock at Adams' apparent dissent from prevailing opinion. Far from considering himself as having taken direction from Burke's *Reflections*, however, Adams seemed to believe that influence, if there were such, had proceeded the other way. He found in the *Reflections*, to the degree he approved of it, largely a reiteration of his own views. In what it is probably safe to designate as a pure fantasy, Adams gave an apparently serious account of the origins of Burke's pamphlet that established in his view the true order of influence. According to Adams, David Hartley had given a copy of the *Defence* to Burke, who up to 1786 was numbered among the "warm enthusiasts for the French Revolution." Adams' volumes "gave [Burke] his first suspicions and diffidence in the French Revolution. They produced an entire change in his views and sentiments . . . A gentleman in company with Burke speaking on General Washington said he was 'the greatest man in the world.' Burke answered him, 'I thought so too, till I knew John Adams.'" [3]

In the *Letters of Publicola* (1791) John Quincy Adams, while tilting at Thomas Paine's *Rights of Man*, offered in passing the judgment that Burke's censures on the National Assembly were as "severe and indiscriminating" as Paine's praise was "undistinguishing." [4] The son's position cannot be taken as conclusive evidence of the father's, but it is at least highly suggestive, considering that John Adams and his son were very often in agreement on political questions. The son's remarks, moreover, fall in with the tendency of the few specific allusions of the father to the *Reflections*.

John Adams was unmoved by Burke's laments for the passing of the age of chivalry,[5] objected violently to Burke's description of the people as a "swinish multitude," [6] and, most of all, was astonished that Burke should have maintained that the French before 1789 possessed the "elements of a constitution very nearly as good as could be wished." [7] On the last point Adams' position is clearly distinguishable from that of Burke. In the light of

Adams' constitutional formalism, the French before as well as after 1789 seemed equally distant from the true path. Nor is it likely that he accepted Burke's assertion that the French did not need a revolution, that, in so engaging, they had made "an unforced choice, a fond election of evil." [8] Despite dismay at the misplaced zeal of the revolutionaries, he never absolved the old regime from complicity in its own overthrow. "The desire of change in Europe is not wonderful. Abuses in religion and government are so numerous and oppressive to the people, that a reformation must take place, or a general decline." [9] Adams' response to the Revolution, the product of distinctively American experience, was very much his own and deviated on major points from both Burke and Paine.

French Democracy: Disgrace of Liberty

After 1791 Adams' attitude to the Revolution underwent a major change in tone and emphasis. Ceasing to regard it as a well-intentioned, if erratic and misguided effort at "breaking the fetters of human reason and exerting the energies of redeemed liberty," he began to anathematize it as a disgrace to "the cause of liberty." [10] The events which provoked him into outright repudiation were first the establishment of the republic and the killing of the King and then the appearance of the terror and open anti-Christianism. His verdict on these developments was that the Revolution had departed wholly from the spirit, principles, and system of rational liberty and subsided into "anarchy, licentiousness, and despotism." [11] Disassociating his own services on behalf of liberty from those of the French revolutionaries, he read the French out of the liberal camp. "The cause of liberty, my dear daughter, is sacred. Your father has spent all his life in it, and sacrificed more to it than millions who now inflame the world. But anarchy, chaos, murder, atheism, and blasphemy are not liberty. The most dreadful tyranny that ever existed upon earth is called liberty by people who know no more about liberty than the brutes." [12]

As the "first empire of the world" dispensed with its king and established republican institutions, the United States was swept with wild enthusiasm for the Revolution. The hatred of George III expanded into a violent antipathy directed against all kings. There was rejoicing when republican troops turned back the arrayed coalition of the great monarchies of Europe.[13] While Jefferson and Madison extenuated the killing of the King as a necessary warning to tyrants, Adams defended the King's conduct during the Revolution and expressed intense dislike for the spirit of crusade against monarchy.[14] Rehearsing an old grudge, he explained that it was not out of any sense of personal obligation to the King of France that he deplored the regicide. "On the contrary, [the King] suffered his name to be used by his minister Vergennes and his base flatterer Franklin to my destruction if it had been in his or their power." Nevertheless Adams confessed himself deeply grateful for Louis' friendship to the United States. "Every vein of my heart sympathizes with him and his family in their afflictions." He repudiated as calumny a letter from the Convention to Washington defending the regicide and charging that the King was no true friend of American liberty and sponsored the American cause only out of base self-interest.[15]

In any case the true ground for deploring the destruction of monarchy in France had nothing to do with the question of Louis' services to the American Revolution. Out of Adams' relativist contrast of American and European circumstances came the insistence that the great states of Europe could not subsist without monarchy. In old countries republicanism must prove destructive to millions and productive of no compensating good. "The nations of Europe, if they become republics, must have laws, and those laws must be executed. Elective kings will not be obtained without continual anarchy, nor will they be able to execute the laws when they are chosen." [16] The French democrats were reaching after an impossibility. "My faith is immovable that after so many trials, the nations of Europe will find that equal laws, natural rights, and essential liberties can never be preserved among them without such an unity of the executive power." If there were undoubted evils in monarchy, there was no way of "getting rid of them but by substituting greater evils in Europe." Without kingship there must be elections to the "first place," and these in old countries would produce "venality, corruption, and distraction." [17]

Looking back over the conduct of the King up to his trial and death, Adams found little to condemn. Republican prejudice falsely attributed many base traits to him, but Louis had honestly occupied himself with establishing concord among the rival interests in France. He had not tried to use troops to intimidate the National Assembly; on the contrary he was sincere in maintaining that he would never allow the blood of Frenchmen to flow. His supposed tyrannies, for which he suffered decapitation, were as nothing compared to the cruelties of the Revolution. The King practiced less duplicity than the National Assembly, which from the beginning carefully masked its hostility to the monarchy. The flight to Varennes was justifiable as "the only way to save his life." Adams found nothing culpable in the plot to escape despite the implied association with émigré enemies of the Revolution and the encouragement of foreign intervention. "The great advocates for the right of expatriation ought not to deny it to a king any more than a subject." No other alternative than flight was open. "Had the king resigned his crown, the Assembly would not and could not have accepted it. Had he asked leave to retire out of the kingdom and taken an oath never to return they would not have consented." Adams appears not to have considered — as the King himself did not — the alternative for the King of acceptance of the Revolution.[18]

Although the National Assembly had granted the King a power of suspensive veto under the new constitution, Adams charged that the purpose of some members all along was to establish a leveling democracy. The delegates originally were restrained from more aggressive acts because "they dreaded . . . the loyalty of the people, and [its] habitual affection for the King."[19] Neither Adams nor the Jeffersonians for that matter did justice to the complex interplay of events that led to the republic. Destruction of the monarchy was not motivated merely by abstract ideological passion for republicanism. What doomed the King was his association with the counter-revolutionary designs of the émigrés and the interventionism of the European powers at the same time that he indicated his acceptance of the constitution and the revolutionary decrees. It is a strange judgment that makes the Assembly's "duplicity" greater than the King's. In 1789 very few dreamed of a republic, and the Assembly was united in wishing to retain the monarchy. "French republicanism was not a ready-made doctrine or programme imported from outside. It was home-made and grew out of the political nature and needs of the country." The agitation for the republic began only after the flight to Varennes, and it arose out of a feeling that the King had betrayed his trust. It was not true that the deputies desired the republic but were held back by deference to the wishes of the people. On the contrary, popular feeling against the King forced the hand of the Assembly despite the fears of many deputies that to dethrone Louis would invite foreign invasion and destroy the constitution of 1791 in its infancy.[20]

In the opening phase of the Revolution Adams appears not to have passed judgment upon the religious policy of the National Assembly. He made no comment on the abolition of the tithe and of monastic vows and the granting of full citizens' rights to Protestants and Jews. There is no indication of his attitude to the Civil Constitution of the Clergy, nor to the nationalization of church property. But he expressed persistent concern that *philosophes* with infidel views had formed the minds of the revolutionaries. "I own to you, I know not what to make of a republic of thirty million atheists." His forebodings led him to suggest with rare prescience that "there are in Europe appearances which indicate such changes that it is not extravagant to say that there may be countries in another century intolerant not only of Christianity but of theism."[21] In the *Discourses on Davila* he felt sufficiently worried to warn against the possibility that

the government of nations may fall into the hands of men who teach the most disconsolate of all creeds, that men are but fireflies, that this *all* is without a father. Is this the way to make man, as man, an object of respect? Or is it to make murder itself as indifferent as shooting a plover, and the exterminating of the Rohilla nation as innocent as the swallowing of mites on a morsel of cheese? . . . A certain duchess of venerable years and masculine understanding, said of some of the philosophers of the eighteenth century, admirably well, — *"On ne croit pas dans le Christianisme, mais on croit toutes les sottises possibles."* ["They do not believe in Christianity, but they believe all possible stupidities."][22]

Beginning in the fall of 1792 and extending into 1793, a fierce anticlericalism made its appearance in France, which seemed bent on destroying the influence of a church identified with counterrevolution. Outright dechristianization was attempted, with the substitution of republican festivals for Sabbaths and saints' days, measures against the clergy, closing of churches, mutilation and destruction of church effects.[23] No single feature of the Revolution caused greater embarrassment to its defenders in the United States than these antireligious expressions. Some Americans who had accepted the killing of the King and extenuated the terror were propelled into opposition by the manifestations of irreligion. A revolutionary sympathizer like Samuel Adams, who was also devout, in a Fast Day Proclamation as governor of Massachusetts implored the French to turn aside from assaults on religion.[24] For John Adams the anticlericalism was the culminating horror in the progress of the Revolution. "Our allies, our only allies, as the demi crazies pathetically call them, have completed their system by turning all their churches into *Je ne sais quoi,* and if they should have any government erected among them either by themselves or others, they may substitute choruses of boys and girls to chant prayers like the Romans." [25]

There was danger that the surge of irreligion, coinciding with destruction of monarchy, would cast permanent discredit upon republicanism. Without "religious principles" the source of morality was undermined. "Religion and virtue [were] the only foundations not only of republicanism and of all free government, but of social felicity under all governments and in all the combinations of human society." [26] Adams was scandalized that some members of the New England clergy, including the highly respected Jeremy Belknap, admired the French republicans and commended their example to the nations of Europe. It was now possible to complete the discomfiture of these divines. "Do they wish to resign all their salaries, and to have their churches turned into riding houses, the Sabbath abolished, and one day in ten substituted to sing songs to the manes of Marat?" [27]

That the venom of the French republicans was directed toward a church which Adams held to be peculiarly hostile to liberty was no ground for excusing their conduct. As he put it unflatteringly, "Atheism is worse than even Catholicism, if we judge by its effects." [28] His indignation at French infidelity was untouched by any new sympathy for the virtues of Catholicism. He would no doubt have been surprised to learn from men like Robespierre that in the worship of the Supreme Goddess Reason they were acknowledging the truth of his principle that atheism could not produce the qualities required by republics. Adams did not regard religion as merely an instrument of civic virtue. By "religious principles" he meant some variety of the Christian faith, not "natural religion" or pagan deification of a merely human faculty.

Adams continued to manifest intense interest in the constitutional experiments of the French through the revolutionary decade. He said little in detail about the stillborn constitution of 1793. He thought that too frequent elections were provided. The assertion of a right of insurrection as inherent in the people was too broad and required qualification.[29] According to his doctrine, when a single assembly chose the executive, the governing power was too variable and weak. The executive that rose out of the Convention actually turned out to be one of the most energetic in France's political history. Adams appeared to believe that his system of balances would have prevented the atrocious struggle among the French parties.

Rejecting Adams' constitutional formalism, the émigré Viscount Noailles told him sadly that a constitution modeled on the English could not last three days in France.[30]

The Thermidorian reaction seemed to Adams a return to moderation and decency. The constitution of 1795 was a turn in the right direction, with its institution of a limited suffrage and a double legislature. But the most unusual feature of the constitution, its plural executive, was a most unfortunate step.

> The French device of five Directors . . . will not answer their end. Among these emulation will soon produce divisions . . . The executive power, in the new constitution, is exactly like Daniel in the den of lions, or Shadrack and Co. in the fiery furnace . . . A hungry wolf will not fly at an innocent lamb, with more certainty than a legislative power at an executive, provided the latter has not a veto with which to defend itself.[31]

He was quite correct in predicting that the Directors would fall out among themselves, but the Directory proved to have little difficulty in maintaining ascendancy over the legislature without a veto power. His condemnation of plural executives was too unqualified and speculative, as the subsequent rise of parliamentary government demonstrates. If the constitutional experiments of the French in the 1790's were hardly raving successes, nevertheless they provided only indifferent support for the validity of some of Adams' most prized constitutional universals.

The "Stupendous Fabric" Threatened

As disquieting to Adams as the deepening of the Revolution within France itself was the enthusiasm it evoked among sections of opinion in Great Britain and the United States. Indeed one of the most alarming characteristics of the Revolution in his view was its faculty for winning adherents among all the nations of the West. Everywhere groups emerged which had caught the contagion of French principles. Among the English liberal Dissenters led by Price and Priestley, the feelings aroused by the Revolution passed beyond quiet satisfaction into millennial expectations and apocalyptic fervors. Price, especially in his famous sermon on the *Love of Country* preached in the Old Jewry Meeting House (November 1789), indulged himself in visions of boundless future felicities. "I see the ardour of liberty catching and spreading; a general amendment beginning in human affairs; the dominion of kings changed for the dominion of laws, and the dominion of priests giving way to the dominion of reason and conscience." [32] In due course Adams received a copy of the work, which was to provoke the magisterial wrath of Edmund Burke. In acknowledging receipt, Adams praised the many excellent sentiments and the zeal for liberty displayed. But the tone of the address already disturbed him. A sentiment or two in it, he said, required explanation, and he took pains to try to check Price's exhilaration. Others in Price's circle spoke of the Revolution as "supernatural." Joseph Priestley saw in it the fulfillment of prophecies in the Book of Revelations.

Adams responded that the hand of Providence was undoubtedly exhibited, but "working . . . by natural and ordinary means." He had learned by "awful experience," he cautioned the Dissenters, to "rejoice with trembling" about even the most promising political events. While the efforts of the age were "enchanting," it was necessary to pause and preserve sobriety. Amidst enthusiasm it must be remembered that there were limits to man's perfectibility. "Cold will still freeze, and fire will never cease to burn; disease and vice will continue to disorder, and death to terrify mankind." [33] In their intense partisanship for the developments in France, the Dissenters were voicing a protest against the religious disabilities from which they were suffering and making a demand for a recasting of the system of English representation. Although an advocate of reform, Price himself spoke with respect of the British constitution. But with the appearance of Paine's *Rights of Man* enthusiasm for France became associated with a challenge to the legitimacy of the traditional political order. [34] Paine created consternation by denying that a British constitution even existed. Adams detested Paine's book, and his son, John Quincy, in the *Letters of Publicola* devoted most of his energies to answering Paine's "libels."

As early as 1791 signs began to appear among the English of a tenacious conservative sentiment that would brook no attacks on the sanctities of the constitution. In July a Birmingham mob expressed its devotion to "King and Church" by burning Priestley's house and destroying nearly all of his books, papers, and apparatus. [35] Adams sent Priestley a copy of the *Defence* to replace the one lost in his library. While expressing sympathy for Priestley's sufferings in the cause of liberty, he did not forbear pointing the obvious moral. In his undiscriminating support of French principles, Priestley had failed to understand that the people could tyrannize as much as kings, and that checks upon the multitude were therefore much required. "Inquisitions and despotisms are not alone in persecuting philosophers. The people themselves we see are capable of persecuting a Priestley, as another people formerly persecuted a Socrates." [36] The people indeed were particularly capable of such persecutions when not discouraged by local authorities.

By 1793 England was at war, and a swell of reaction

engulfed the admirers of France. The governing classes were swept by fear. The movement for constitutional reform and elimination of religious disabilities was overwhelmed by public opinion and government action. A repression began that reached its apogee in the closing years of the revolutionary decade, with the destruction of clubs and reform societies, the prohibition of public meetings, suspension of habeas corpus, and prosecutions for sedition.[37] Adams sympathized in a limited way with the cause of parliamentary reform in England, but he showed mixed feelings about the rebuffs it was meeting. He deeply regretted the inconveniences to which the Dissenters were subjected, and he was not "well able to account for the violent attachment in the people of England to the Establishment of the Church." But he could not censure their attachment "to the monarchical part of their constitution," being convinced "by facts, authorities, and reasonings," that appeared to him "equivalent to a mathematical demonstration that both their liberties and prosperity would be totally destroyed" without the monarchy. He would prefer, he said, that the whole body of Dissenters were driven to America, where they "would be kindly received and infinitely happier than they can be in England," rather than that "the sublime and beautiful fabric of the English constitution in three branches should be lost out of Europe to whose liberties it is essential." [38]

His remarks carried the implication that the Dissenters in some way threatened the "sublime fabric." Adams was in fact worried that the reform movement in England was tainted with French principles and the extremist doctrines of Paine. His regret that reform was in abeyance and dissenting clergymen severely harassed was therefore highly qualified. He was unmistakably relieved that Eng-

lish opinion showed itself deeply attached to the constitution and that republican doctrine was rebuffed. It was
a point gained that the English had proved immune to
the contamination of French ideas, although he regretted
(without intense indignation it must be admitted) the
atrocious manifestations of popular support for King and
Church. He gave some countenance to the reaction in
Great Britain, and made no unequivocal condemnation
of this sad chapter in the history of English liberty. His
relief that "Jacobinism" in England was stemmed must
be understood against the background of his persistent
fear that English society stood on the brink of revolution.
In their unrestrained admiration for France the Dissenters
had been doing dangerous work, even though they disclaimed revolutionary intentions, and most made the required obeisances to the constitution. Years afterward
Adams was still blaming the Dissenters for propagating
in the 1790's a democratic fury which came close to producing a revolution in England similar to that of France.[39]

Federalist Fundamentalism

Adams early concluded that in his own country the
enthusiasm for France was also manifesting itself in mischievous forms. He began the publication of his *Davila*
in the hope of persuading his fellow countrymen "to ab-
jure foreign example." Americans had established a rational and ordered liberty and had nothing to learn from
inexperienced reformers who pursued rash courses in constitution-making and were addicted to equalitarian leveling. An eruption of democratic clubs alarmed him. Such
self-constituted associations had already contributed
enough to the evils besetting France and caused serious
concern to the authorities in Great Britain. The immense
outpouring of sentiment for the French Republic's first

ambassador, Genêt, almost persuaded him that French principles were about to engulf American institutions. As he recalled to Jefferson,

> You certainly never felt the terrorism, excited by Genêt, in 1793, when ten thousand people in the streets of Philadelphia, day after day, threatened to drag Washington out of his house, and effect a revolution in the government, or compel it to declare war in favor of the French Revolution, and against England. The coolest and firmest minds . . . have given their opinions to me, that nothing but the yellow fever, which removed Dr. Hutchinson and Jonathan Dickinson Sargent from this world, could have saved the United States from a total revolution of government.[40]

Most of the time during the decade Adams interpreted the threat from the French partisans in less horrendous terms. In intense ideological attachments to another nation inhered the danger that American policy would be swayed from its true course and based upon considerations having little to do with national interests rightly understood. So the Francophiles, out of gratitude for past services and general attachment to the cause of liberty, wished the United States to depart from strict neutrality in the war between revolutionary France and the armed coalition. The true interests of the nation required it to stand aside from such collisions. Adams even considered that Washington should have carried his neutrality policy further than the Proclamation, to the point of not receiving Genêt.[41] In extending recognition to the government of the Convention, the United States might involve itself in difficulties with the nations who were supporting the pretender to the vacant throne of France.

The American enthusiasts saw in the French Revolution a vindication and extension of the principles of their own revolution. For those like Adams who detested the French Revolution a necessary strategy in combatting adherence to it was to deny the identity in purposes or means or results of the two revolutions. Anti-Jacobins believed it essential to rescue the American Revolution from the "disgraceful imputation" of having proceeded from the same principles as the French. Although it was axiomatic that the French had acquired their whetted appetite for liberty from the American example — Samuel Adams' "Boston town meetings and . . . Harvard College have set the universe in motion" [42] — Adams was certain that they had not profited from their lesson. That the French had caught their delirium from the Americans was a matter for chastened pride. It showed that evil might ensue even from good intentions, and it was a lesson to avoid contributing to the artificial propagation of revolutionary enthusiasm in other lands. "Have I not been employed in mischief all my days? Did not the American Revolution produce the French Revolution? And did not the French Revolution produce all the calamities and desolations to the human race and the whole globe ever since?" [43]

If the American Revolution could not disclaim this offspring, the offspring was yet not cast in the image of the parent and must be ruled illegitimate. Adams' elaborate citation of the many ways in which the French liberals departed from American example implied plainly that legitimacy in his eyes depended upon conformity to such example. The leading men in the American Revolution had practical knowledge, were experienced in popular assemblies, and were not mere theorists. They did not aim at perfection or base their hopes on a vain belief in man's disinterestedness. In the French Revolution the advocates of republicanism were "theatrical actors, romance writers," and hack journalists.[44] The Americans had not practiced violence against religion, nor had the patriots divided into parties which engaged in ferocious, internecine slaughter. The Americans did not presume to proselytize for their system by subverting the governments of other nations. The French, animated by zeal to set oppressed nations free, had overturned the governments of half of Europe, erecting military despotisms "under the delusive names of representative democracies." [45] The American Revolution had been a defense of established rights against ministerial encroachments, not a wild career of unbridled reform. "For a long course of years . . . I was called to act with your fathers in concerting measures the most disagreeable and dangerous, not from a desire of innovation, not from discontent with the government under which we were born and bred, but to preserve the honor of our country, and vindicate the immemorial liberties of our ancestors." [46]

The idea of the American Revolution as a movement to conserve existing liberties was upheld also by John Quincy Adams, who in 1800 translated and published an essay by Friedrich Gentz which contrasted the American and French revolutions on this very point. How a revolution called upon to create the conditions for a recovery of "lost liberties" could conform to the pattern of one which sought merely to defend liberties already enjoyed was not easily explained. To condemn the French revolutionaries out of hand for departures from American standards of what constituted rational and ordered liberty was to lose sight of American singularity of circumstances.

In observing the different parts enacted by the common people in the two revolutions, Adams recovered the benevolent image of the American people submerged in the universalism of the *Defence*. Popular violence in France had assumed ungovernable proportions because especially in the major cities there existed a multitude of indigent and desperate persons ready for every mischief, who once excited could not be easily reduced to subordination. The rabble (by no means all of the people) of Paris as in every metropolis of Europe could acquire more by plunder than by industry and was therefore sanguinary and turbulent. In America the mass consisted of farmers and mechanics, industrious and settled, absorbed in their own affairs and paying attention to political matters only intermittently. Adams passed over lightly the question as to whether there had been victims of popular fury during the American Revolution. The condition of the people was for him the largest factor limiting liberal hopes in Europe, as it was the most potent consideration permitting their fulfillment in America.

The urge to distinguish the ordered liberty of the Americans from the licentious democracy of the French was but one expression of the anti-Jacobinism bred by the threat to established values posed by a revolution with messianic claims. Dread of revolution inspired its own frenzies all over the Atlantic civilization. In the United States a fundamentalist reaction against the contamination of French principles reached the high mark of intensity in the last years of the decade, during the eighteen months of undeclared war with the Directory. The continuing popularity of an opposition party identified with sympathy for France brought out high levels of anxiety and aggression from the Federalist "friends of government."

Adams' role in the reaction of the period was a characteristically individual one. In general, he encouraged and abetted it. But in a few crucial respects he resisted the "terrorism of the day" and parted company from the hyper-Federalists. Some expressions of his anti-Jacobinism he later repudiated; others remained a permanent legacy of the impact of the great Revolution upon his mind. Examination of these expressions reveals everywhere a common theme. Whether in surge of feeling against French irreligion, intensified distrust of intercourse with foreign intellectuals, support for alien and sedition laws, or refusal to abet revolution abroad, the impulse in each instance is one of withdrawal into insularity in the reinforced conviction of the basic opposition between American and European operative principles. Adams' criticisms of the French Revolution in their universalist imposition of his own nation's patterns on another reflected belief in the self-evident validity of American norms. The more genuine messianism of the French, however, brought out the relativist side of this same American absolutism in the form of fierce assertion of American uniqueness and heightened sensitivity to the perils of alien subversion.

The horror inspired by attempted dechristianization in France produced a rally around the established religions and a proscription of infidelity. Adams, whose own Christianity had grown steadily more "liberal," always sternly reprobated infidelity. Verging on Unitarianism, he approved of efforts through Biblical criticism to restore Christianity to its "primitive simplicity"; but he did not approve of attacks on the authority of revelation — a subtle but essential distinction. While abroad, he had been shocked by the prevalence of religious indifference among the upper classes in England and France, and so he noted with dry satisfaction that the English aristocracy had turned "very demure since . . . the Jacobins so impudently insulted religion." [47] During the 1790's he strongly supported the application of social pressures to discountenance deism and "natural religion." He was pleased to learn that Harvard College authorities had distributed to their young scholars copies of Watson's reply to Paine's *Age of Reason*.[48] He participated in the general tendency to place all the varieties of infidelity beyond the bounds of social toleration.

At the height of party passions in the late 1790's, Adams played a certain part also in the Federalist effort to associate the opposition party with irreligion. During the undeclared war with France he issued a Fast Day Proclamation which aroused the wrath of some Jeffersonians because it appeared to suggest that some persons in the country pushed their attachments to France to the point of espousing infidelity.[49] In the election of 1800 Adams made no objection to the charges of irreligion directed at Jefferson by Federalist divines. After his falling-out with the High Federalists and subsequent reconciliation with the Jeffersonians, Adams denounced the political uses to which religion was put in the Federalist decade. "The pious and virtuous Hamilton, in 1790, began to teach our nation Christianity, and to commission his followers to cry down Jefferson and Madison as atheists in league with the French nation, who were all atheists." [50]

In one manifestation of the rally around the established faiths, Adams was very much in the forefront. Paine's *Age of Reason,* appearing at a time when priests had been guillotined and churches were in ruins, shocked opinion in the English-speaking world and produced an orgy of vituperation for which there are few parallels.[51] It became a badge of respectability to shriek at Paine. In heaping abuse upon Paine, Adams let himself go without restraint. Paine was an "insolent blasphemer of things sacred, and transcendent libeller of all that is good," "a mongrel between pig and puppy, begotten by a wild boar on a bitch wolf." [52] His efforts against revelation would never discredit Christianity; the perfections of the Christian religion could never have been discovered without revelation.[53] Paine's libels induced feelings of latitudinarian fellowship with all varieties of Christian denomination. "Ask me not . . . whether I am a Catholic or Protestant, Calvinist or Arminian. As far as they are Christians, I wish to be a fellow disciple with them all." [54]

The fervors of Adams' anti-Jacobinism found expression also in what amounted to a repudiation of the cosmopolitanism of the eighteenth century and a secession from the republic of letters. He denounced the *philosophes* as an "accursed crew," preaching about the progress of reason and the improvement of society but contributing by their wild speculations to the experiment in France.[55] With their foreign allies they had come very near producing similar experiments in the rest of Europe.[56] He engaged in recriminations against European liberal intellectuals as a "black regiment" of "disorganizers," who had taught the common people "treachery . . . against their own countries" and to seek "revenge against all whom they have been in the habit of looking up to . . . at every expense of misery to themselves." [57]

His reproaches extended to European academies and learned societies, in which he refused membership. After returning letters and packets from one such academy, he explained, "I am not much charmed with the honour of being a member of any society in Europe." [58] During his presidency a group of French academicians led by Dupont de Nemours applied for permission to pass through the United States with the intention of forming an establishment for scientific investigations high up on the Mississippi River in then Spanish territory. Adams declined to give any encouragement to the mission.

I shall not be guilty of so much affectation of regard to science, as to be very willing to grant passports . . . in the present situation of our country. We have had too many

French philosophers already, and I really begin to think, or rather to suspect, that learned academies, not under the immediate inspection and control of government, have disorganized the world, and are incompatible with social order.[59]

While he was still nursing the wounds of electoral defeat, he learned that Jefferson was at the head of a subscription to promote a circulating library of the works of modern philosophers. Jefferson, he thought, placed himself in the role of Frederick of Prussia in seeking to win credit from "that part of the world of science, called Academicians," who were regrettably too prone to Epicureanism.[60] Almost a quarter of a century later, Adams was still of the opinion that foreign scholars ought to be received with caution: in 1825 he advised Jefferson against stocking his Virginia faculty with European men of learning, because they were addicted to ecclesiastical and temporal ideas incompatible with "liberal science." In the intervening years reaction had replaced revolution as the dominant force in European politics and as the main object of his animus, but the essential ground of Adams' reserve about a full and free intercourse with European intellectuals remained unchanged. A tenacious American insularity expressed itself in his relativist dictum that the "Europeans are all deeply tainted with prejudices . . . which they can never get rid of." [61] Whether in revolutionary or reactionary manifestations, the "plague of Europe" could seem equally threatening to the American way.

The apparent successes of the French in overturning European governments intensified Adams' belief that Americans should avoid revolutionary proselytism in foreign lands out of abstract zeal for liberty. During his administration he rejected an opportunity to contribute to revolutionary activity in Spanish America. Influenced by Francisco Miranda, a Venezuelan patriot, the British government was considering an expedition to break off the Spanish colonies from the mother land. Hamilton desired the United States to join in the enterprise. For a variety of reasons Adams refused to embark upon the adventure. He was reluctant to draw too close to Great Britain or to encourage Hamilton's dreams of military glory, and he was concerned about the possible impact upon the settlement of unresolved territorial issues with Spain. Certain that the independence of these colonies must come at some point, he did not regard himself or the United States as duty-bound to sponsor republican liberty everywhere in the world. He was not so enamored with revolutions, "so delighted with these electric shocks," as to be "ambitious of the character of a chemist who could produce artificial ones in South America." Events in France had not made him desirous "of engaging . . . in most hazardous and expensive and bloody experiments to excite similar horrors in South America." [62]

The Federalist reaction in the United States reached its high point in the Alien and Sedition Acts. Although these laws were passed in his administration, Adams did not initiate them, and afterwards, when they had come to be held in a general odium, he disclaimed responsibility for them. He argued that since Jefferson was vice president at the time, obloquy, if merited, was rightly shared. [63] His point would have gained in consistency if there were any evidence that the Sedition Act was intended to protect the vice president as well as the president from seditious libels. At the time of passage Adams certainly regarded the measures as constitutional and salutary.

Although at least on one occasion he spoke of the opposition to the Federalists as arising out of a difference of sentiment on public measures and not an alienation of affection to the country, after the XYZ affair he was as oppressed by the fear of faction and a licentious press as any of the High Federalists. In April 1798 he alluded to a "spirit of party, which scruples not to go all lengths of profligacy, falsehood, and malignity in defaming our government." [64] An acute suspicion of aliens appeared in his conviction that it was necessary to prevent them from taking advantage of lenient naturalization laws to become citizens and voters. Commenting after the election of 1800 on the proposals of the South Carolina Federalist John Rutledge to confine voting rights exclusively to the native-born, or, failing that, to set a ten years' residence requirement for naturalization, he agreed in principle that America's too easy admission of strangers to the privileges of citizenship was a fault, which had contributed to tumbling the "friends of government" from power.[65] Although he threw the mantle of his protection over Joseph Priestley, his remarks on that occasion about the great savant, who had sought advice from him about emigration to the United States after being victimized by one outbreak of anti-Jacobin fury, were a singular breach of the mutual respect that had prevailed in their relations. In restraining the eager Pickering, Adams referred to Priestley as "weak as water, as unstable as Reuben, or the wind. His influence is not an atom in the world." [66]

To his eternal honor, however, Adams did not indulge the mood which produced the statutes to the point of permitting it to determine his foreign policy. When in 1799 various signs indicated that the Directory had tired of the undeclared war, over the opposition of the Hamiltonian wing of his party, he sent a fresh peace mission to France. At the cost of splitting his party, he avoided an unnecessary war by remaining faithful to his guiding idea in foreign policy, that the correct course for the country was a system of "perfect neutrality," if possible, in all the wars of Europe.[67] The mission to France was the decision of his administration of which he was always most proud; it remains an action for which he has never received his due meed of praise.

Bonapartism and the Bourbon Restoration

In his early discussions of the National Assembly Adams expressed forebodings that the constitutional decisions made, if persisted in, must lead straight to despotism. A constitution without sufficient checks to contain the rivalries of the few and the many would produce violent dissensions for which there would be no remedy but absolutism. "If they fail in [obtaining a balance], simple monarchy, or what is more to be dreaded, simple despotism . . . will infallibly return." Echoing an idea of Montesquieu's, he asserted that, in destroying intermediate orders, the French were removing an essential security for liberty. "The destruction of privileged orders in Europe is taking away all the limitations of despotism. And France without the restoration of these orders will be no less a despotism than Turkey or Morocco." [68] Adams was less specific about the nature of the despotism he foresaw than Burke, who drew the outlines of a coming military autocracy. "Some popular general," Burke wrote, "who understands the art of conciliating the soldiery . . . shall draw the eyes of all men upon himself. The moment in which that event shall happen, the person who really commands the army is your master." [69]

Adams' penetration and independence of mind are nowhere better displayed than in his evaluation of the career of Napoleon. Jefferson expressed the more common view among Adams' contemporaries in concluding simply that Napoleon was a "great scoundrel." Jefferson denounced Napoleon as the

Attila of the age . . . the ruthless destroyer of ten millions of the human race, whose thirst for blood appeared unquenchable, the great oppressor of the rights and liberties of the world . . . in civil life a cold-blooded, calculating, unprincipled usurper, without a virtue, no statesman, knowing nothing of commerce, political economy, or civil government.[70]

Adams, while agreeing that Napoleon was "a military fanatic" like Alexander or Caesar, whose enterprises were "rash, extravagant, mad," felt also the need to go beyond the urge "to blacken him." He pierced deeper than Jefferson into the causes and effects of Napoleon's career. Violent prejudices against Bonaparte had been insinuated into men's minds by the English to serve their national purposes. Jefferson was not "strict" to call Napoleon a usurper. "Was not his elevation to the Empire of France as legitimate and authentic a national act as that of William III or the House of Hanover to the throne of the three kingdoms." [71] For the sake of the liberties of Europe, Napoleon's preponderance had to be opposed, and it was essential that French influence not be extended from land to sea. But it was not accurate to represent Napoleon as the great oppressor seeking to destroy an England that was fighting for its own existence. On balance England was a more powerful nation than France.

Britain is carrying her arms all over the globe and conquering every spot that is worth having, every place that can yield any profit, and what does France get by her conquests? She only lays herself under the necessity of raising and maintaining more immense armies in order to secure them.[72]

In Napoleon's conquests Adams saw something that reached beyond extension of French power. In Italy and Germany Napoleon was weakening the power of the Popes, Austria, and Spain.[73]

Adams' conception of Napoleon's role in the internal

affairs of France was equally free of conventional horror; it reflected some of the same feelings which had led the French bourgeoisie to turn with relief to the despot. Napoleon's emergence was required to put an end to reigns of terror, the insubordinations of the Paris rabble, intolerable insecurity of life and property. Adams saw him as a providential judgment upon the errors and crimes of the Revolution. "He has been employed as an instrument to defend . . . the human race from that inundation of bloody Jacobinical democracy which was overwhelming all liberty, property, religion, and morality among men." [74] Napoleon was a rebuff to, as well as a product of, the excesses of the Age of Reason.[75] Adams did not agree with Jefferson that Napoleon knew nothing of civil government (a judgment Jefferson partially retracted). To the contrary Napoleon's criticisms of the ideology of the French Revolution appeared to Adams to manifest unusual political astuteness. In a speech which won Adams' admiration, Napoleon had castigated the liberals who spoke of insurrection as a duty, who flattered the people by proclaiming for them a sovereignty they could not exercise, and who founded legislation upon obscure metaphysics.[76]

Adopting a view of Napoleon different from Jefferson's, Adams nevertheless shared his friend's relief at the accession of Louis XVIII. "I agree with you that the milk of human kindness in the Bourbons is safer for mankind than the fierce ambition of Napoleon." He was gratified at the restoration of his "old friends, the Bourbons, from whom I received invariably the most kind and condescending treatment." [77] His rejoicing was characteristically mingled with fears of the future. The Stuarts, too, had been restored.[78] Was it possible that the French people could be reconciled to the dynasty after so great a lapse of time? He was bothered that the French had not freely chosen Louis, and he wondered whether they might not still regret Napoleon. In any case the problem of a stable executive power — "who can they find for a head?" — promised to continue as a source of vexation.[79]

The Charter granted by Louis XVIII, he noted approvingly, approximated more closely to the balance than any of the innumerable French constitutions since 1789. "The French have a King, a Chamber of Peers, and a Chamber of Deputies. *Voila! les ossemen[t]s* [the bones] of a constitution of a limited monarchy; and of a good one, provided the bones are united by good joints, and knitted together by strong tendons." He doubted, however, whether the lower house was in a position to make itself respected by peers and king. The limits of the franchise were too strict. "A fair representation of the body of the people by elections sufficiently frequent is essential to a free government." The Charter was deficient in not providing adequately for liberty of press and thought.[80] In his criticisms he was unconsciously anticipating the dissatisfactions and program of the advocates of the coming "bourgeois monarchy." When Napoleon broke out of Elba and set Louis on his travels again, Adams in common with Jefferson considered that it was the obscurantism of the new regime that had given the Emperor his opportunity.[81] This time Napoleon was a judgment not upon sans-culotte democracy but the reactionary policy of restored monarchy. A brief experience of restoration and reaction was sufficient to evoke in Adams a strong reassertion of the more radical side of his Whig politics.

Retrospect

In his retirement Adams' interest in the Revolution remained unflagging. He returned to the subject repeatedly in his correspondence, attempting now a retrospective judgment upon the entire course and issue of the Revolution. He was concerned particularly to vindicate the pessimistic opinion of the revolutionary prospects, held unvaryingly ever since the Assembly of Notables in 1787. He was proud that he had never even momentarily yielded to the enthusiasm that had swept over liberal circles in England and the United States. As he read again in 1816 the comments on the Revolution written to Richard Price in 1790, they seemed, "scambling" as some of his expressions had been, to have contained "nothing but the sure words of prophecy." [82]

In his Quincy years, stretching from 1801 to 1826 and spanning the successive periods of Napoleonic dictatorship and Bourbon monarchy, Adams was undoubtedly encouraged in his conviction that the French revolutionaries had been attempting impossibilities in seeking "to abolish their monarchy and all their ancient institutions and erect a levelling democracy." [83] Indeed this long period in which liberal hopes in France seemed under a cloud depressed the spirits of men like Jefferson, who at the outset had adopted a different opinion from Adams', and led some of these repentant "Jacobins" to make their obeisance to his political penetration. Jefferson was not merely being polite in praising Adams' somber prophecies as proceeding from the "sober dictates of a superior understanding, and a sound calculation of effects from causes well understood." [84]

At a moment when military adventure abroad and authoritarianism at home were the order of the day in France, Adams scored heavily in recalling the millennial fervors of the early revolutionary years. "Where are now in 1813 the perfection and the perfectability of human nature? . . . Where is the amelioration of society? Where the augmentations of human comforts? Where the diminutions of human pains and miseries?" [85] The object that the French liberals held in view was

> to form a free constitution for twenty-five millions of French-men. Three hundred years would be well spent in procuring so great a blessing, but I doubt whether it will be accomplished in three thousand. No one of the projects of the Sage of La Mancha was more absurd, ridiculous, or delirious than this of a revolution . . . from a monarchy to a democracy. I thought so in 1785 when it was first talked of. I thought so in all the intermediate time, and I think so in 1812. [86]

A republican government was as little pertinent in France as in the royal menagerie at Versailles. [87] It was hardly possible to expect the millions of Frenchmen who had never known or thought of any law but the king's will to rally around any constitution.

Although usually condemning the Revolution as having utterly failed to achieve anything that might compensate for the massive evils it had unleashed upon the world, Adams conceded one or two ameliorations traceable to it, which he hoped might prove lasting. "Such is the destiny of man in his terrestrial existence that nothing good is to be obtained but by much tribulation. The overthrow of the horrors of papal superstition, and the introduction of religious liberty in France have been produced amid all the horrors of the last twenty years." [88] One other gain had accrued: it had contributed to the emancipation of the "Africans."

If Adams seemed to imply that these improvements could have been obtained only at the cost of vast upheavals, and so to approach justifying the Revolution, his more central belief was that major improvements had been possible in Europe at the end of the eighteenth century without revolution. "The nations of Europe appeared to me, when I was among them, from the beginning of 1778 . . . to the commencement of the troubles in France, to be advancing by slow but sure steps toward an amelioration of the condition of man, in religion and government, in liberty, equality, fraternity, knowledge, civilization, and humanity." The Revolution dispelled the atmosphere of humane tolerance created by the Enlightenment and blighted the promise of the eighteenth century. "The French Revolution I dreaded; because I was sure it would, not only arrest the progress of improvement, but give it a retrograde course, for at least a century, if not many centuries." [89]

Whether one concedes Adams' verdict that the Revolution failed of its object to be correct depends in the final instance on whether one shares his understanding of what that object was. For Adams the object was the institution of republican government on a basis of universal suffrage. Certainly the French appeared very far from that state in the years of Bonapartist autocracy and Bourbon restoration. But in his concentration on narrowly political results, Adams seemed not to take account of the immensity of the changes that had occurred in the life of France as a result of the Revolution. If the émigrés had returned, if a Bourbon sat again on the throne in 1815, France in that year was separated by an impassable gulf from the France of 1789. Major alterations of civil and social life had taken place. The rage and violence of the Ultras, even when in power, was a recognition of how far France had strayed from their ideal.

One might lament the passing of the old regime and believe that an incomparable *douceur de vivre* had departed with it, but it was useless to maintain that the Revolution had been futile. The hereditary privileges had disappeared, and with them an ancient corporate structure of society. The Bourbon Charter might speak of Catholicism as the religion of the state, but the clergy, without tithes, with great properties gone, salaried personnel of the state, were no longer a great separate corporate entity. If the old elites had returned with the Bourbons, their importance had shrunk, and they were now rudely jostled by competitor elites from the professions and business. In the country the manorial system had been swept away, and a great peasant mass had won unencumbered title to its soil. The symbols and myths of the old regime had lost efficacy. When Charles X insisted upon a coronation at Rheims according to ancient ritual, he was the object of barbed witticisms.

In the political sphere itself the changes were formidable. Restoration France, though there was no republic and no bill of rights and the suffrage was confined to under one hundred thousand persons, had still to be regarded as the most liberal of the great states of continental Europe.[90] Ideas of natural right and equality had taken firm root. The fact that the Charter provided for a Chamber of Deputies and a Chamber of Peers, such as Adams had desired for France in 1789, might strengthen his conviction that the Revolution had little to show for its mighty efforts. Could not this constitution have been obtained at the beginning without all the horrors of the intervening twenty-five years? The answer can only be that a constitution in the English style two decades after the privileges were destroyed was one thing; in 1789 it would have preserved the old order. To maintain with Adams that whatever gains the Revolution accomplished might have been obtained by gradualist means, one must assume that the interests it assailed would have given way peacefully, and that they had no vision of the future which challenged the purposes of the Revolution.

If one defines the object of the Revolution as that of

creating the social and civil foundations of a regime of liberty in France, then there would be more doubt that the Revolution failed. Adams despaired too easily and proved correct only in the short run. In many ways the Revolution did not fulfill the expectations it aroused or the hopes that went into it; some of its consequences might be held dubious. But one result for the long term was that it made the institution of republican government on a basis of universal suffrage inevitable in that country. Adams approached the problems of political change in France with the conviction, born of his relativist contrast of America and Europe, that a "corrupted" nation seeking to surmount its historical inheritance and make the leap into freedom would confront insuperable difficulties. The French could not hope to duplicate American liberal successes because the Americans were a peculiar nation endowed with special advantages and exemptions not to be found in any great European state. In effect, by making these advantages and exemptions into absolutes, Adams came close to consigning the Europeans to political perdition and reserving the blessings of liberty to the Americans.

Wiser than most in his generation in grasping how arduous the transition from servitude to free institutions could be, he exhibited also a less fortunate lack of openness to the new possibilities of history. If he became quickly alienated from the French revolutionaries and ended by denying them recognition as friends of liberty, a key reason was that he never pursued the consequences of his relativist perspective ruthlessly enough. With European and American social-historical conditions so disparate, the French Revolution, having both to create and destroy in a fashion never required in America, assumed of necessity a different shape than the American. Instead of conceding to relativity of circumstance, Adams, when he reacted to major developments of the Revolution, imposed standards and preoccupations he assumed to be universally applicable but which in fact largely reflected America's special experience. The judgment that the French Revolution had failed represented in itself a projection of an American criterion of what constituted success without due regard for the difference in nature and scale of problems encountered by the two revolutions implicitly being compared.

With his characteristic generosity Jefferson admitted freely that Adams foresaw difficulties in the path of the French Revolution that his own more sanguine mind overlooked. In 1789 Jefferson did not believe that the Revolution could produce convulsions that would last so long and cost so much blood. Nevertheless he did not really think that Adams had said the last word on the outcome of the Revolution. "Although your prophecy has proved true so far, I hope it does not preclude a better final result." At the cost of civil war, massacre, exile, the Revolution had cleared the stage of everything but the multitude; the land had come into its hands. The people had acquired a sense of its own rights and power, to which even its masters found it necessary to concede. Jefferson's confidence remained: "Even France will yet attain representative government," by which he meant something more evidently than the measure of it already provided by the Restoration Charter.[91] Indeed Adams himself, in raising his doubt that the French people and the Bourbons could ever be reconciled, admitted that it was perhaps too soon to speak of a final result of the great Revolution.

CHAPTER SEVEN

STRAIT IS THE GATE
THAT LEADS TO LIBERTY

*T*HE AUTHORS of a recent study of John Adams in retirement express surprise that a figure whom they were accustomed to regard as a major American conservative should have voiced such liberal views in his comments on political developments after 1815 in Europe.[1] There is less reason for puzzlement, however, if one keeps in mind that what is called American conservatism, when considered within the wider context of European political ideas, is itself a variant of the liberal creed. The Whig tradition of liberalism to which Adams belonged represented both defense against radical democracy and challenge to traditionalism and the ramparts of privilege.[2] In social terms Adams' opposition to the French Revolution reflected his belief in the wisdom of preserving key institutions of the old regime as bulwarks against leveling democracy. When Europe entered upon a period of rampant reaction in the post-Napoleonic era, what has been called the "positive side of [the Whig] personality"[3] can be observed in full resurgence in Adams. The shift of emphasis is hardly to be explained, however, as the replacement of his former "conservatism" by a new "liberalism." The dualism inherent in his Whiggery meant that although in 1823 he denounced the "proud oppressors" of the Spanish Patriots, in the same period he deplored the radicalism of parliamentary reformers in Great Britain and opposed revisions of the system of representation in his native state.

Eclipse of Reason

If Adams in 1815 shared Jefferson's relief that with the "usurper" at last caged on Saint Helena, the era of French assault upon the liberties of Europe was over, he was also dismayed by the policies adopted by the combined powers who were now in the ascendancy on the continent. With mounting indignation he witnessed the "relapse of Europe into the principles of monkery and despotism" under the tutelage of the "victims and final vanquishers" of the French Revolution. "Sovereigns, who modestly call themselves legitimate, are conspiring in holy and unhallowed leagues against the progress of human knowledge and liberty." [4]

Adams shared to the full the nineteenth century liberal inclination to condemn without reservation the political and territorial settlements made or ratified by the "grand council at Vienna." [5] He was incensed that the rights of self-government and nationality were largely disregarded and therefore little inclined to praise the work of the diplomats in adjusting the balance of power and restoring general peace. Nor did he give them credit for the relative magnanimity of the terms imposed upon France. Although in respect to France he was compelled to agree that there was little alternative to a return of the Bourbons, he was appalled that the "votaries of legitimacy" presumed to reestablish previously repudiated ruling families on their thrones all over western Europe without any consultation of the wishes of the people concerned. His dislike of this procedure was reinforced when as in Spain the restored monarch promptly extinguished all vestiges of representative government. Napoleon in Adams' view was rightly execrated for imposing sovereigns at will upon Europe; the Quadruple Alliance, however, in retaliation appeared to be following in the tyrant's footsteps. "These are all abominable examples, detestable precedents. When will the rights of mankind, the liberties and independence of nations be respected?" [6] The European peoples had been treated by the Alliance as so many pawns in the game of dynastic aggrandizement. Long before the term came into general usage, Adams was a zealous advocate of the self-determination of nations. Thus he was outraged at the annexation by the Hapsburgs of the richest parts of Italy. "Neither France, Austria, or Spain ought to have a foot of land in Italy." [7]

The changes in the religious atmosphere of Europe in the post-Napoleonic period jarred Adams' sensibilities even more profoundly than the triumph of reaction in politics. He was confronted by the multiplying signs of a great Catholic revival. The governing classes, formerly indifferent, had become pious and united in bringing the Catholic Church back to its former prominence. A new deference was paid to the Pope, even by Protestant monarchs. The Inquisition was functioning again in Spain, and the Index had reappeared at Rome.[8] In France the principle of secular education was under attack, and some Protestants had been murdered by Royalist mobs. "The priests are at their old work again. The Protestants are denounced and another St. Bartholomew's day threatened." [9] If Adams still held the view that "Platonic, Pythagoric, Hindu, and cabballistical Christianity which is Catholic Christianity . . . has received a mortal wound of which the monster must finally die," [10] he was now compelled to acknowledge that this institution had shown more endurance than was expected at the end of the eighteenth century, when it was widely assumed to be tottering on the brink of extinction.

A resurgence of deplorable forms of religious enthusiasm was discernible even in the Protestant world. In Great Britain the Methodists were winning converts by the thousand, whereas the more rationalist sects were withering on the vine. In the United States evangelical religions were making giant strides, while the cool sobrieties of Unitarianism were demonstrating only limited appeal.

Exasperated by this seemingly universal trend toward "unreasoning illuminism," Adams took refuge in philosophical explanation. The violence and extremism of the French Revolution had bred their own counterresponse alike in politics and religion. "Awakenings and revivals of religion always attend the most cruel extremities of anarchy, despotism, and civil war. They have brought again the Pope and all his train of Jesuits, Inquisitions, Sorbonnes, massacres, etc. The pendulum swings as far on one side as on the other." [11]

For Adams the most characteristic note of the new age was struck by the papal decision to reconstitute the Society of Jesus. In the 1760's the Jesuits had been expelled from several Catholic countries, and in 1773 the society was dissolved by the Pope. In 1814 the Jesuits were again in high favor at Rome and were reorganizing their forces all over Europe. Adams took down from his shelves and read through the four volumes of a violently hostile Jansenist history of the Jesuits published in Amsterdam shortly before the expulsion of the society from France. This work — "very particular and very horrible" — although written by "true Catholics," showed that "if ever any congregation of men could merit eternal perdition

on earth and in hell . . . it is this company of Loyola."
Adams was alarmed at the prospect that the Jesuits would
soon spread their influence into the United States, where
already, he hinted darkly, they were "more numerous than
everybody knows." Swarms of them, "in many shapes and
disguises," could be expected to locate in America. Committed to religious liberty, the nation must afford them a
refuge, but there was danger that they would put the
"purity of our elections to a severe trial." [12]

Jefferson disliked the rebirth of the Jesuits as much as
Adams, considering it a retrogression from light to darkness, but he did not share Adams' fears of the order's
possible impact in the United States.[13] Here education
and free discussion, he was confident, would present effective barriers against the follies of bigotry. Adams' son
ventured to differ from him even more fundamentally
than Jefferson. John Quincy thought the danger from the
Jesuits greatly exaggerated even for Europe. It was not
possible in his view to revive "exanimated impostures," or
to bring back the "monkeries and mummeries" of a past
age. Europe was tyrannized in reality not by priests but
by bayonets. Catholicism's revival had been propagated
artificially by the privileged orders and could not be sustained without the protection of soldiers.[14]

The father agreed in part with the son that much of the
reawakened enthusiasm for Catholicism was mere "political religion," encouraged by European governments that
felt fires "kindling under their seats." Monarchs and aristocrats had joined the clergy to combat revolution. "The
priests of all nations imagined they felt approaching such
flames as they had so often kindled about the bodies of
honest men. Priests and politicians, never before, so suddenly and so unanimously concurred in re-establishing
darkness and ignorance, superstition and despotism." [15]

Nevertheless, it had to be acknowledged that a new and genuine devotion to the faith had appeared, not to be dismissed as a thinly disguised fear of liberal reform. The most ancient of Europe's institutions was demonstrating renewed vitality, if one judged by its ability to attract the allegiance of distinguished men of letters. Adams had read with delight a recent travel book by Chateaubriand, which he pronounced to be a "work of infinite learning, perfectly well-written, a magazine of information." Yet the Frenchman was an "enthusiastic, bigoted, superstitious Roman Catholic throughout," and appeared to believe in the "system of holy lies and pious frauds" as sincerely as "St. Austin." [16] Chateaubriand ardently defended papal claims and celebrated the Church for the great variety of its positive contributions to civilization. The mystery and miracle which Adams was accustomed to denouncing were the objects of Chateaubriand's veneration. Chateaubriand took delight in just those pagan incrustations upon primitive Christianity which in Adams' view it was essential to prune away to restore the faith's native purity.

Adams' old friend Van Der Kemp, out of the depths of his unhappy obscurity on a New York farm, had produced a sketch for a proposed history of the rise of the revolutionary spirit in the eighteenth century. Adams was dubious about the prospect of obtaining its publication abroad. Showing an acute awareness of a major change in the intellectual climate of Europe, he explained that the eighteenth century had become "so odious and unpopular in England and France that I do not believe it possible to make the sketch known in either." [17] Twenty-five years before, in an opening statement in the *Defence*, Adams had expressed the consensus of men of learning in singling out his own century for conspicuous achievements in the advancement of civilization. In the early nineteenth century, however, the Age of Reason "lay under the shadow of a great disillusionment." The eighteenth century had become "ce vilain siècle," denounced, not always consistently, by Chateaubriand because it believed in everything except the existence of God, and by Madame de Staël because it denied everything.[18] It was despised and feared for its love of bold ideas. The ideals of the pre-revolutionary thinkers were repudiated. To their political dogmas were attributed the abominations of Jacobinism. The great catchwords of the century had issued only in bloodshed and misery.

The odium in which the century was held appeared to be accompanied in some minds by a rancorous dislike for the United States. If Adams' son, who wrote from abroad, is to be credited, the newly restored governments were deeply hostile to the United States, because the very existence of the republic across the seas was an unpleasant reminder to them that the ideals of the Enlightenment had a visible embodiment and were realizable.[19] To uphold the worth of the American experiment without commitment to the values of the Enlightenment was therefore hardly possible.

With due allowance for its "errors and vices," Adams in 1815, despite the Jacobins and Napoleon, still eulogized the eighteenth century as "of all that are past, the most honorable to human nature. Knowledge and virtues were increased and diffused, arts, sciences, useful to men, ameliorating their condition, were improved more than in any former equal period." [20] In voicing such sentiments, Adams showed himself to be, in the philosophical sense, an archaic survivor from a past age. Through the first quarter of the new century, he remained firmly fixed in the perspectives of the eighteenth century, as one small instance may indicate. An omnivorous reader, even as a very old man, he tried to keep up with the books that were in vogue. Accordingly, he sampled some of Walter Scott's narrative poems. He enjoyed them enormously, without in the least catching their point. He did not enter at all into the mood of romantic idealization of the feudal past that Scott's works were intended to evoke. Instead he read them as instructive lessons in the horrors of un-mixed governments and "barons' wars." At a time when neomedievalism was becoming rampant, he retained the Enlightenment view of the feudal period as the epitome of superstition and barbarism.[21]

There is very little in Adams' works to indicate the nature of his responses to the political ideas of the Re-action. But it is a matter of unusual interest that during this last period of his life Adams voiced his most un-equivocal condemnations of Burke, the oracle of the Reaction. He conveyed unmistakably at last the tenor of his view of the *Reflections* in speaking on one occasion of Burke's "musical insolence . . . against Dr. Price." More definite still was his observation that Burke had uttered and published very absurd notions of the principles of government. He pronounced Burke's and Johnson's re-ligious views those of "superstitious slaves," who were as much "political Christians as Leo X." In the context of his repeated scurrilities against the Church it is hardly likely that he meant to be complimentary in noting with con-siderable perception that Burke was more a Catholic than a Protestant at heart.[22]

As these expressions make overwhelmingly clear, Adams was always closer to the liberalism of the *philosophes* at whom he directed angry polemics than he ever was to the traditionalism and romanticism of Burke. He never for a moment shared Burke's ardor for the privileged or-ders of Europe, even if he deplored the ill-considered

effort by the French revolutionaries to destroy them. If
he thought kingship and "artificial aristocracy" necessary
in Europe, this did not represent admiration for these
institutions so much as condemnation of the corruption
in manners and morals that made them indispensable.
The hereditary principle was a punishment for sin; it was
not the finest flower of high civilization. Its justification
was that it barred the way in Europe to the onset of worse
evils — the unleashing of the mob, the fury of leveling
democracy. Regrettably, it was the necessary means for
upholding authority, order, and property in ancient,
opulent, and "contaminated" lands. For Burke the French
Revolution was a disruption of organic processes; it represented an insane refusal to use the materials at hand in
making reforms. Adams stood aside both from the radicalism of the Revolution and from the depths of the reaction
to it which in Burke precipitated an entirely new set of
categories of political thought. For Adams the revolutionaries had failed because they tried to do too much and too
quickly, and because they stubbornly refused to understand the principles of political construction. Adams deplored the Revolution for its excesses; for Burke the Revolution was in itself an excess.

For a certain kind of an apostate from the value com-
mitments of the eighteenth century — for the reactionary
type who in Hazlitt's phrase "missed the road to Utopia
and landed in Old Sarum" — Adams had a special loath-
ing. He did not admire Gibbon's undermining of Christianity in the otherwise great history, but he disliked even
more that Gibbon was enough frightened by the French
Revolution to end as an "advocate for the Inquisition." [23]
Adams richly enjoyed Robert Southey's tormented writh-
ings when Southey's Jacobin poem *Wat Tyler*, written in
1794, was published without authorization in 1817, na-

kedly exposing the gap between the poet laureate's current High Toryism and his earlier republican sentiments.[24]

Under the impact of the Reaction Adams moved discernibly in the direction of a partial reconciliation with the *philosophes*. He remained fixed in his opinion that the members of the Turgot circle were blindly infatuated with a chimera when they embraced the doctrine of unified sovereignty. Their error was traceable to a lack of experience of free government and to a misplaced appetite for originality, which led them to disregard the settled tradition of Western political thought that testified overwhelmingly in favor of mixed government. Adams was as unwilling as ever to connect their inclination for simple government with the strategic requirements of their reform program. If these adverse judgments appear essentially similar to the ones pronounced in the decade of the Revolution, there was nevertheless a marked alteration in the tone of his references to Turgot's circle, which suggests that he had readmitted the group into the fraternity of the friends of liberty. Perhaps this implication is conveyed by no more than his willingness to call to mind again that long ago he had been "personally treated with great kindness by these . . . great and good men." [25]

A clearer indication of the movement of his sympathies is afforded by the extraordinarily high estimate that he began to place upon the value of the work of Voltaire, despite his dislike of the "wretch's" infidel libels upon Christianity. "I should have given my reason for rejoicing in Voltaire etc. It is because I believe they have done more than even Luther or Calvin, to lower the tone of that proud hierarchy that shot itself up above the clouds, and more to propagate religious liberty than Calvin or Luther, or even Locke." [26] The former anti-Jacobin fervors which had led him into violent denunciations of the anti-

Christianism of the *philosophes* gave way to a mood of angry exasperation at the religious obscurantism fostered by the restored governments, which he observed bitterly was "enough to make the best Christians pray for another Voltaire" [27] or engage even in lamentations for the death of Robespierre. In the context of the Reaction perspectives altered so that the Jesuits appeared a greater calamity to mankind than either the French Revolution or Napoleon's despotism, having "obstructed the progress of reformation and the improvement of the human mind in society much longer and more fatally." [28]

The Persistence of Revolution

The combined powers of Europe had grouped themselves into a Holy Alliance whose major intention appeared to be to wage a ceaseless war on liberalism. Adams was entirely confident that the effort to imprison the revolutionary impulse would fail. The frenetic efforts to reverse the trend of events and return to the pre-revolutionary world were manifestations of weakness and fear. The age of constitutions and revolutions, which began with the American struggle for independence, was not at an end. The "wave of liberality" would undoubtedly rise again. A century of civil wars might conceivably lie ahead for Europe, because rival principles of legitimacy were in collision, between which no compromise was possible. An awesome question confronted mankind: "whether authority is from nature and reason, or from miraculous revelation; from the revelation from God, by the human understanding, or from the revelation to Moses and to Constantine, and the Council of Nice." [29]

From the days when as President he had refused to lend the assistance of the United States to the filibustering expedition of Francisco Miranda, the fate of the Spanish colonies in the Western Hemisphere had been the object of Adams' anxious attention. The power of the Holy Alliance to contain the spirit of revolution was surely at its weakest in this vast region, loosely held by an exhausted Spain and the object of covetous attentions from British merchants. As long ago as his embassy in London he had observed intrigues of individuals to set South America free from Spain, and he was even then certain that the object would be pursued until obtained.[30] About the general principles that were applicable to the problem he had no doubts. The "system of colonization" of the European powers could not endure. "Colonies universally, ardently breathe for independence. No man, who has a soul, will ever live in a colony under the present establishments one moment longer than necessity compels him." [31]

Inevitable as the emancipation from Spain must be and natural as the sympathy for this cause was among his fellow citizens, Adams held tenaciously to the view, which had inspired him during his administration, that the United States should be very circumspect about hastening the result. Although some overexcited persons in the United States saw an affinity between anticolonialist aspirations in North and South America, he thought that the parallel was dangerously overdrawn. The real difference lay in the capacities of the people of the two regions to make use of the opportunities afforded by national independence. It was hardly to be expected that the inhabitants of "new Spain" would follow in the footsteps of the United States and establish an ordered liberty.

Adams drew back appalled when he considered the future prospects of a South America detached from Spain. A clue was afforded by past events in Santo Domingo. During his administration the slaves on that island, encouraged by incendiary ideas propagated among them by the French, had broken loose and won independence. In result, the "mass of African bones and sinews" had hardly gained anything from their emancipation.[32] They had fallen under the sway of "aristocrats" of their own color like L'Ouverture under whom they neither lived better nor were more free than before.[33] Adams envisaged similar unhappy consequences in South America. Military despotism or simple monarchy would probably replace subjection to Spain. South America "will be governed by a dozen royalists independent of each other, and each of them seeking alliances in Europe, and in the United States. Suppose a confederation of these little sovereigns, will it not be a perpetual struggle which shall be first?"[34]

What other consequences could be envisaged from revolutionary efforts among a people so sunk in "general ignorance"? Long ago he had settled firmly into the judgment that a free government and Roman Catholicism could not exist together in any nation,[35] and he was certain that all projects for reconciling them "in old Spain or new" were "utopian, Platonic, and chimerical."[36] The Spanish Americans were

the most superstitious of all the Roman Catholics in Christendom. They believe salvation to be confined to themselves and the Spaniards in Europe. They can scarcely allow it to the Pope and his Italians, certainly not to the French; and as to England, English America, and all other Protestant nations, nothing could be expected or hoped for any of them, but a fearful looking for of eternal and unquenchable flames of fire and brimstone. No Catholics on earth were so abjectly devoted to their priests, as blindly superstitious as themselves, and these priests had the powers and apparatus of the Inquisition to seize every suspected person and suppress every rising motion.[37]

He was surprised and gratified on learning that a Spanish edition of the *Defence* had actually been printed in

Latin America.[38] But it was a case of unrequited devotion, for he had no advice to give these people. Their cause seemed too utterly hopeless. He consigned them to a perdition so complete that he did not even bother to go through the motions of admonishing them to establish a balance in their constitutions. In France or Holland there were genuine liberals to instruct in the principles of political architecture, but the inhabitants of new Spain, so far as could be determined, seemed not to possess even the rudiments of the idea of liberty. On no other people's political future was his perspective more unwaveringly and consistently bleak.

National revolutions against the territorial settlements of the Congress of Vienna did not make their appearance in Europe in significant degree until after Adams' death, but on the few occasions when he witnessed nationalist forces at work on the continent, he gave them his blessing. He had followed closely the Spanish insurrection against Napoleon. Although the power of France was at its height at the time, he grasped very quickly the potential significance of the fierce resistance of the Spanish to foreign occupation and imposition of an alien king. He wondered whether Napoleon might not have roused an emotion in Spain that could consume him. Other "humbled" nations might be tempted by the contagion of the same emotion to avenge their disgrace. He applauded the Spanish rising because it was essential to prevent the domination of the continent by a single power.

But there were certain ambiguities in the Spanish situation that bothered him. The difficulty was that the nationalist and liberal impulses appeared to coincide only imperfectly in this case. The intruder, Joseph Bonaparte, had, after all, imposed certain liberal reforms upon Spain, which went beyond anything that even the boldest Spaniards envisaged. Napoleon's brother established freedom of conscience, abolished torture, attacked entailed estates. Some Spanish liberals had even rallied to his side, their ideological sympathies outweighing their sense of national identification. On the other hand, the Spanish resistance, although there were liberal elements in it also, was accompanied by a resurgence of absolutist and clerical influences. Although a Cortes was summoned by some of the resistants, the Jesuits and the Inquisition were reinstated in places where the priests rallied the people against the French.[39] With appropriate qualifications acknowledging the complex and ironical interplay of contradictory elements, Adams admitted that dominantly he felt the deepest admiration for the desperate struggle of the Spanish. "Whatever proportion of loyalty to an established dynasty of kings, or whatever taint of Catholic superstition there may be in the present sensations of the Spanish people, or however their conduct may have been excited by British or Austrian gold, I revere the mixture of pure patriotism that appears to be in it." [40]

On one other occasion a national rising stirred him to the roots. In 1821 the revolt of the Greeks against the Ottomans broke out. He felt immediately a "kind of missionary enthusiasm" [41] for the Greeks, who appeared to be "rising like a phoenix from their ashes." Committees were formed all over the Christian world to solicit funds in aid of the insurgents. Adams was pleased and proud to contribute to the general collection organized in Boston. Stirred by the philhellenic excitement he regarded it as a badge of civilization to feel ardent sympathy for the sufferings of the Greeks "in the great cause of liberty and humanity." [42]

Years before, Adams had engaged in a spirited interchange with his friend Benjamin Rush, who held that excessive attention was paid to the dead languages in the schools. Rush was of the opinion that classical studies, because they raised artificial communication barriers between the educated and the rest of the community, were unsuited to the requirements of democratic republics. The learned used Latin and Greek "as the scuttlefish emit their ink, on purpose to conceal themselves from an intercourse with the common people." [43] In reply Adams insisted that the classics were indispensable precisely in republics. Had not the apologist of absolutism, Hobbes, calumniated the classics because they filled men's heads with ideas of liberty and excited them to rebellion against Leviathan? "God forbid that Greek should ever be forgotten on this globe, to which it is the greatest honor; the glory of all other nations since it, having been derived from it." [44] With almost one hundred volumes of ancient authors in his library, many in sixteenth or seventeenth century editions acquired in England, France, and Holland, this eighteenth century gentleman and country Yankee in his last years, as if to make the conclusive response to Rush, resumed the study of Greek with the aid of lexicon and grammar.[45]

Inevitably the struggle of the "people of Hellas" against the infidel Turk stirred reverberations in his mind. So much so, that the Greeks afford the one instance in which this congenitally cautious observer, immune to enthusiasm, gave himself completely to a foreign revolution, despite the fact that in its course there was much that ordinarily might have been expected to enlist his usual reserve, including the prospect of the extension of Russian influence into the Balkans, the savagery of the fighting on both sides, and the internal dissensions among the Greeks. The customary roles of Jefferson and Adams in the discussion of foreign developments were reversed in this case, with Jefferson worrying out loud that even if the poor Greeks escaped the Turk, they must fall under the sway of the "hypocritical Autocrat."[46] On his part Adams was uniquely content to go "by feelings rather than reasonings," even though his information, as he admitted, was not sufficiently extensive to enable him to foresee the result.[47]

Adams' expectation that the pressures to establish constitutional regimes in Europe would prove persistent, despite the reinstatement of legitimacy, was fulfilled even earlier than he anticipated. In 1820 liberal revolutions erupted in Spain, Portugal, Naples, and finally Piedmont. The nations of southern Europe, to whose cultures and institutions his feelings were so profoundly antipathetic, constituted in Adams' view one of the least likely corners of the continent in which liberal reforms might be successfully effected. In the case of the Italian risings Adams had little more than become aware that they had occurred before their brief flickering light was extinguished. Within a few months in Piedmont and within a year in Naples the vigorous intervention of Austrian troops produced the debacle of the liberals. "The Piedmontese revolution scarcely assumed a form; and the Neapolitan bubble is burst."[48]

Although the liberal regime in Spain, not snuffed out until the French intervention in 1823, appeared to have some chance to achieve stability, Adams discounted its possibility of survival from the first, unlike Jefferson who persistently hoped that the Spanish would settle down in "a temperate representative government."[49] The Spanish liberals had to contend with the nation's inveterate Catholicism, which would baffle and defeat their purposes.

Riding his hobbyhorse about constitutional mechanics to the end, Adams, furthermore, could not forgive the

Spanish liberals for their gross errors in constitution-making. They had reinstated the constitution of 1812, the one adopted during the war with Napoleon and suspended by Ferdinand VII in 1814. This document, which appeared to exert a fatal attraction to all the liberals of southern Europe, was modeled on the first revolutionary French constitution. "The Cortes is in one assembly, vested with the legislative power. The king and his priests, armies, navies, and all other officers are vested with the executive authority of government. Are not here two authorities up, neither supreme? Are they not necessarily rivals, constantly contending, like law, physic, and divinity for superiority? Are they not two armies drawn up in battle array just ready for civil war?"[50] The constitution perpetuated a French error in providing for rotation of members of the Cortes after one term of office. Unlike Jefferson Adams disliked the most unusual feature of the constitution, its provision of a literacy test for voting. In a nation where the vast majority could neither read nor write, a literacy test was an unduly oligarchic measure that would disenfranchise far too many people. In 1823 when the French stood at Cadiz, having occupied most of the country, and the Spanish revolution was *in extremis,* he expressed warm sympathy for the plight of the Patriots, but he was still shaking his head over their primitive notions of the machinery of a free government. "What rational being can have any well-grounded confidence in such a constitution?"[51]

The triumph of the Reaction on the continent left no other alternative for liberal movements there except to take the path of revolution, but what of England, where, despite the long, unbroken tenure of Tory ministries and the deep-dyed corruptions of its politics, the elements of a free government were still maintained? In Adams' view the English alone among the peoples of Europe had a political system worth preserving. Adams' admiration for the British constitution had remained undiminished since the days of the *Defence,* but in the post-Napoleonic era his chronic anxiety that the nation stood on the brink of a precipice revived. His son, who was in England as the American ambassador in 1816–17, wrote home graphic accounts of the sickness of trade, the distresses of the population, and the renewal of agitation for parliamentary reform.[52] On many occasions in the past Adams had anticipated that the British were near "dangerous convulsions" and that their constitution was "tottering to its base." [53] During the War of Independence it had been a popularly held American opinion, fully shared by Adams, that the English were running fast into ruin. The Lord Gordon riots gave evidence that the common people in England were as distressed and unruly as any in Europe.[54] In the 1790's he was full of apprehension that the English might succumb to the contagion of French principles. "In case of a revolution in England, a wild democracy will probably prevail for as long a time as it did in France." [55] The return of general peace had not brought relief from the danger. "Half a million of people in England have petitioned Parliament for annual parliaments and universal suffrage. Parliament is unanimous against them. What is this state of things short of a declaration of war between the government and people?" [56]

When he exchanged views on England with Jefferson, a chasm was revealed. Jefferson's bitterness toward the English was fierce and colored his judgments about their political future. The government of England, Jefferson considered "as the most flagitious which has existed since the days of Philip of Macedon." It was not only founded "in corruption itself, but insinuates the same poison into the bowels of every other." Jefferson looked forward, therefore, to "their revolution with great interest," wishing it to be as moderate and bloodless as would "effect the desired object of an honest government." In reconstituting their system the English might even be disposed to tread in America's footsteps. "There is no part of our model to which they seem unequal, unless perhaps the elective presidency."[57]

Adams doubted all of Jefferson's conclusions. The constitution, which Jefferson believed had ruined them, was in Adams' opinion "the source of all their power and importance." It was a wild notion to hold that the English would ever follow the republican example of the United States. He agreed that there were deep evils in the British system. Elections appeared to be "a mere commercial traffic; mere bargain and sale." A revolution, he was willing to concede, "might destroy the boroughs and the inequalities of representation and might produce more toleration, and these acquisitions might be worth all they would cost." But he frankly dreaded the experiment. He clearly hoped, although all the portents seemed to belie him, that the English would hold tenaciously to their institutions, while finding the means to purge them of their glaring defects.[58] The governing classes had shown on occasion a limited willingness to concede reform. Even under a Tory ministry the position of the Dissenters had been improved by passage of a measure for the relief of anti-Trinitarians.[59] Conceivably the British with their "sense and knowledge of liberty" would avoid falling into the extremes of despotism or Jacobin democracy, hitherto the fate of the European nations that had embarked upon the road of revolution.

Parliamentary reform was indispensable, but the great difficulty was that the cause of reform had fallen into the hands of immoderate persons, newly designated as Radicals, whose following, furthermore, consisted of the most insubordinate part of the population. The leadership of reform was typified for him by Major Cartwright, who appeared to have an ardent love of liberty but "never understood the system necessary to secure it — one of those ardent spirits whose violent principles defeated all their benevolent purposes." [60] The Radicals espoused universal suffrage, an idea "as dangerous, as plausible, and pernicious" as the exploded notion of government in a single center. The French Revolution furnished an "experiment perfect and complete in all its stages and branches of the utility and excellence of universal suffrage." In Great Britain there were twenty persons who had no property to one that had. "If the Radicals should succeed in obtaining universal suffrage, they will overturn the whole kingdom, and turn those who have property out of their houses. The people in England in favor of universal suffrage are ruining themselves." Men were born not with equal property, "but with equal rights to acquire property. The great object is to render property secure," as "the foundation upon which civilization rests." [61] Even in the United States, where property was widely diffused, a majority of persons did not possess any. If the decision were left to mere numbers, the "party of the pennies" would despoil the "party of the groats." In the constitutional convention of 1820 in his native state, Adams argued for retention of the constitutional provision whereby the state senators were apportioned according to the taxable property in each district rather than in accordance with population. If the advocates of universal suffrage required to be restrained even in America, how much greater must the need be in England.[62]

Implicit in Adams' entire analysis of the English situation was the hope that the cause of parliamentary reform would be rescued from the Radicals and taken up by the solid and respectable elements in English society. The revival of Whig liberalism and the rally of the middle classes to it, a development which he did not live long enough to witness, answered his need.

The "Awful Prospect of Europe"

For almost forty years Adams had followed the fortunes of revolutionary liberalism in western Europe and Latin America. Virtually without exception, from the Dutch Patriot movement in the late 1780's, to the Spanish liberals in the early 1820's, the efforts to establish or extend representative institutions had crashed in ruins. In several instances revolution had ended in the re-establishment of a harsher and more restrictive regime than the one which had called forth the original protest, and wholesale proscriptions of the defeated had ensued. The overwhelming fact of persistent failure of repeated struggles to enlarge the area of constitutional government beyond the United States and Great Britain had to be faced and assimilated by the friends of liberty. The age of revolutions and constitution-making inaugurated by the Americans had disorganized the world, exposed it to countless horrors and untold misery, all unhappily with little apparent positive result for the amelioration of mankind. Europe for the foreseeable future appeared doomed to an inconclusive struggle between rival principles of legitimacy, neither of which could command enough consent to pacify or govern the continent.

A detestable Reaction confronting an incompetent Revolution — such was in effect Adams' summary evaluation of the political position in Europe after 1815. For its encouragement of religious obscurantism, its suppressions of national rights, as well as a myriad of other crimes and misdemeanors, the Reaction was an offense to mankind. If Adams' rejection of the Reaction was violent and complete, he was unable to give his heart without reservation to the proponents of revolutionary liberalism in Europe. His identification with Europe's liberals was so limited that he could pass condemnation evenhandedly on them and their reactionary enemies, as on the occasion when he remarked that the return of legitimacy with the Congress of Vienna meant only that the "old deceivers have triumphed over the new." [63] Responsive to the personal plight of the liberals when they met disaster, he was yet a harsh and censorious critic of their political performance.

When he applied his relativist perspective, Adams concluded that the essential mistake of the foreign liberals lay in their failure to grasp how heavily the incubus of an inherited social order could weigh upon the present and circumscribe the possibilities of change. One wing of the liberals made war on hereditary institutions without recognizing their absolute necessity in Europe if decency, order, and security of property were to be preserved. The more appropriate course to have followed would have been to modify, restrain, and correct these institutions instead of attempting to extirpate them.[64] Only in a new country like the United States were the conditions propitious for a full trial of the republican experiment. The liberals had engaged in "rash enterprises" out of a vast overconfidence about the ease of transition to free institutions. They imagined it possible to convert the multitudes of ignorant people in their nations into materials capable of conducting constitutional government.[65] Whole nations could not be readily changed in their "principles, opinions, habits, and feelings," however credulous and barbaric these might be. It was indispensable to consider the "force of early education" on millions of minds which had scarcely been exposed to the Enlightenment.[66]

Europe's liberals had drawn great encouragement from the success of the American Revolution. Gratified by their devotion to the American cause, Adams nevertheless thought that they made disastrously wrong inferences about the meaning for Europe of American successes. Hardly allowing at all for the singular situation and character of the Americans, the European liberals conceived that the proper object of their aspiration ought to be to achieve American degrees of freedom in their own countries. During a crucial decade abroad Adams learned to define the prospects of liberty in Europe in much more restricted terms.

In the comparative perspective in which Adams viewed Europe's problems, the gulf between American and European circumstances appeared on occasion so overwhelmingly wide as to raise even a fundamental doubt in his mind as to whether the old continent could ever recover any significant measure of its lost freedom. Although in making his elaborate defense of the mixed constitutions of the revolutionary states he appeared to forget the special conditions of American life, his awareness of this uniqueness revived when he offered advice to Europe's liberals. What the Americans could safely do, he warned, afforded no criterion of what was possible in Europe. Efforts to bring fully liberal societies into existence in Europe would be wildly visionary and would end in disaster. This was his settled judgment before 1789, and nothing that happened in that fateful year or thereafter suggested any need for revision of his opinion. Europe's liberals should have been content with small gains, ideally avoiding any resort to revolution. His admonitions emphasized caution and the avoidance of bold leaps. The twin tyrannies of the feudal and canon law could not be swept away all at once, affronts as they undoubtedly were to the dignity of human nature. He thought that the liberals should make their compromise with the institutions of the old regime. The amount of change which he was willing to envisage in Europe was so limited that he was easily alienated by all but the most moderate liberals. So the leaders of the French National Assembly whose views made the most sense to him were already joining the emigration by September 1789.

In his relativist mood Adams accused the liberals in effect of blind disregard of the appropriate conclusions to be drawn from the separateness of American and European circumstances. But in reality the liberals did not so much ignore relativism as derive different applications from it than he did. If comparative analysis suggested to Adams that Europe must follow behind America at a safe and respectful distance, some European liberals drew instead the inference that because the conditions of freedom were so much less favorable in the Old World, a work of creation and destruction would be required that was never found necessary among the Americans. Jefferson's friend Mme. d'Houdetot, in appealing for his acceptance of that very boldness on the part of the French liberals which Adams condemned, invoked also a comparative perspective: "The characteristic difference between your revolution and ours is that having nothing to destroy, you had nothing to injure." [67]

Adams found no incompatibility in denying first that American political experience was directly relevant to Europe's problems and then condemning Europe's revolutionaries for the many ways in which their path diverged from American patterns. When Europe's liberals rejected his constitutional universalism, as they were compelled to do because of its irrelevance to their situation, he found in their rejection self-confirming evidence of his earlier conclusion that Europe was not equipped to institute free government. Because America had never experienced the feudal oppressions of the Old World, Whig liberals like Adams never had to shoulder the task of doing battle against the privileged orders. Without the enemy from above to worry about, American middle class liberalism after the Revolution came to be exclusively preoccupied with its fears of the enemy from below. In the absence of sheltering hereditary institutions, the system of balances was Adams' answer to the problem of providing for the safety of property against the potentially wild leveling proclivities of the multitude. That his constitutional solution was applicable also in European nations seemed self-evident to him, given the fact that the European populace could be expected to be even more unruly than American artisans and farmers. European liberalism, however, had to wage a struggle against two antagonists, neither of which, furthermore, was a phantom. In pressing the balance upon the liberals, Adams was in effect asking them to temporize with the privileged orders in order to hold the multitude in check. In its revolutionary age European liberalism was obsessed rather with its hatred of the feudal privileges. Fearing the mob, the liberals had to make common cause with it against the hereditary enemy. They rejected the balance, because if it would contain the multitude, it would do so at the cost of surrender to the privileged orders.

Adams' balance was designed for a far simpler and happier world than the one in which European liberalism had to make its way. The irony of history was exhibited in the fact that complex government could fit the simpler condi-

tions of American life, while simple government would
seem required in the more complicated circumstances of
Europe. Whether Adams applied his comparative perspective, or forgot about it in preaching a constitutional universalism, the European liberals were not likely to fare
well in his hands; in either case they were equally likely
to be damned. In the first instance, when he paid attention to relativity of circumstances, the result was to con-
strict the possibilities open to the liberals and make them
seem hopelessly visionary if they formulated their goals
boldly. In the second instance, when he ignored relativism, Europeans appeared not to possess even an elementary knowledge of the institutional basis and the
appropriate strategy of freedom.

In the period of Napoleon's despotism and the succeed-
ing Reaction, Adams marveled at the gulf between the
completeness of the triumph of the liberal cause in America and its submergence in Europe. In the United States
the party struggles of the 1790's were dying away to be
replaced by an era of good feeling. Despite the recent
disaffection of the seaboard areas of New England, the
great body of Americans had grown steadily more fixed
in their attachment to the federal constitution. Amendment of the revolutionary constitutions was being accomplished in the older, more populous states with order and
decency in constitutional conventions whose members
were persons of respectable weight and learning. If a
tendency to an extreme of representative democracy was
discernible, Adams was content with the constitutional
revisions, which on the whole seemed salutary.[68] The
slavery issue remained to provoke disquiet,[69] but it had
been resolved at least temporarily by compromise. All
this unparalleled felicity was in shocking contrast to the
state of Europe, as Adams surveyed it in 1820: "The pol-

iticians stand aghast at the awful prospect of Europe; it looks like a vast ocean scattered over with innumerable water spouts or an immense region interspersed everywhere with volcanoes smoking and bursting under the feet of mankind . . . May God avert the scenes of carnage, blood, and devastation which appear but too dangerous and probable in prospect." [70]

In part, Adams reconciled himself to the catastrophes suffered by European liberalism by a transference of his hopes into the future. Europe's efforts must be viewed as experiments from which ultimately lasting improvements would result.[71] The form in which these expectations of future ameliorations were cast, however, reflected Adams' characteristic propensity to attach an absolute significance to American political experience. In his mind Europe's failures were the result of blind, unaccountable rejection by the liberals of the lessons which that experience had to teach. Lasting improvements he was confident would come, but only when the foreign liberals adopted more rational systems of politics, that is, surrendered their unreasoning commitment to unified sovereignties.

More persistently Europe's inconclusive social struggles stimulated feelings of alienation in Adams. "I hope our country will have wisdom enough to stand aloof from them all, come out from among them and keep ourselves separate from all their wars and politics." The American people alone among the nations of the Atlantic civilization had passed with happy result through the fiery trials of revolution. He was expressing a root conviction, when he distinguished America's revolutionary effort from all the others: "I cannot believe from anything I have seen or read that any other nation is capable of it. In all other nations a revolution will be only an exchange of one absolute government for another." In the American political

tradition no one has phrased the antithesis between Old
and New Worlds in such fierce terms. In America an opportunity was presented to fulfill certain higher human
possibilities: "Strait is the gate and narrow is the way that
leads to liberty, and few nations, if any, have found it."
But from Europe there was little to be anticipated: "Have
you ever found in history one single example of a nation
thoroughly corrupted, that was afterwards restored to virtue, and without virtue, there can be no political liberty." [72]

Long before he had ever dreamed of going abroad, he
had contrasted Europe, groaning under the feudal and
canon law, and America, happily spared the knowledge
of the twin tyrannies. If the frustration of his impulse to
impose an American constitutional absolutism upon revolutionary Europe — Adams' own form of messianism —
in result chiefly intensified his original conception of the
separation of American and European destinies, the ambivalence in Adams' outlook upon America's relationship
to the outside world remained unresolved. On the one
hand, America's experience was special to the point of
being unique, and not properly a subject of imitation; on
the other hand, it was universally applicable, so that other
peoples might find political salvation in adopting it as a
guide. America remained more than ever a "city set upon
a hill," at once removed from all other nations and called
to contribute to their emancipation by the radiance of its
example.

Concluding Assessment

This work has been concerned with the permutations
in Adams' vision of the relative and universal in American
experience as they appear in his definitions of American
social reality and his responses to Europe's revolutions.

Although the contradictory nature of Adams' perspectives, whether in resultant views of the United States or the demands made on the foreign revolutionaries, has received special attention throughout, that is only in part the point of the book. Adams was not the first or last American political writer in whom conflicting purposes gave rise to conflicting perspectives. "Franklin, who in 1787 saw Americans struggling with each other because of the 'love of power,' had only a few years before, when he was in Ireland and Scotland, spoken lyrically of the 'happiness of New England, where every man is a freeholder.'" [73] Americans have always been prone to see diametrically opposed attributes in their own society, depending on the vantage point from which they surveyed it. A student of American labor points to the contradiction of American labor leaders abroad praising the free enterprise system for enabling the worker to obtain a fair and rising share of the country's wealth while at home excoriating the American businessman as profiteer, monopolist, and exploiter. [74] The more fundamental argument is that not only was there in each of Adams' perspectives an exclusive concentration on either the particular or the shared elements in American experience, but that more especially the particular and the shared were mistaken for one another with the consequence that misunderstanding of self bred misunderstanding of others.

In Europe when rallying support for the American revolutionary cause from liberals and conservatives alike, Adams dwelt on the remarkable contrast between America and Europe. But in the political doctrine and accompanying social analysis that he elaborated in answer to French liberalism's critique of the emergent American constitutional order, Adams asserted the basic affinity between the two worlds. American differences from Europe were conceived as the peculiarities of a new country, as secondary in importance and in any case likely to prove temporary. Postrevolutionary disturbances indicated that America already faced common problems with Europe in maintaining order and security of property.

The strategy of Adams' argument was largely determined by the position pre-empted by his adversaries. Turgot and Condorcet, having absorbed the lesson taught by French visitors to the United States and American revolutionaries in Europe like Adams, rested their case against the necessity of balanced powers on the uniqueness of American social patterns. They professed astonishment that the Americans, who enjoyed equality of condition, slavishly imitated political institutions that presupposed the European class hierarchy. In reply Adams chose to minimize or even explain away American particularity. The consequence for his political doctrine was the founding of the American preference for dispersing power into several competing centers not on the special benign features of American social reality but on the presumed stern necessities that America confronted in common with Europe. An organization of public powers more properly understood as a luxury that Americans could afford because of their peculiar social solidarity was derived from the need to tame class passions and social struggles envisaged as likely to rage with similar intensity in America and Europe.

The misinterpretation of American institutional norms which consisted in rooting them in shared rather than particular elements in American experience was compounded in Adams' view of the foreign revolutionaries. Nothing could have been more special to the Americans than the revolutionary process by which they attained their freedom and the constitutional formulas in which they embodied it. But if one forgot American social and historical exemptions, one might not easily see why other peoples struggling for their emancipation moved along a different revolutionary path and adopted other constitutional solutions. What was in actuality the product of unique experience became transformed into requirements for others. The connection between the two halves of Adams' universalism proves to be an intimate one. What began as universalist imposition of European categories on America turned by seeming paradox but inevitable logic into universalist imposition of American categories on Europe.

The deficiency of Adams' universalism considered as a mode of social analysis was that it obscured the crucial differences between societies. In making this observation there is no intention to quarrel with the accepted view that Adams belongs among the few really significant American political thinkers. There is every reason to suppose that the failing to which we have alluded was widely shared by his compeers. Madison's celebrated argument in *Federalist Number 10* makes scarcely any distinctions about the character and intensity of faction in different societies. Adams' faculty for trenchant social observation was often brilliantly displayed, as in the letters that he wrote in his old age to John Taylor. He called attention to some genuine universals. With a deep feeling for the structural prerequisites of society, he was endlessly alert to the persistence of the forces that make for social differentiation. His stubborn independence of mind on occasion gave him a singular freedom from the conventional dogmatisms to which others were enslaved. But at the same time few political theorists have been as much a prisoner of their own fixed idea. A social vision, capable of an admirable hard clarity, was cramped within the confines of an obsessive commitment to the mechanistic schematism of the balance. In combining American experiences with European concepts, Adams was constantly assimilating distinctive American patterns to those of Europe.

The mixture of blindness and insight that appears in his social analysis is beautifully epitomized in the curious episode of his struggle to persuade the Senate in 1789 to adopt formal address for the officers of the new national government. His argument for titles showed a rare understanding, well beyond the grasp of his adversaries, of the importance of symbolism as inherent in the very texture of human life. He formulated a genuine universal in observing that in all societies nonrational factors have to be enlisted to enhance authority and elicit obedience. But where he was incredibly myopic was in urging symbolism whose content was to be no different than that of Europe. A congenitally republican society — his opponents understood this better than he — required a symbolism that embodied belief not in subordination of classes but in the doctrine of human equality.[75]

The same confusion between particular and universal occurs everywhere in his social analysis. When he observed that a differentiation between few and many was found in all societies, he was on tenable ground; but even if so, it did not mean that the motivations of few and many were identical everywhere, nor that the relations between them would assume the same character. The proposition that a balance among the significant elements in society was indispensable to liberty was an important insight; the error lay in believing that the same unvarying constitutional formula could be applied without reference to differences in situation to create the necessary balance.

If Adams' universalist perspective obscured the particularity of American experience, his relativist perspective diminished the significance of the shared elements in it. The delineation of the distinguishing features of the American social world in his relativism possesses some of the quality of perception of national differences missing in his universalism. But the sense of the opposition between America and Europe was pursued so far as to make American particularity synonymous with the substance of liberty itself. What else was the meaning of the confident assertion that Catholic peoples would never be able to become free, that the sexual morality of the French, the absence of general literacy in that nation, made the attainment of republican institutions an impossibility? In these judgments the circumstances of one's own nation have been raised to the level of prerequisites for the enjoyment of a universal value — a form of blindness one hastens to add not confined to Adams or to the Americans. (A good case in point is afforded by the currency of dark speculations in the West, as parliamentary institutions have given way to "tutelary democracy" in many of the new countries, as to whether liberty is not so grounded in the unique circumstances of European culture as to be unrealizable in the non-European world.)

Adams' awareness of American particularity gave him a sense of the difficulties, in his view dangerously minimized by some foreign liberals, which would be encountered by European societies seeking to move toward new degrees of freedom and equality; but it led him also to confine the potential reach of these values too narrowly. What was peculiar to the Americans was not devotion to liberty so much as an unusually favorable situation for its realization. Commitment to liberty was a value shared with Europe; it was in fact one of the signs that America was in the largest sense an extension of Europe, indissolubly linked to it by a common heritage. The Adams image of Europe as a region of domination was unidimensional; Europe represented also a tradition of revolt and experiment. In both Adams' relativism and universalism, whether the external world was consigned to outer darkness or America became the norm for it, there is the same deep-dyed parochialism of vision.

Although in recent times the United States has come to share some of the predicaments of Europe, and western Europe at least has come to participate in achievements formerly conceived as distinctive to the United States, neither the issue of American likeness nor unlikeness to the external world nor Adams' perspectives upon it has lost pertinence. It remains as difficult as ever for the Americans to define themselves except by reference to Europe. For the social analyst the penalty of mixing American illustration and European concepts, confusing the particular and the shared, is still misunderstanding of American social reality.[76] Definitions of the conditions of freedom that reflect insularity retain in some minds the force of dogma.[77] To seek in other peoples for the reflection of one's own preoccupations continues to be an American way of not seeing others at all.

With the graduation of the United States to world power and responsibility, the problem of discriminating the universal and the relative in American experience has acquired an importance that it could never possess in the long period of American isolation. In defining their role especially in a new age of revolution, Americans have to decide what about their own achievement may be transferable and what is rooted in their own peculiar circumstances. With nations as well as with individuals, understanding of self is the path to understanding of others. It is meant as no disrespect to the memory of a classic

American to offer the concluding judgment that although Adams grappled with a central problem in the American experience, his resolutions of it require more than ever to be surmounted. Two of Adams' great compeers, Jefferson, with his acknowledgment — however intermittent — of plurality of paths to liberation, and Franklin, at his ease in two worlds, a quintessential Yankee who could accept Europe on its own terms as well, point toward what is required: an American openness to what one writer has called the "multiple possibilities of decency" [78] in the world.

NOTES

INDEX

NOTES

Chapter I. Relativism and Universalism: Dual Perspectives

1. A sensitive treatment of the polarities in the American response to Europe is found in Philip Rahv's introduction to his anthology *Discovery of Europe* (Garden City, N.Y., 1960). See also Daniel J. Boorstin, *America and the Image of Europe* (New York, 1960), pp. 19–39, and Louis J. Halle, *Dream and Reality* (New York, 1958), pp. 1–12.

2. See Louis Hartz, *The Liberal Tradition in America* (New York, 1955), p. 83.

3. John Adams, *Works*, ed. Charles Francis Adams (Boston, 1850–1856), I, 669. (Hereafter cited as *Works*.)

4. To the President of Congress, Oct. 15, 1781, *Works*, VII, 474; Katherine Metcalf Roof, *Colonel William Smith and Lady* (Boston, 1929), p. 32.

5. *Diary and Autobiography of John Adams*, ed. L. H. Butterfield (Cambridge, Mass., 1961), IV, 123.

6. The rhythm has appeared on other occasions in American history. The turns in the Wilson-Harding era from isolation to involvement and then back to reinforced isolation are a case in point.

7. Joseph E. Johnson, "Helping to Build New States," *The United States and the United Nations*, ed. Francis O. Wilcox and H. Field Haviland, Jr. (Baltimore, 1961), pp. 3–26.

8. Quoted in Zoltán Haraszti, *John Adams and the Prophets of Progress* (Cambridge, Mass., 1952), p. 257.

9. Bernard Kieran, "Limitations of United States Policy toward the Underdeveloped World: A Note on the Sociology of Revolution," *American Scholar*, 31:208–219 (Spring 1962).

10. Oct. 28, 1813, *The Adams-Jefferson Letters*, ed. Lester J. Cappon (Chapel Hill, N.C., 1959), II, 391.

11. *Works*, III, 448–464.

12. *Works*, VII, 279, 283, 309.

13. *Works*, VII, 305.

14. To George Washington, Aug. 29, 1790, *Works*, VIII, 498.

15. Nov. 11, 1807, *Old Family Letters*, copied for Alexander Biddle, Series A (Philadelphia, 1892), p. 173. (All letters cited in this work are addressed to Benjamin Rush.)

16. July 28, 1789, *ibid.*, p. 48.

17. Peter Viereck, *Conservatism: From Burke to Churchill* (Princeton, 1956), p. 88.

18. On his return home from Europe briefly in 1779 the town of Braintree promptly made Adams a delegate to the convention which, after the failure of the proposed constitution of 1778 to secure ratification, was about to try to give the state a permanent frame of government. The task of preparing a preliminary draft devolved on Adams, and he proceeded to provide for a tripartite sovereignty in a two-house legislature and a governor with an absolute veto. The constitution as finally adopted in the following year retained all his essential ideas about the appropriate machinery of a free government with the exception that the governor's veto could be overridden by two-thirds votes in the legislature. Although Adams accepted the substitute apparently with good grace, he continued to hold the view that an exact adjustment of the balance required the executive to be vested with an absolute veto.

Chapter II. Correct Principles of Political Architecture

1. Maurice Cranston, *Freedom: A New Analysis* (New York, 1953), p. 65.
2. Thomas Jefferson to John Adams, Oct. 28, 1813, *Adams-Jefferson Letters*, II, 388.
3. Haraszti, *Prophets of Progress*, p. 20.
4. R. R. Palmer, *The Age of the Democratic Revolution* (Princeton, 1959), pp. 239–240, 266.
5. *Ibid.*, pp. 263–282. Palmer gives the best account of the international controversy over the American state constitutions.
6. John Stevens, *Examen du gouvernement d'Angleterre* (Paris, 1789), p. 68.
7. *Works*, IV, 559–560.
8. Haraszti, *Prophets of Progress*, pp. 145–147; *Works*, IV, 280.
9. Haraszti, *Prophets of Progress*, p. 145; *Works*, IV, 55–56, 221.
10. To Henry Channing, Nov. 3, 1820, *Works*, X, 392–393.
11. Haraszti, *Prophets of Progress*, pp. 143, 147.
12. *Ibid.*, p. 148.
13. *Works*, IV, 288–289.
14. Baron de Montesquieu, *The Spirit of the Laws*, ed. Franz Neumann (New York, 1949), pp. xix–xxix (editor's introduction).
15. *Works*, IV, 279, 389.
16. Marquis de Condorcet, *Sketch for a Historical Picture of the*

Progress of the Human Mind, trans. June Barraclough (New York, 1955), p. 145.

17. *Works*, IV, 401.

18. *Works*, IV, 300.

19. *Ibid.*

20. *Works*, IV, 358.

21. *Works*, IV, 359.

22. *Works*, IV, 358, 468; Thomas Jefferson, *The Life and Selected Writings*, ed. Adrienne Koch and William Peden (New York, 1944), p. 126.

23. Marquis de Condorcet, *Lettres d'un bourgeois de New Haven* in Filippo Mazzei, *Recherches historiques et politiques sur les États-Unis* (Paris, 1788), I, 351.

24. J. Salwyn Schapiro, *Condorcet and the Rise of Liberalism* (New York, 1934), pp. 122–124.

25. *Works*, IV, 406.

26. *Works*, V, 40.

27. *Works*, V, 40; IV, 521; IV, 390; VI, 218.

28. *Works*, IV, 400.

29. *Works*, VI, 7, 10, 114.

30. *Works*, VI, 109–114, 122–127.

31. *Works*, VI, 64, 114–115, 211.

32. *Works*, VI, 218.

33. Condorcet, *Lettres*, I, 361, 363.

34. *Works*, IV, 491, 587.

35. *Works*, IV, 587–588.

36. *Works*, VI, 8, 185, 464, 280.

37. *Works*, IV, 379; Haraszti, *Prophets of Progress*, p. 205.

38. *Works*, IV, 290, 336.

39. *Works*, VI, 66, 89.

40. Thomas Jefferson to John Adams, Oct. 28, 1813, *Adams-Jefferson Letters*, II, 388.

41. *Works*, IV, 585; VI, 186; V, 214.

42. *Works*, IV, 360, 392–393, 395, 397.

43. Thomas Jefferson to John Adams, Oct. 28, 1813, *Adams-Jefferson Letters*, II, 389.

44. *Works*, VI, 508.

45. *Works*, V, 24.

46. *Works*, VI, 507.

47. Stevens, *Examen du gouvernement d'Angleterre*, p. 2.

48. Thomas Jefferson to John Adams, Oct. 28, 1813, *Adams-Jefferson Letters*, II, 391.

49. *Works*, IV, 392, 524.

50. *Works*, V, 454–460.

Chapter III. On the Eve

1. *Diary and Autobiography*, IV, 63; *Works*, IV, 297.

2. Quoted in H. J. Morgenthau and K. W. Thompson, *Principles and Problems of International Politics* (New York, 1950), p. 8.

3. *Diary and Autobiography*, II, 387.

4. June 25, 1786, *Adams-Jefferson Letters*, I, 136; *Diary and Autobiography*, III, 109.

5. *Diary and Autobiography*, II, 299.

6. *Ibid.*, III, 100.

7. *Works*, I, 660; to James Warren, Dec. 5, 1778, *Warren-Adams Letters* (Boston, 1925), II, 74.

8. *Works*, I, 660–662.

9. *Diary and Autobiography*, IV, 81; Alexis de Tocqueville, *The European Revolution*, trans. and ed. John Lukacs (New York, 1959), p. 34.

10. *Diary and Autobiography*, IV, 81.

11. *Ibid.*

12. Crane Brinton, *Anatomy of Revolution* (New York, 1957), p. 46.

13. *Works*, IV, 283.

14. Brinton, *Anatomy of Revolution*, p. 46.

15. *Works*, IV, 283.

16. *Works*, IV, 297.

17. *Works*, V, 96.

18. *Works*, IV, 288.

19. *Works*, IV, 355.

20. R. R. Palmer, "The Dubious Democrat: Thomas Jefferson in Bourbon France," *Political Science Quarterly*, 72:388–404 (September 1957), pp. 402–403.

21. Brinton, *Anatomy of Revolution*, p. 53.

22. *Works*, IV, 288.

23. Hartz, *Liberal Tradition*, p. 51.

24. Ernest Barker, *Essays on Government* (Oxford, 1945), p. 211; *Diary and Autobiography*, IV, 131.

25. *Works*, IV, 551, 332, 335, 355, 585; V, 454–459.

26. *Works*, V, 457.

27. *Works*, IV, 288.

28. *Works*, IV, 395, 288.

29. *Works*, VI, 94–95.

30. *Works*, III, 449–450; *Diary and Autobiography*, II, 419, 425, 431.

31. To James Warren, Aug. 4, 1778, *Warren-Adams Letters*, II, 39–40.

32. *Works*, III, 453.

33. *Works*, IV, 587; *Works*, VI, 516; *Diary and Autobiography*, II, 296.

34. June 17, 1780, *Familiar Letters of John Adams and His Wife Abigail Adams during the Revolution* (Boston, 1876), pp. 382–383.

35. *Works*, IV, 538.

36. To John Jay, Sept. 23, 1787, *Works*, VIII, 454.

37. Tocqueville, *European Revolution*, p. 85.

38. Hartz, *Liberal Tradition*, pp. 50–66.

Chapter IV. Advent of Revolution

1. *Works*, IV, 284.

2. To James Lloyd, March 29 and 30, 1815, *Works*, X, 149.

3. *Works*, VI, 130.

4. To Count Sarsfield, Jan. 21, 1785, *Works*, VIII, 369–370.

5. To Thomas McKean, June 2, 1812, *Works*, X, 13.

6. Nov. 13, 1815, *Adams-Jefferson Letters*, II, 457.

7. *Works*, IX, 106; VII, 281; II, 421.

8. *Works*, IV, 283.

9. To T. Digges, May 13, 1780, *Works*, VII, 168; Rahv, *Discovery of Europe*, p. 10.

10. Dec. 18, 1781, *Familiar Letters*, p. 403.

11. To Mercy Warren, Jan. 29, 1783, *Warren-Adams Letters*, II, 188–189; to Lafayette, May 21, 1782, *Works*, VII, 593.

12. Rahv, *Discovery of Europe*, p. 10.

13. Lewis Rosenthal, *America and Europe* (New York, 1882), pp. 86–87.

14. To Benjamin Rush, Aug. 28, 1811, *Works*, IX, 635.

15. *Diary and Autobiography*, III, 138.

16. *Works*, II, 420–421.

17. To William Tudor, Dec. 18, 1816, *Works*, X, 233; to John Winthrop, June 23, 1776, *Collections of the Massachusetts Historical Society* (Boston, 1878), vol. IV, series 5, p. 310; to Benjamin Hichborn, May 29, 1776, *Works*, IX, 380.

18. *Works*, VI, 202.

19. June 21, 1811, *Old Family Letters*, p. 287.

20. To Mercy Warren, July 20, 1807, *Collections of the Massachusetts Historical Society*, vol. IV, series 5, p. 347.

21. Palmer, *Age of the Democratic Revolution*, p. 365. In what follows I lean heavily upon Palmer's treatment of the Dutch Patriot Movement in the same work, esp. pp. 323–340, 364–370.

22. John T. Morse, *John Adams* (Boston, 1884), pp. 190–191.

NOTES TO CHAPTER IV

23. Palmer, *Age of the Democratic Revolution,* p. 252.
24. To Richard Cranch, Jan. 15, 1787, *Works,* I, 432.
25. Palmer, *Age of the Democratic Revolution,* p. 251.
26. Palmer, "The Dubious Democrat," p. 396.
27. Thomas Jefferson to John Jay, Aug. 6, 1787, *Papers of Thomas Jefferson,* ed. Julian P. Boyd (Princeton, 1955), XI, 696.
28. To Mercy Warren, July 30, 1807, *Collections of the Massachusetts Historical Society,* vol. IV, series 5, p. 390; Oct. 28, 1787, *Adams-Jefferson Letters,* I, 204; to John Jay, Sept. 23, 1787, *Works,* VIII, 454–455; Nov. 10, 1787, *Adams-Jefferson Letters,* I, 210.
29. To John Jay, Nov. 30, 1787, *Works,* VIII, 462.
30. March 14, 1788, *Letters of John Adams, Addressed to His Wife,* ed. C. F. Adams (Boston, 1841), II, 112.
31. To John Jay, Nov. 30, 1787, *Works,* VIII, 462.
32. Louis Gottschalk, *Lafayette between the American and French Revolution, 1783–1789* (Chicago, 1950), p. 340.
33. To C. W. F. Dumas, Sept. 22, 1786, *Papers of Thomas Jefferson,* X, 397.
34. Palmer, *Age of the Democratic Revolution,* pp. 368–369.
35. *Ibid.,* p. 334.
36. *Ibid.,* pp. 365, 368.
37. To Francis Van Der Kemp, Feb. 23, 1815, Adams–Van Der Kemp letters, Historical Society of Pennsylvania.
38. Lafayette to Adams, Oct. 12, 1787, *Works,* VIII, 456.
39. Quoted in Palmer, "The Dubious Democrat," p. 402.
40. To Lafayette, Jan. 12, 1787, Adams Papers, Massachusetts Historical Society.
41. To John Jay, Sept. 22, 1787, *Works,* VIII, 451; to Thomas Jefferson, Dec. 10, 1787, *Works,* VIII, 465.
42. Georges Lefebvre, *The Coming of the French Revolution,* trans. R. R. Palmer (New York, 1957), pp. 22–34.
43. To John Jay, Sept. 22, 1787, *Works,* VIII, 451.
44. To Thomas Jefferson, Dec. 10, 1787, *Works,* VIII, 466; to John Jay, Sept. 22, 1787, *Works,* VIII, 451.
45. To Lafayette, Oct. 27, 1787, Adams Papers.
46. To Thomas Jefferson, Dec. 10, 1787, *Works,* VIII, 465–466.
47. Lefebvre, *Coming of the French Revolution,* pp. 44–45.
48. Quoted in Leo Gershoy, *Era of the French Revolution, 1788–1799* (Princeton, 1957), p. 27.
49. To Thomas Jefferson, Dec. 10, 1787, *Works,* VIII, 465–466.
50. *Ibid.*
51. Quoted in Haraszti, *Prophets of Progress,* p. 342.
52. Sept. 30, 1805, *Old Family Letters,* p. 82.
53. Palmer, "The Dubious Democrat," pp. 388–404; Dumas

VICTORY OF THE BOURGEOISIE

Malone, *Jefferson and the Rights of Man* (Boston, 1951), pp. 180–202, 214–237.

Chapter V. Victory of the Bourgeoisie

1. To Count Sarsfield, Feb. 3, 1786, *Works*, IX, 546; Sept. 16, 1789, Adams Papers.
2. Lefebvre, *Coming of the French Revolution*, p. 76.
3. To Count Sarsfield, Sept. 16, 1789, Adams Papers.
4. To Francis Van Der Kemp, March 27, 1790, Adams–Van Der Kemp letters; Feb. 2, 1790, *Old Family Letters*, pp. 54–55; to Richard Price, April 19, 1790, *Works*, IX, 565; to Thomas Brand-Hollis, June 1, 1790, *Works*, IX, 569; to Count Sarsfield, Sept. 16, 1789, Adams Papers.
5. *Works*, VI, 429–431.
6. Quoted in Haraszti, *Prophets of Progress*, pp. 207, 223.
7. Palmer, *Age of the Democratic Revolution*, p. 497.
8. *Ibid.*, p. 494.
9. *Ibid.*, p. 495.
10. *Ibid.*, p. 498.
11. Haraszti, *Prophets of Progress*, p. 207.
12. Palmer, *Age of the Democratic Revolution*, p. 493.
13. *Ibid.*, p. 498.
14. *Works*, VI, 411–412.
15. To Alexander Jardine, June 1, 1790, *Works*, IX, 568.
16. To Francis Van Der Kemp, March 27, 1790, Adams–Van Der Kemp letters.
17. Palmer, *Age of the Democratic Revolution*, pp. 281, 495.
18. *Ibid.*, p. 282.
19. Quoted in Haraszti, *Prophets of Progress*, p. 234.
20. Brinton, *Anatomy of Revolution*, p. 38.
21. Quoted in Haraszti, *Prophets of Progress*, p. 204.
22. Palmer, *Age of the Democratic Revolution*, p. 495.
23. *Works*, VI, 274.
24. Palmer, *Age of the Democratic Revolution*, p. 498.
25. *Works*, VI, 399.
26. *Works*, VI, 252.
27. *Works*, VI, 274.
28. To Francis Dana, Aug. 16, 1776, *Works*, IX, 429.
29. To Francis Van Der Kemp, March 27, 1790, Adams–Van Der Kemp letters.
30. *Works*, VI, 299, 395–396, 417.
31. *Works*, VI, 300.
32. Palmer, *Age of the Democratic Revolution*, p. 479.

33. *Works*, VI, 251–252.
34. *Works*, VI, 256.
35. Lefebvre, *Coming of the French Revolution*, p. 11.
36. Quoted in Haraszti, *Prophets of Progress*, p. 190.
37. *Ibid.*, p. 188.
38. *Ibid.*, pp. 200–201.
39. *Works*, VI, 273.
40. *Works*, VI, 271.
41. Dec. 18, 1780, *Familiar Letters*, pp. 388–389.
42. *Works*, IV, 428.
43. Quoted in Haraszti, *Prophets of Progress*, p. 233.
44. *Works*, VI, 271.
45. Lefebvre, *Coming of the French Revolution*, pp. 10–11.
46. To Thomas Brand-Hollis, June 11, 1790, *Works*, IX, 570.
47. *Works*, VI, 285.
48. Haraszti, *Prophets of Progress*, p. 169, where Adams' observations in the *Discourses on Davila* on emulation and the passion for distinction are shown to consist of paraphrase or straight quotation from a single chapter of Adam Smith's *Theory of Moral Sentiments*.
49. *Works*, VI, 275.
50. *Works*, VI, 271–272.
51. *Works*, VI, 285–286; to Richard Price, April 19, 1790, *Works*, IX, 564; to Thomas Brand-Hollis, June 11, 1790, *Works*, IX, 570.
52. *Works*, VI, 280.
53. To Thomas Brand-Hollis, June 11, 1790, *Works*, IX, 571.
54. *Works*, VI, 280.
55. Lefebvre, *Coming of the French Revolution*, pp. 137–138, 156.
56. July 6, 1774, *Familiar Letters*, p. 14.
57. *Works*, V, 456–457.
58. Palmer, *Age of the Democratic Revolution*, p. 517.

Chapter VI. American Anti-Jacobin

1. To Thomas Brand-Hollis, June 11, 1790, *Works*, IX, 570.
2. *Journal of William Maclay*, intro. by Charles A. Beard (New York, 1929), p. 243.
3. To Francis Van Der Kemp, July 5, 1814, Adams–Van Der Kemp letters.
4. *Selected Writings of John and John Quincy Adams*, ed. Adrienne Koch and William Peden (New York, 1946), p. 226.
5. Haraszti, *Prophets of Progress*, p. 339.

6. *Ibid.*, p. 209.
7. *Ibid.*, p. 213; Barker, *Essays on Government*, p. 217.
8. Quoted in Palmer, *Age of the Democratic Revolution*, p. 311.
9. To Alexander Jardine, June 1, 1790, *Works*, IX, 568.
10. *Works*, VI, 279; to Francis Van Der Kemp, Feb. 18, 1794, Adams–Van Der Kemp letters.
11. Feb. 9, 1794, *Letters of John Adams, Addressed to His Wife*, II, 142.
12. To Abigail Smith, Jan. 7, 1794, quoted in Roof, *Colonel William Smith*, p. 222.
13. Charles D. Hazen, *Contemporary American Opinion of the French Revolution* (Baltimore, 1897), p. 171.
14. To Jeremy Belknap, Feb. 18, 1793, Belknap Papers, Massachusetts Historical Society.
15. To Francis Van Der Kemp, March 19, 1793, Adams–Van Der Kemp letters.
16. To Jeremy Belknap, Feb. 18, 1793, Belknap Papers.
17. Quoted in Roof, *Colonel William Smith*, p. 217.
18. Haraszti, *Prophets of Progress*, pp. 189, 199, 216, 224–227.
19. *Ibid.*, p. 215.
20. J. M. Thompson, *The French Revolution* (Oxford, 1947), pp. 214, 217.
21. To Richard Price, April 19, 1790, *Works*, IX, 564; to Peter Thacher, Feb. 25, 1791, Adams Papers.
22. *Works*, VI, 281.
23. Thompson, *French Revolution*, p. 442.
24. Hazen, *Contemporary American Opinion*, p. 271.
25. Feb. 9, 1794, *Letters of John Adams, Addressed to His Wife*, II, 141.
26. To Benjamin Rush, Aug. 28, 1811, *Works*, IX, 636.
27. Feb. 9, 1794, *Letters of John Adams, Addressed to His Wife*, II, 142.
28. Quoted in Haraszti, *Prophets of Progress*, p. 194.
29. Marginal notes in Adams' hand in his copy (now in Boston Public Library) of *An Impartial History of the Late Revolution in France* (Philadelphia, 1794), I, 162, 167.
30. Dec. 5, 1793, *Letters of John Adams, Addressed to His Wife*, II, 131.
31. Dec. 11, 1795, "Une Lettre inédite à Sir Francis d'Ivernois," *Revue historique de la révolution française*, 5:346–348 (1914).
32. Quoted in Elie Halévy, *The Growth of Philosophic Radicalism*, trans. Mary Morris (New York, 1949), p. 156.
33. To Thomas Brand-Hollis, June 11, 1790, *Works*, IX, 570; to

NOTES TO CHAPTER VI

Richard Price, April 19, 1790, *Works,* IX, 563–565; *Works,* VI, 279.

34. George M. Trevelyan, *History of England* (Garden City, N.Y., 1952), III, 87.

35. *Ibid.,* 85.

36. To Joseph Priestley, Feb. 19, 1792, Adams Papers.

37. Trevelyan, *History of England,* III, 87–92.

38. To Joseph Priestley, May 12, 1793, Adams Papers.

39. Dec. 22, 1808, *Old Family Letters,* p. 208.

40. June 30, 1813, *Adams-Jefferson Letters,* II, 346–347.

41. Dec. 19, 1793, *Letters of John Adams, Addressed to His Wife,* II, 133.

42. *Works,* VI, 411.

43. Aug. 28, 1811, *Old Family Letters,* p. 352.

44. Haraszti, *Prophets of Progress,* p. 202.

45. *Works,* IX, 191.

46. *Works,* IX, 187.

47. Feb. 11, 1810, *Old Family Letters,* p. 254.

48. *Diary and Autobiography,* III, 231.

49. *Works,* IX, 172.

50. Sept. 4, 1812, *Old Family Letters,* p. 423.

51. Leslie Stephen, *History of English Thought in the Eighteenth Century* (London, 1876), I, 463–464.

52. *Diary and Autobiography,* IV, 5; Oct. 29, 1805, *Statesman and Friend, Correspondence of John Adams with Benjamin Waterhouse, 1784–1822,* ed. W. C. Ford (Boston, 1927), p. 31.

53. To Benjamin Rush, Jan. 21, 1810, *Works,* IX, 627.

54. Jan. 21, 1810, *Old Family Letters,* p. 251.

55. To Francis Van Der Kemp, Sept. 28, 1802, Adams–Van Der Kemp letters.

56. *Works,* I, 404.

57. To Oliver Wolcott, Oct. 27, 1797, *Works,* VIII, 559; *Works,* IX, 227.

58. To Timothy Pickering, Sept. 4, 1797, Pickering Papers, Massachusetts Historical Society.

59. To Timothy Pickering, Sept. 16, 1798, *Works,* VIII, 596.

60. To William Cranch, June 29, 1801, Adams Papers.

61. To Thomas Jefferson, Jan. 22, 1825, *Works,* X, 415.

62. To James Lloyd, March 6 and March 29, 1815, *Works,* X, 135, 148; June 22, 1806, *Old Family Letters,* p. 102.

63. John C. Miller, *Crisis in Freedom* (Boston, 1951), pp. 71–72; to Thomas Jefferson, June 14, 1813, *Works,* X, 42.

64. *Works,* IX, 182, 184.

65. To Christopher Gadsden, April 16, 1801, *Works,* IX, 584.

66. To Timothy Pickering, Aug. 13, 1799, *Works*, IX, 14.

67. To John Jackson, Dec. 30, 1817, *Works*, X, 269; to Livingston, Nov. 11, 1782, *Works*, VIII, 9.

68. *Works*, VI, 299; to Francis Van Der Kemp, Feb. 20, 1806, Adams–Van Der Kemp letters.

69. Quoted in Barker, *Essays on Government*, p. 217.

70. Thomas Jefferson to John Adams, July 5, 1814, *Adams-Jefferson Letters*, II, 431.

71. July 16, 1814, *ibid.*, 435–436.

72. To Francis Van Der Kemp, Nov. 30, 1810, Adams–Van Der Kemp letters.

73. April 22, 1812, *Old Family Letters*, p. 376.

74. *Ibid.*

75. May 26, 1817, *Adams-Jefferson Letters*, II, 517.

76. *Works*, VI, 402–403.

77. July 16, 1814, *Adams-Jefferson Letters*, II, 436; June 25, 1814, "Some Unpublished Correspondence of John Adams and Richard Rush, 1811–16," ed. J. H. Powell, *Pennsylvania Magazine of History and Biography*, 61:50–51 (Jan. 1937).

78. To Richard Rush, May 30, 1814, *Works*, X, 98.

79. July 16, 1814, and Aug. 24, 1815, *Adams-Jefferson Letters*, II, 436, 456.

80. Oct. 10, 1817, *ibid.*, p. 521.

81. June 20, 1815, *ibid.*, p. 446.

82. Nov. 13, 1815, *ibid.*, p. 458.

83. To G. W. Adams, Oct. 10, 1808, Adams Papers.

84. Thomas Jefferson to John Adams, Jan. 11, 1816, *Adams-Jefferson Letters*, II, 460.

85. July 15, 1813, *ibid.*, p. 358.

86. Quoted in Haraszti, *Prophets of Progress*, pp. 221–222.

87. *Ibid.*, p. 219.

88. Aug. 17, 1812, *Old Family Letters*, p. 422.

89. July 15, 1813, *Adams-Jefferson Letters*, II, 357.

90. Frederick B. Artz, *France under the Bourbon Restoration, 1814–1830* (Cambridge, Mass., 1931), pp. 9–37.

91. Thomas Jefferson to John Adams, Jan. 11, 1816, *Adams-Jefferson Letters*, II, 459–460.

Chapter VII. Strait Is the Gate That Leads to Liberty

1. Donald H. Stewart and George P. Clark, "Misanthrope or Humanitarian? John Adams in Retirement," *New England Quarterly*, 28:216–236 (June 1955).

2. Sheldon Wolin, *Politics and Vision* (Boston, 1960), p. 294.

3. Hartz, *Liberal Tradition*, p. 97.
4. To James Madison, June 17, 1817, *Works*, X, 267.
5. To Thomas McKean, July 6, 1815, *Works*, X, 167.
6. Aug. 24, 1815, *Adams-Jefferson Letters*, II, 455–456.
7. March 10, 1823, *ibid.*, p. 590.
8. Frederick B. Artz, *Reaction and Revolution, 1814–1832* (New York, 1934), pp. 10–22.
9. Nov. 13, 1815, *Adams-Jefferson Letters*, II, 457.
10. July 16, 1814, *ibid.*, p. 435.
11. To Thomas McKean, Nov. 26, 1815, *Works*, X, 181.
12. May 6 and Aug. 9, 1816, *Adams-Jefferson Letters*, II, 474, 486.
13. Aug. 1, 1816, *ibid.*, p. 484.
14. Aug. 1, 1816, *Selected Writings of John and John Quincy Adams*, p. 287.
15. Feb. 2, 1816, *Adams-Jefferson Letters*, II, 462.
16. Dec. 3, 1813, *ibid.*, p. 405.
17. To Francis Van Der Kemp, Nov. 10, 1815, Adams–Van Der Kemp letters.
18. Artz, *Reaction and Revolution*, p. 49.
19. Aug. 1, 1816, *Selected Writings of John and John Quincy Adams*, p. 288.
20. Nov. 13, 1815, *Adams-Jefferson Letters*, II, 456.
21. Dec. 27, 1810, *Old Family Letters*, p. 269; to Francis Van Der Kemp, Feb. 20, 1811, Adams–Van Der Kemp letters.
22. To J. Morse, Dec. 5, 1815, *Works*, X, 190; Dec. 25, 1813, and June 20, 1815, *Adams-Jefferson Letters*, II, 410, 445; Sept. 27, 1809, *Old Family Letters*, p. 242.
23. June 20, 1815, *Adams-Jefferson Letters*, II, 445.
24. May 26, 1817, *ibid.*, p. 518.
25. To James Madison, April 22, 1817, *Works*, X, 256.
26. Dec. 25, 1813, *Adams-Jefferson Letters*, II, 410.
27. To John Quincy Adams, Jan. 5, 1818, quoted in Samuel Flagg Bemis, *John Quincy Adams and the Foundations of American Foreign Policy* (New York, 1949), pp. 342–343.
28. Nov. 4, 1816, *Adams-Jefferson Letters*, II, 494.
29. To Francis Van Der Kemp, July 13, 1815, *Works*, X, 169.
30. To James Bowdoin, May 9, 1786, Bowdoin-Temple Papers, Massachusetts Historical Society.
31. To William Tudor, June 17, 1818, *Works*, X, 321.
32. To Benjamin Stoddert, May 8, 1799, *Works*, VIII, 642.
33. *Works*, VI, 511.
34. To John Quincy Adams, Jan. 5, 1818, quoted in Bemis, *Adams and the Foundations of American Foreign Policy*, pp. 342–343.

35. Jan. 28, 1818, *Adams-Jefferson Letters,* II, 523.
36. Feb. 3, 1821, *ibid.,* p. 571.
37. To James Lloyd, March 27, 1815, *Works,* X, 144.
38. To Richard Rush, Nov. 28, 1821, *Works,* X, 402.
39. Henry Butler Clarke, *Modern Spain, 1815–1898* (Cambridge, England, 1906), pp. 10–28.
40. To Benjamin Rush, Sept. 3, 1808, *Works,* IX, 600.
41. Dec. 29, 1823, *Adams-Jefferson Letters,* II, 602.
42. To William Bayard, Dec. 29, 1823, Adams Papers.
43. To John Adams, July 21, 1789, Benjamin Rush, *Letters,* ed. L. H. Butterfield (Princeton, 1951), I, 524.
44. Feb. 10, 1812, *Old Family Letters,* p. 454.
45. Dorothy M. Robathan, "John Adams and the Classics," *New England Quarterly,* 19:91–98 (March 1946).
46. Sept. 12, 1821, *Adams-Jefferson Letters,* II, 574.
47. Dec. 29, 1823, *ibid.,* p. 602.
48. May 19, 1821, *ibid.,* p. 572.
49. Sept. 4, 1823, *ibid.,* p. 597.
50. May 19, 1821, *ibid.,* p. 573.
51. Sept. 18, 1823, *ibid.,* p. 599.
52. Dec. 3, 1816, and Jan. 14, 1817, John Quincy Adams, *Works,* ed. W. C. Ford (New York, 1913–1917), VI, 123–124.
53. To John Jay, Nov. 24, 1785, *Works,* VIII, 347; to the President of Congress, Aug. 4, 1779, *Works,* VII, 103.
54. To Mercy Warren, June 23, 1780, *Warren-Adams Letters,* II, 133–134; to the President of Congress, Feb. 27, 1779, *Works,* VII, 87.
55. To the Heads of Department, Jan. 24, 1798, *Works,* VIII, 561–562.
56. To James Madison, June 17, 1817, *Works,* X, 267.
57. Nov. 25, 1816, *Adams-Jefferson Letters,* II, 497–498.
58. Dec. 16, 1816, *ibid.,* pp. 501–502.
59. Sept. 14, 1813, *ibid.,* p. 373.
60. Feb. 25, 1825, *ibid.,* p. 610.
61. *Journal of Debates and Proceedings in the Convention of Delegates Chosen to Revise the Constitution of Massachusetts, November 15, 1820–January 9, 1821* (Boston, 1821), pp. 134–135.
62. To James Madison, June 17, 1817, *Works,* X, 268.
63. Feb. 2, 1816, *Adams-Jefferson Letters,* II, 462.
64. To James Madison, June 17, 1817, *Works,* X, 268.
65. Aug. 15, 1823, *Adams-Jefferson Letters,* II, 595.
66. March 2, 1816, *ibid.,* pp. 464–465.
67. Sept. 23, 1790, quoted in Dumas Malone, *Jefferson and the Rights of Man,* p. 265.

NOTES TO CHAPTER VII

68. To Richard Peters, March 31, 1822, *Works*, X, 403; May 19, 1821, *Adams-Jefferson Letters*, II, 573.

69. Feb. 3, 1821, *Adams-Jefferson Letters*, II, 571.

70. To Francis Van Der Kemp, Oct. 10, 1820, Adams–Van Der Kemp letters.

71. Sept. 24, 1821, and Sept. 18, 1823, *Adams-Jefferson Letters*, II, 576, 598.

72. To Francis Van Der Kemp, Oct. 10, 1820, Adams–Van Der Kemp letters; to Richard Sharp, Feb. 27, 1811, Adams Papers; to Richard Rush, May 14, 1821, *Works*, X, 397; Dec. 21, 1819, *Adams-Jefferson Letters*, II, 550.

73. Hartz, *Liberal Tradition*, p. 81.

74. Daniel Bell, *The End of Ideology* (New York, 1961), p. 211.

75. June 9 and July 5, 24, 28, 1789, *Old Family Letters*, pp. 36–38, 41–43, 44–51; *Journal of William Maclay*, pp. 1–2, 9–12, 26–27.

76. See Bell, *End of Ideology*, pp. 57–60, where C. Wright Mills' *Power Elite* is criticized on the ground that the illustrations used are drawn from American life and the key concepts from European experiences.

77. See Clinton Rossiter, "The Paradox of India's Democracy," *New York Times Magazine*, July 3, 1962, p. 15, for a comment on the parochialism of American political science when it treats the problem of the prerequisites of democracy.

78. Boorstin, *Image of Europe*, p. 38.

INDEX

"Abolition of feudalism," 135, 146
Academies (Europe), Adams and, 177–178
Adams, John Quincy, 158, 168, 173, 195, 197, 209
Adams, Samuel, 107, 164, 172
Alien and Sedition Laws, 175, 179–180
American exceptionalism, 62
American Revolution, 160; Adams on, 6–8, 17, 75, 83, 96, 101–102, 105; French liberals on, 16, 33–34, 82; Condorcet on, 17, 108; religion in, 18; special nature of, 20, 22, 28–29, 31, 81, 99, 103, 106, 107–108, 114, 172–173, 214–215, 218–219, 221–222; influence of, 103–104; Dutch Patriots and, 109–110, 111; and Jefferson, 125; mobs in, 152–153
Anti-Federalists, 157
Aristocracy: Adams' theory of, 5, 12–13, 19, 23, 29, 87–88, 121, 141–142, 148, 154; in France, 14, 42; in England, 88. See also Louis XVI; Nobility
Articles of Confederation, 38
Assembly of Notables, 116, 185; Adams on, 117–118, 120–122
Atheism, 163, 165, 176; Adams on, 91
Autobiography, 105
Auvergne Assembly, 119

Babouvists, 16
Balanced government: applied in Europe, 10–12, 126–127, 129, 156, 165, 199–200, 207–208, 216–217, 219; Adams' defense of, 24, 44–45, 47–48; critique of, 25–27, 29, 32, 46–47, 48, 51, 56,

69–70, 72, 221; French liberals and, 32, 41–44; Condorcet on, 52–53, 56–57; and human nature, 54–55; colonial experience of, 67; in National Assembly, 132–133, 135–138; and despotism, 181
Barlow, Joel, 102
Beard, Charles A., 25
Belknap, Jeremy, 164
Bicameralism: Adams on, 46, 53, 64–65, 142; Condorcet on, 57, 65–66; in France, 129; in National Assembly, 132
Bonaparte, Joseph, 204–205
Boulainvilliers, Henri de, 148
Bourgeoisie (France), 118; class feelings of, 84, 88–89, 94, 104–105, 144–145, 147, 151; and Napoleon, 183. See also Middle class
Brissot de Warville, 122–123, 124
Burke, Edmund, 167, 181; Adams' divergence from, 26–27, 48–49, 85, 157–159, 198–199; *Reflections on the Revolution in France*, 27, 157, 158, 198. See also Reaction

Calonne, Charles Alexandre de, 19, 116, 117
Carr, E. H., 1
Cartwright, Major, 211
Catholic Church, 186, 187–188, 205, 224; Adams on, 5, 18, 89–91, 165, 203; in Spain, 89–90; French liberals on, 91; revival of, 193–201
Charles X, 188
Charter of 1814, *see* Restoration Charter

INDEX

Chateaubriand, François René de, 196, 197

Church and state: Adams on, 36–37; Jefferson on, 36

Church of England, 168–170

Civil Constitution of the Clergy, 163

Class conflict: Adams' theory of, 23–24, 64; in ancient world, 25, 45, 58, 71; in America, 45, 70–72; in France, 136–137, 151

Classical studies, Adams on, 206

Colonialism, 202

Condorcet, 18, 70, 104, 134, 221; constitutional preferences of, 10, 41–44, 52–53, 57; on American Revolution, 17, 108; differences with Adams, 31–33; and English constitution, 41, 51–53; and American state constitutions, 41–42; affinities with Adams, 49; on balanced government, 56–57; on bicameralism, 57, 65–66; and history, 60–61; and property, 66; on nobility, 148. *See also* Liberals (France); Turgot

Constitution (England), 11, 32, 88, 167, 168; Montesquieu on, 33; Turgot on, 40; Condorcet on, 41, 51–53; Adams on, 49, 53, 169–170, 209; defects of, 50–51; opinion in France, 132, 136–137

Constitution, French: of *1791*, 153, 163; of *1793*, 165; of *1795*, 166

Constitution, Spanish, of *1812*, 208

Constitution, U.S., 129–130, 217

Convention (France), 160, 165, 171

Cooper, Samuel, 103

Cranston, Maurice, 30

Declaration of Independence, 103, 105, 106

Defence of the Constitutions of Government of the United States of America, 22–29 (passim), 34, 41, 45, 50, 54, 55, 58, 61, 64, 67, 71, 92, 96, 110, 116, 119, 121, 126, 133–134, 142, 143, 147, 158, 168, 173, 196, 203, 209

Deism, 165, 175; Adams on, 91

Directory, 166, 174, 180

Discourses on Davila, 126, 137, 138, 142, 157, 163, 170

Dissenters, 124, 167–170, 210. *See also* Price; Priestley

Dissertation on the Canon and Feudal Law, 21, 83

Dupont de Nemours, Pierre Samuel, 70, 134, 177

Dutch Patriot Movement, 2, 14, 19, 108, 121, 142, 212; and American Revolution, 109–110, 111; Adams' relation to, 110; development of, 110–112; Adams on, 112–116; Lafayette on, 113, 114

Elections, Adams on, 57–58

England, 4, 77; revolution in, 74, 170, 209–210; Adams in, 116

Enlightened despotism, Adams and Turgot on, 38–39

Enlightenment, 33, 34, 76, 77, 90, 100, 196, 214; Adams on, 197–198

Equality: Adams' views, 14, 15, 28, 148–149, 152–154; French liberals on, 14–15; in America, 21–22, 71; and French Revolution, 149

Estates General, 80, 118, 121, 123, 143; organization of, 43; seating in, 120; Adams on, 128

Executive power, Adams' theory of, 23, 24, 66–67, 134–135, 166

Executive veto: in English constitution, 53; Adams' theory of, 66–67; in France, 129–131; in U.S. constitution, 129–130

Federalism, 9–10; Turgot and, 35–36; Adams and, 38

Federalist, The, 222

Federalists, 157, 174, 176, 179–180

Fenno, John, 157

Ferdinand VII, 208

Ferguson, Adam, 92

INDEX

Fisher, H. A. L., 73
Founding Fathers, 95
Franklin, Benjamin, 33, 40, 74, 75–76, 102, 103, 109, 129, 139, 160, 220, 226
Frederick the Great, 178
French Revolution, 5, 6; anticlericalism in, 18, 163–165, 176; Adams' assessment of, 18–20, 98–100, 104, 118–119, 123, 124–125, 126, 154–155, 156, 159–160, 167–168, 185–190, 191, 194, 199, 201; Jefferson on, 125; reunion of orders in, 127–128, 129; and property, 147, 148–149; and equality, 149; American opinion of, 160, 171

Genêt, Edmond, 171
Gentz, Friedrich, 173
George III, 17, 160
Gibbon, Edward, 199
Gordon riots, 92, 209
"Great chain of being," 148
Greek Revolution, 8, 205–207

Hamilton, Alexander, 51, 176, 179
Hapsburgs, 193
Harrington, James, 147
Hartley, David, 158
Hawley, Joseph, 106–107
Hazlitt, William, 199
History: Adams and, 25, 48, 60; Condorcet and, 60–61; classical analogies in, 61–62
Hobbes, Thomas, 206
Holland, 69, 116, 146–147, 204; Adams in, 108–110
Holy Alliance, 192–193, 201
Houdetot, Madame d', 215
House of Commons, 51, 52, 53, 64
House of Lords, 50, 51, 53, 64, 132
House of Representatives, 65
Human nature: Adams' concept of, 23, 24, 54–56; and tyranny, 59
Hume, David, 27, 34, 51
Hutchinson, Thomas, 107

Index, 193
Inquisition, 193, 194, 199, 203, 205
Intellectuals (Europe), Adams and, 177–178
Isolationism, 4, 8–9, 225

Jansenism, 194
Jefferson, Thomas, 51, 106, 125, 133, 141, 171, 176, 178, 179, 215, 226; on Europe, 2; on America, 20; on balanced powers, 32; on church and state, 36; on human nature, 54; on bicameralism, 65; and land tenure, 68; on class conflict, 70–71; on France, 74, 75, 80, 81, 95, 98, 117, 124, 185; on Dutch Patriots, 113, 114; on Burke, 157; on Louis XVI, 160; and Napoleon, 181–183, 192; on French Revolution, 190; on Jesuits, 195; on Greek Revolution, 206–207; on Spanish Revolution, 207–208; on England, 209–210
Jeffersonians, 162, 176
Jesuits, 194–195, 201, 205
Johnson, Samuel, 27, 198

Lafayette, Marquis de, 102, 113, 117, 119, 120
Laissez-faire, Adams and, 37–38
Lally-Tollendal, Marquis de, 136
Laski, Harold, 25
Latin America, revolutions in, 97, 178–179, 201–204
Leo X, 198
Leonard, Daniel, 36
Liberals (Europe), 99, 103; Adams on, 4–8, 213–218; on balanced government, 10–11; on middle class, 13–14; and the people, 177
Liberals (France), 30–33, 124, 157; on American Revolution, 16, 33–34, 82, 103; as revolutionaries, 19, 99–100, 172–173; state of mind, 76–78, 80, 82, 88–89; on English constitution, 82; on nobility, 84, 87, 95; class feelings of, 86, 94; anticlericalism of, 90–

INDEX

91, 201; reform program of, 95; Adams on, 200–201. *See also* Bourgeoisie; Condorcet; Middle class; Turgot

Literacy test for voting, Adams and Jefferson on, 208

Locke, John, 106, 200

Louis XV, 73

Louis XVI, 17, 18, 66, 67, 74, 121, 128, 130, 131, 134, 135, 159; Adams on, 160–162. *See also* Aristocracy; Nobility

Louis XVIII, Adams and Jefferson on, 183–184

L'Ouverture, Toussaint, 203

Loyalists, 36, 44

Mably, Gabriel Bonnet de, 75

Machiavelli, Niccolò, 141

Maclay's *Journal*, 157

Madison, James, 54, 160, 176, 222

Malone, Dumas, 124

Massachusetts, 67, 105–106; constitution of *1780*, 28, 36, 109, 230n; constitutional convention of *1820*, 37, 211

Middle class, 16; in Europe, 4, 13–14; in America, 12, 29, 71, 84–85, 94–95; Adams on, 85–86, 147; in England, 212. *See also* Bourgeoisie

Mirabeau, Comte de, 130, 131, 132, 138

Miranda, Francisco, 178, 201

Mob, *see* People

Monarchy, 17–18; in Europe, 4–5; Adams and, 12, 13, 29, 49–50, 85; in France, 78–79, 82. *See also* Republicanism

Monroe, James, 8

Montesquieu, Baron de, 33, 40, 41, 181; Adams' divergence from, 48

Mounier, Jean Joseph, 131, 132, 134, 138

Napoleon, 123, 184, 185, 197, 201, 204, 217; Adams and Jefferson on, 181–183, 192, 193

National Assembly, 181, 215; and balanced government, 11–12, 132–133, 135–138; and equality, 14, 149–150, 153; Adams' criticism of, 66, 126, 128–129, 139–140, 146, 156, 161; constitutional debates in, 130–132; and privilege, 131–132, 134, 140–141; and property, 152–153; and Louis XVI, 162–163

National Guard (France), 150

Needham, Marchamont, 49

Neomedievalism, 198

Neutrality, Proclamation of, 171

Newton, Sir Isaac, and Adams' political thinking, 27, 55–56

Noailles, Viscount, 166

Nobility (France): privileges of, 19, 75, 82, 83, 93–94, 128, 134, 150, 151, 153; Adams on, 84–89, 94, 95, 120–122, 123, 141–145; and wealth, 87, 146–147; as reformers, 118; Condorcet on, 148. *See also* Aristocracy; Louis XVI

Novanglus, 37

Old Regime, 191; Adams on, 13, 74–75, 78, 80, 99, 159, 215; political conflict in, 39–40; foreign observers on, 73–74; crisis of, 75–78; reform of, 78–84; and religious toleration, 90

Oligarchy, Adams on, 68–69

Orange, House of, 109, 110, 111, 113, 115

Paine, Thomas, 102, 158, 159, 168, 169, 176–177; *Rights of Man,* 158, 168

Palmer, R. R., 80, 84, 124

Parlements, 10, 42, 57, 74, 79–80, 121

Parliament, 21, 31, 107, 209. *See also* House of Commons; House of Lords

Parliamentary reform, 50, 126, 168, 169, 192, 209–212

Parrington, Vernon L., 25

INDEX

Peasantry, 188; in France, 14, 143, 150, 151; in Spain, 90

Pennsylvania: constitution of *1776*, 34, 40, 47, 129; constitution of *1790*, 138–139

People, the: in America, 12, 22, 29, 99; in Europe, 13–14, 85, 99, 119, 174; in Paris, 14, 92, 151, 183; Adams on, 22–23, 91–95, 153, 154, 168, 216; in ancient world, 92, French middle class on, 94; in Holland, 115; in France, 118, 142, 143, 150, 173–174, 190; in American Revolution, 152–153

Pickering, Timothy, 180

Price, Richard, 40, 41, 124, 137, 138, 167, 185, 198; letter from Turgot, 34, 38. *See also* Dissenters

Priestley, Joseph, 124, 167, 168, 180. *See also* Dissenters

Property: distribution in America, 22, 68, 71, 211; and bicameralism, 65; Condorcet on, 66; distribution in Europe, 91; influence of, 146–147; and French Revolution, 147, 148–149; and National Assembly, 152–153

Prussia, 111, 112, 116

Radicals (England), 211, 212

Rahv, Philip, 1

Rational Dissenters, *See* Dissenters

Reaction, 3, 27, 101, 161, 187, 198, 217; Adams on, 16, 192–201, 212–213; in England, 168–170; in America, 174–180. *See also* Burke

Reformation, 100

Relativism (Adams'): definition of, 2; critique of, 219–226

Republicanism, 223; Adams and, 49–50, 161, 164; in Europe, 83, 93, 102, 103, 213; in France, 120, 162–163, 186. *See also* Monarchy

Restoration Charter, 187, 188, 190; Adams on, 184

Revolutions (Europe), 96, 212; Adams on, 2–3, 5–8, 10, 98–100

Revolutions (non-European), 8, 9, 225

Revolutions of *1820*, 207–208

Robespierre, M. F. M. I. de, 165, 201

Roman Catholic Church, *see* Catholic Church

Rush, Benjamin, 205–206

Russia, 1, 2, 101, 206

Rutledge, John, 180

Santo Domingo, revolution in, 202

Sarsfield, Count, 128

Schwartz, Delmore, 1

Scott, Sir Walter, 198

Self-determination of nations, Adams on, 193

Senate (U.S.), 65

Shays' Rebellion, 12, 15, 28, 45, 54, 94

Sieyès, Abbé, 84, 86–87

Slavery, 19, 186, 202–203, 217

Smith, Adam, 149

Social structure, Adams' concept of, 63–64, 67–68, 222–223

South America, *see* Latin America

Southey, Robert, 199

Spain, 193, 201, 202; Adams in, 89–90; uprising against Napoleon, 204–205; revolution of *1820*, 207–208, 212

Spanish Patriots, 192, 208, 212

Staël, Madame de, 197

Stamp Act controversies, 12, 21

Stevens, John, 133, 134

Suffrage, *see* Universal suffrage

Taylor, John, 63, 68, 222

Third Estate, 86–87, 127, 145; Adams on, 83, 89, 91, 93, 128, 139–140, 142; and nobility, 88; in French Revolution, 94, 134, 135, 144

Thoughts on Government, 97

Titles, Adams on, 223

Tocqueville, Alexis de, 21, 76–77

INDEX

Turgot, 10, 11, 38, 200, 201; reform efforts of, 19; differences with Adams, 30–34, 200; and American state constitutions, 34, 40; religious and economic views of, 35, 36–38; and federalism, 35–36; on enlightened despotism, 39; constitutional preferences of, 41–44; critique of, 46–47; affinities with Adams, 49; Adams on fall of, 74. *See also* Condorcet; Liberals (France)

Tyler, Wat, 15

Tyranny of the majority, 58

Universal suffrage, 65, 187, 189; in Europe, 93; in Massachusetts, 106, 192; in England, 209–211

Universalism (Adams'): definition of, 2; critique of, 219–226

Utrecht, 111, 115

Van Der Kemp, Francis A., 112, 196

Varennes, flight to, 161, 162

Veto, *see* Executive veto

Vienna, Congress of, 192–193, 204, 213

Virginia, oligarchy in, 69

Voltaire, François Marie, 41, 200, 201

Warren, Dr. Joseph, 107

Washington, George, 23, 98, 158, 160, 171

Watson, John, 176

Whig tradition, Adams and, 191

XYZ affair, 179